VISUAL QUICKSTART GUIDE

K E Y N O T E

FOR MAC OS X

Tom Negrino

D1501165

 Peachpit Press

Visual QuickStart Guide
Keynote for Mac OS X
Tom Negrino

Peachpit Press
1249 Eighth Street
Berkeley, CA 94710
510/524-2178
800/283-9444
510/524-2221 (fax)
Find us on the World Wide Web at: www.peachpit.com
Peachpit Press is a division of Pearson Education

Editor: Nancy Davis
Production Coordinators: Myrna Vladic, Becky Winter
Compositors: Rick Gordon, Deborah Roberti
Tech Editor: Brian A. Peat
Proofreader: Suzie Lowey, Anne Gillick
Indexer: Joy Dean Lee
Cover Design: The Visual Group
Cover Production: Nathalie Valette

ISBN 0-321-19775-5

9 8 7 6 5 4 3 2

Printed and bound in the United States of America

Dedication

This one goes out to my big sister,
Marie Bevins. Just because.

Special Thanks to:

The folks at Peachpit

Once again, I am indebted to my editor, Nancy Davis, for her fabulous editing skills, and for being more patient than I probably deserve.

Thanks to Myrna Vladic for her production skills.

Thanks to Kim Lombardi and Scott Cowlin for that promotional pizzazz.

Thanks to Marjorie Baer and Nancy Ruenzel for believing that I was the right guy for the project.

The Keynote community

I'm not the only person who thinks that Keynote is pretty cool; a vibrant community quickly sprang up to offer themes, news, and help. My thanks to the following members of the Keynote ecosystem:

Brian Peat, of KeynoteUser.com (`www.keynoteuser.com`), served as the technical editor for this book, provided his themes for screenshots, and wrote the first draft of Chapter 14.

John Driedger, proprietor of Keynote Theme Park (`www.keynotethemepark.com`), allowed me to use his excellent themes.

Brad Taylor, KeynoteHQ.com (`www.keynotehq.com`), built the first site dedicated to Keynote, and let me use his themes as examples.

Keith Manegre and Brenda Epp, Keynote Gallery (`www.keynotegallery.com`), debuted their site as the book was going to press, and allowed me to use their themes.

Everybody else

Thanks to my wife Dori, and my son Sean, for living with me through another book project without strangling me in my sleep.

My agent, David Rogelberg, of StudioB.

Thanks to the following people and vendors for their help and the use of their products:

Apple Computer's Suman Mariyappa, the Keynote Product Marketing Manager.

Kim Dixon, of Hemera Technologies, Inc.

Linda Sharps, Marketing Manager, The Omni Group.

Naomi Pearce, of Pearce Communications.

Kevin Mallon, of FileMaker, Inc.

Gary Lewis, proprietor of PowerPoint Art.com (`www.powerpointart.com`).

Tony Rennier, of Blacksmith.

The soundtrack for this book (hum it along with me!) was graciously provided by Evanescence, Patty Griffin, Caitlin Cary, Toad the Wet Sprocket, Kim Richey, Lucy Kaplansky, and U2. Thank goodness (and Apple) for iTunes.

CONTENTS AT A GLANCE

TABLE OF CONTENTS

GETTING STARTED WITH KEYNOTE

Welcome to Keynote! Apple's Keynote is an exciting new presentation program that can help you create compelling presentations with a minimum of effort. Keynote's gorgeous presentation themes, superior text handling, attractive animations, and excellent graphics capabilities allow you to deliver your ideas with the maximum visual impact.

This visual power doesn't come at the price of complexity; it's easy to build a Keynote presentation, whether you're a novice speaker or a polished presenter. But don't be fooled into thinking that because Keynote is easy to use, it lacks power; there's a lot of substance behind that pretty face.

As the newcomer on the block, Keynote does an excellent job of getting along with the competition, namely Microsoft's venerable PowerPoint. Keynote imports from and exports to PowerPoint format, so you're able to share your Keynote presentations with other Mac users who have Microsoft Office, or with your Windows-using colleagues.

In this chapter, you'll learn how to install and start Keynote, see an overview of the program's workspace, customize Keynote's interface, and ask the program for help. Let's get started with Keynote.

Installing Keynote

Installing Keynote is as straightforward as installing any of Apple's software. After just a few clicks of the mouse, you'll be done.

To install Keynote:

1. Insert the Keynote CD into your Mac.

2. Double-click the CD icon to open it.

3. Double-click the Keynote.pkg file on the CD.

   This file is an Installer document. The Installer program will launch and ask you to enter your passphrase to authenticate that you have permission to install software (**Figure 1.1**).

4. Enter your passphrase, then click OK.

   The first Install Keynote screen appears (**Figure 1.2**).

5. Click Continue.

6. On the second Installer screen, read the Read Me information, then click Continue.

   The Software License Agreement screen appears.

7. Click Continue, then click Agree.

Figure 1.1 Enter your passphrase to start the installation process.

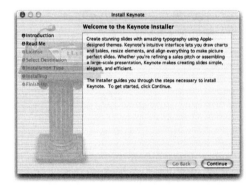

Figure 1.2 The Keynote Installer walks you through the process of installing the program.

Figure 1.3 Choose the disk on which you want to install Keynote.

8. On the Select a Destination screen (**Figure 1.3**), click the disk on which you want to install Keynote, then click Continue.

The destination disk must contain Mac OS X 10.2 or later to install Keynote.

9. At the Easy Install screen, click Continue.

The installation process commences. When it is complete, click Close to quit the Installer. The program will be installed into the */harddisk/*Applications/ folder on your computer.

✔ Tips

■ It's a good idea to copy the Keynote User Guide and Keynote Quick Reference Guide folders to your Documents folder for later use.

■ Keynote must be installed on your startup volume (the partition of your hard disk that contains a System folder for Mac OS X version 10.2 or later).

INSTALLING KEYNOTE

Starting Keynote

Starting Keynote for the first time will require a brief registration process, then you can jump right into creating presentations.

To start Keynote:

1. Open your Applications folder.

2. Double-click the Keynote application icon (**Figure 1.4**).

    The program launches.

3. The first time you use Keynote, you'll be asked to fill out a short registration form (**Figure 1.5**).

4. Fill out the form, then click Register Now.

    Keynote connects to the Internet and sends your registration information to Apple.

5. An untitled document appears, and asks you to select a theme for your presentation (**Figure 1.6**).

6. Select a theme, make a choice from the Presentation Size pop-up menu, and click Choose Theme.

    Keynote builds the theme and prepares the first slide for editing. You'll find more information about selecting themes and creating presentations in Chapter 2.

Figure 1.4 Double-click the Keynote application icon to launch the program.

Figure 1.5 Don't forget to register your copy of Keynote with Apple.

Figure 1.6 Every Keynote presentation has to have a theme, so choose one to create a new Keynote document.

Exploring the Keynote Workspace

The Keynote workspace is made up of one main window and a variety of tool windows that you can show or hide (**Figure 1.7**). Let's look at the pieces one by one.

Toolbar   Slide Canvas   Inspector window

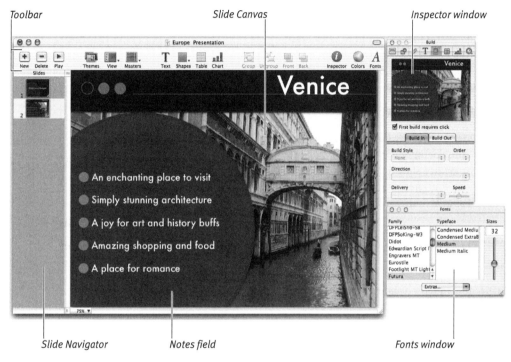

Slide Navigator   Notes field   Fonts window

Figure 1.7 The Keynote workspace has one main document window, and several floating windows. Not shown in this picture is the floating Colors window.

The Slide Canvas

This is the main Keynote document window; it's where you will be editing your slides and placing graphics, tables and charts. You can zoom into (or out of) the action with the Zoom pop-up menu at the lower-left corner of the Slide Canvas window (**Figure 1.8**).

✔ Tip

■ You can also zoom in or out on a slide by choosing View > Zoom > Zoom In or View > Zoom > Zoom Out. If you prefer keyboard shortcuts, you can use ⌘⃞> to zoom in, and ⌘⃞< to zoom out.

The Slide Navigator

The Slide Navigator is the pane at the left edge of the document window. It actually does triple duty, showing three different aspects of your presentation. In *Navigator View*, it shows thumbnails of your slides.

You can organize and group slides in this view by dragging slide thumbnails to the right so they are indented in the list, as shown in **Figure 1.9**. The parent slide of a group of indented slides has a disclosure triangle; clicking the triangle allows you to hide or show the indented slides. This makes it easier to organize the presentation, especially with longer shows. You can also drag the parent slide to another place in the presentation, and the indented slides move along with it.

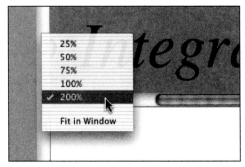

Figure 1.8 Select the magnification of the slide with the Zoom pop-up menu in the Slide Canvas.

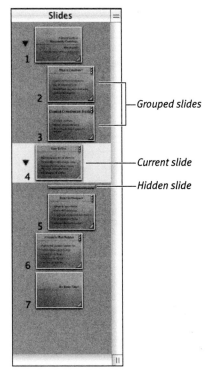

Figure 1.9 You can group and organize slides in the Slide Navigator.

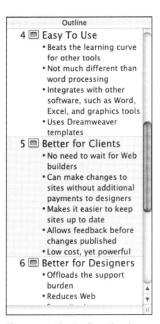

Figure 1.10 The Outline View is best to get an overview of the content of your presentation.

Another thing you can do in Navigator View is skip slides; skipped slides won't appear when you give the presentation, and will "collapse" in Navigator View, appearing as a line.

The second function of the Slide Navigator is *Outline View*; in this view the content of your slides appears (**Figure 1.10**). You can create, write, edit, and rearrange your slides and their content in this view. In fact, that's one of the best ways to create a presentation; more on that in Chapter 2.

The Slide Navigator can also show you the master slides associated with the presentation's theme; in this view, the Slide Navigator is split into two panes, with the top pane showing the master slides and the bottom pane your presentation's slides (**Figure 1.11**). You'll find more information about master slides in Chapter 3.

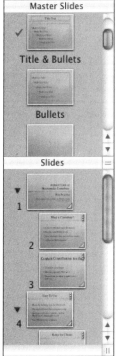

Figure 1.11 When you view master slides, the Slide Navigator splits into two panes, showing both the master slides and your presentation slides.

EXPLORING THE KEYNOTE WORKSPACE

The Notes field

The Notes field (**Figure 1.12**) is where you can enter speaker notes that help you give the presentation; these won't appear on the presentations screen, but they can be viewed on a second display. For example, if you are presenting using a PowerBook and a projector, the notes can appear on the PowerBook's screen while the presentation runs on the projector.

This is one of Keynote's advantages over PowerPoint. PowerPoint can't show speaker notes on a second monitor; the speaker and the audience see exactly the same view.

If you prefer, you can print speaker notes.

The Toolbar

Like most programs, Keynote has a toolbar that provides the tools you need to create, edit, and play presentations (**Figure 1.13**). You can change the buttons in the toolbar to suit your way of working; see "Customizing the Toolbar," later in this chapter.

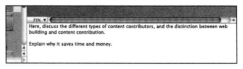

Figure 1.12 You enter your speaker notes in the Notes field.

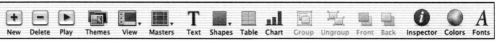

Figure 1.13 With Keynote's Toolbar you get access to most of the tools that you need to create, edit, and play presentations.

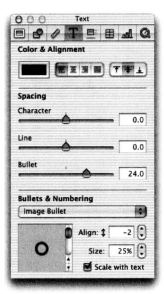

Figure 1.14 The Inspector window gives you eight different sets of controls to modify your presentation.

The Inspector

The Inspector window (**Figure 1.14**) is actually eight windows in one; it has a toolbar that lets you change between its eight panes:

◆ **Slide Inspector** allows you to change the master slide associated with the current slide; apply slide backgrounds; and apply animated transitions between slides.

◆ **Graphic Inspector** allows you to adjust the fill, stroke, shadow, and opacity of graphic elements on a slide or slide master.

◆ **Metrics Inspector** allows you to adjust the size, position, and angle of slide elements.

◆ **Text Inspector** gives you control over the color, alignment and spacing of slide text, and lets you set bullet types.

◆ **Build Inspector** controls animated builds for slide content. For example, this is the Inspector you will use to make each bullet point within a slide appear as you get to it.

◆ **Table Inspector** allows you to adjust table rows, columns, alignment, background, and borders.

◆ **Chart Inspector** lets you change chart types and presentation formats.

◆ **Media Inspector** gives you control over dynamic media, such as QuickTime & Flash movies, animated GIFs, and music.

✔ Tips

■ You're not limited to just one Inspector window; you can have multiple Inspector windows on the screen by choosing View > New Inspector. If you have the screen real estate, it's a good way to keep all the tools that you want near at hand.

■ You'll see how to use each of the above Inspectors as you work through the book.

The Colors window

Like the Inspector window, the Colors window (**Figure 1.15**) has several modes; it gives you five different ways to choose colors: Color Wheel, Color Sliders, Color Palettes, Image Palettes, and Crayons.

The Fonts window

The Fonts window allows you to choose the font family, the typeface, and the size for any selected type (**Figure 1.16**).

✔ Tip

■ Be sure to check out the Extras pop-up menu at the bottom of the Fonts window. It allows you to show a preview area so you can see fonts before you apply them to your own text. It lets you change the way that you display font sizes. It even lets you set some fonts as favorites so that you don't always have to scroll through the dozens of fonts included with Mac OS X. See Chapter 4 for more information about using the Fonts window.

Figure 1.15 Keynote gives you five different ways to choose colors. Here are the Color Wheel and Crayons choices.

Figure 1.16 The Fonts window can show you a preview of your font selection.

Customizing the Toolbar

Like many other Mac OS X applications, Keynote allows you to customize its toolbar, which lets you put the tools you use often within easy reach.

To customize the Toolbar:

1. With a Keynote document open, choose View > Customize Toolbar.

   The Customize Toolbar sheet slides down from the Toolbar (**Figure 1.17**).

2. Drag the item or items that you want from the Customize Toolbar sheet into the Toolbar.

   or

   Drag items off the Toolbar and release the mouse button; the item will disappear in a puff of animated smoke.

   or

   Drag the default tool set into the Toolbar.

   or

   Use the Show pop-up menu to choose between showing icons and text in the Toolbar, just icons, or just text.

   or

   Click the Use Small Icons check box to make the toolbar icons take up less space.

3. Click Done.

Figure 1.17 Use the Customize Toolbar sheet to arrange your Toolbar as you like it.

Using Rulers and Guides

When you are placing text and graphics on slides, you'll often want to make sure that objects on slides are aligned to each other, or to the boundaries of the slide. Similarly, you might want to make sure that objects are a particular size, especially if you have the objects on more than one slide. This helps you create a consistent-looking presentation. Keynote gives you on-screen rulers and "smart" alignment guides to help you get the job done.

Rulers

The horizontal and vertical rulers can be shown or hidden, and are customizable. You can change their measurement units and adjust the zero point (or *origin*) of the ruler from the left or top end of the rulers to the center.

You can also set tabs and indents using rulers. See "Setting Text and Bullet Tabs" in Chapter 4 for more information.

To turn on rulers:

1. Choose View > Show Rulers, or press ⌘R.
   The rulers appear.

2. To hide the rulers, choose View > Hide Rulers, or press ⌘R.

To adjust ruler properties:

1. Choose Keynote > Preferences.
   The Preferences window appears (**Figure 1.18**).

2. In the Ruler Units section, choose the units that you wish to use from the pop-up menu.

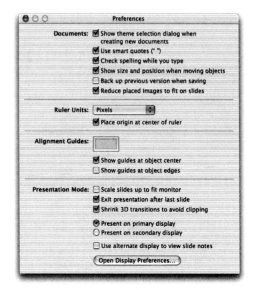

Figure 1.18 The Keynote Preferences window.

Text box boundary   Position tag

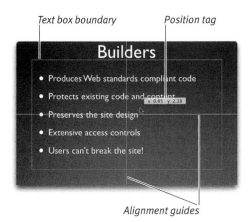

Alignment guides

Figure 1.19 Alignment guides and position tags appear as you move objects around on the Slide Canvas.

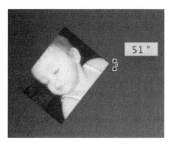

Figure 1.20 The angle tag appears when you free rotate a graphic.

Figure 1.21 When you resize a graphic, the size tag appears.

3. If you prefer, click "Place origin at center of ruler."

4. Close the Preferences window to save your changes.

Alignment guides

Keynote's yellow alignment guides appear when you need them; you'll notice them appearing and disappearing as you move objects around the Slide Canvas (**Figure 1.19**). The guides are part of the master slides for your presentation, and they help you center and align objects on the canvas. The guides appear whenever the center or edge of an object aligns with the center or edge of another object, or with the center of the Slide Canvas.

You'll also see *position tags* that appear along with the guides. These tags display the X and Y coordinates of the top-left corner of each object as you move it around the Slide Canvas.

The position tag changes into an *angle tag* when you free rotate a graphic object. You can do that by selecting the object, holding down the Command key, and moving one of the object's handles (**Figure 1.20**).

Similarly, the position tag changes into a *size tag* when you resize a graphic (**Figure 1.21**).

You can also set up your own alignment guides that remain on a slide. See "Using Rulers and Alignment Guides" in Chapter 5 for more information.

You can change the appearance and behavior of the alignment guides in Keynote's Preferences.

USING RULERS AND GUIDES

To set alignment guides preferences:

1. Choose Keynote > Preferences.

   The Preferences window appears.

2. In the Alignment Guides section, click the color swatch to change the color of the alignment guides. The Colors window will appear. Make your choice and close the window.

   or

   Click either (or both) "Show guides at object center" or "Show guides at object edges."

3. Close the Preferences window to save your changes.

✔ Tips

■ If you checked "Place origin at center of ruler" in the Ruler Units section of the Preferences, the position tags will also use that center as the origin.

■ You can turn position and size tags off if you like. Check out the Documents section in Keynote's Preferences.

Getting On-Screen Help

Besides the Keynote User Guide and Keynote
Quick Reference Guide that come on the
program's CD-ROM, Keynote also has on-
screen Help files that use the Mac OS X Help
Viewer application. You'll find a general Help
file and a list of keyboard shortcuts.

To get help with Keynote:

1. Choose Help > Keynote Help, or
   press ⌘?.
   The Help Viewer launches, and the
   Keynote Help file appears.

2. Click the topic you want, or enter search
   text in the Ask a Question field, then
   press Return.

To get a list of Keynote keyboard shortcuts:

◆ Choose Help > Keynote Keyboard
   Shortcuts.
   The Keynote Keyboard Shortcuts
   file appears.

✔ Tip

■ You can print any page of Keynote's
   Help files by choosing File > Print in
   Help Viewer, including the Keynote
   Keyboard Shortcuts.

GETTING ON-SCREEN HELP

CREATING A
PRESENTATION

A Keynote file includes all of the items that make up your presentation, including text, images, and dynamic media such as QuickTime movies and Flash animations. It also includes the set of *master slides* for the presentation. Master slides are templates for slides that you can use throughout your presentation. Master slides contain slide backgrounds and boxes for text and graphics that you'll fill in with your show's content. Master slides help your presentation look more polished and consistent.

You'll use each different sort of master slide for a particular purpose in your show. For example, a common master slide type for the beginning of a presentation is Title & Subtitle, which gives you a large line of type for the presentation's title, centered horizontally and vertically on the slide. Underneath is a smaller line of type for a subtitle, if you want one. A group of master slides makes up a *theme*, which is the basic building block of a Keynote presentation.

In this chapter, you'll see how to choose a theme for your presentation; add and organize slides; and find the best ways to write a successful presentation.

Choosing a Theme

All Keynote presentations begin with a theme. A theme provides a set of master slides and a graphic look for a presentation. Think of a theme as a template from which you can build your presentation.

When you first create a Keynote document, you must choose a theme.

To choose a presentation theme:

1. Launch Keynote.

   or

   If you're already in Keynote, choose File > New, or press ⌘Ⓝ.

   A new window appears, and a sheet that allows you to choose a theme for your presentation slides down from the top of the window (**Figure 2.1**).

2. Click to select one of the available themes from the scrolling area of the sheet.

   Apple provides twelve themes with Keynote, but you can easily download and install additional themes.

3. From the Presentation Size pop-up menu, choose the size that you want your slides to be.

   Keynote presentations come in one of two sizes: 1024 × 768 or the smaller 800 × 600 pixels. You can decide which size to use based on the output device you'll be using for your presentation. In some cases, such as presentations for small groups, you'll be using a monitor to show your presentation, so you can use the larger size. If you'll be using a video projector, you should check to see which display resolutions the projector supports. Most newer projectors can show 1024 × 768, but older projectors will be limited to 800 × 600. If you're not sure what the

Figure 2.1 Choose the theme for your new presentation from the Themes sheet.

Using Custom Themes

Keynote's built-in themes are pretty good, but they're hardly the last word in presentations. A small cottage industry of Keynote theme makers has sprung up in the months since Keynote's release. These folks have created many Keynote themes; some are free for downloading, and some are for sale.

After you obtain these custom themes (or create your own), you must put them in one of two places on your hard disk so that Keynote can display them in the "Choose a theme" sheet. You can put them in *harddisk*/Library/ Application Support/Keynote/Themes or in *home*/Library/Application Support/Keynote/Themes. Either location will work fine. If you use the first choice, the themes will be available to all users of your machine (assuming that you have multiple users enabled on your machine). The second choice makes the themes available only to your user account, which can be useful in some cases. For example, if you have multiple people using your Mac, each of whom is creating Keynote presentations, putting custom themes under the *home* directory allows each user to have their own set of custom themes.

You don't actually have to put a theme file in one of these locations to use it in Keynote. If you have a theme file elsewhere on your hard disk, you can simply double-click on it and work in the new file to create your presentation. This file will not appear in the "Choose a theme" sheet, however.

projector can handle, it's safer to use the smaller size. All of Keynote's built-in themes allow you to choose from either of the two sizes. Additional themes that you download or purchase may or may not have both sizes available.

4. Click Choose Theme.

Keynote takes a moment to build the theme, then creates the new document window, using the first slide master in the theme. This is almost always the Title & Subtitles slide master.

✔ Tips

- Keynote's built-in themes will always appear first in the "Choose a theme" sheet. Any themes that you add will show up in alphabetical order after the built-in themes. See the "Using Custom Themes" sidebar to learn where to put themes that you've created or downloaded so that Keynote can use them.

- Custom themes can come in sizes other than the two standard sizes. For example, you could have a theme that fits a wide-screen monitor, at 1440 × 900.

- See Appendix A for a list of sites where you can find Keynote themes for free download or purchase.

- If you don't want the theme sheet to automatically appear every time you create a new Keynote document, choose Keynote > Preferences, and uncheck "Show theme selection dialog when creating new documents."

CHOOSING A THEME

Adding Slides

Once you have created a presentation and applied a theme, you'll want to add additional slides. You need to first add the slide, then choose the master slide you want for that slide.

To add slides:

1. Click the New button on the toolbar (**Figure 2.2**).

   or

   Choose Slide > New Slide.

   or

   Press ⌘ Shift N.

   The slide appears below the currently selected slide in the Slide Navigator.

2. Choose the master slide for the new slide from the Masters pop-up menu in the toolbar (**Figure 2.3**).

   Subsequent slides that you create will continue to use the same master slide, until you change it.

3. Double-click in a text box placeholder to add text to the slide (**Figure 2.4**), or add graphics.

   See Chapter 4 for more about working with text on slides, and see Chapter 5 for details on working with graphics.

Figure 2.2 Create a new slide with the New button on the toolbar.

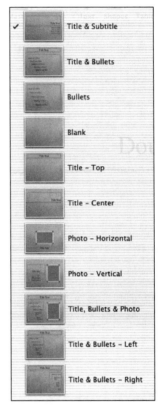

Figure 2.3 The Masters pop-up menu shows you all of the available master slides for the theme that you've selected.

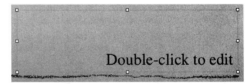

Figure 2.4 Enter text in the text box; the instructional text will disappear once you begin typing.

Deleting Slides

Deleting unwanted slides is easy; just select the slide and get rid of it.

To delete slides:

1. In the Slide Navigator, click to select the slide you want to delete.

2. Click the Delete button in the toolbar.
   or
   Choose Edit > Delete.
   or
   Press the Delete key.

✔ Tips

■ If you accidentally delete a slide, immediately choose Edit > Undo, or press ⌘Z.

■ Another way to roll back to an earlier version of your Keynote file is to choose File > Revert to Saved, which will restore the last saved version of your file.

■ If you delete the first slide in a group of slides (see "Grouping Slides" later in this chapter), all the slides indented below it will also be deleted. Be careful!

Changing Slide Navigator Views

The Slide Navigator allows you to view the slides in your presentation in three different views, *Navigator View*, *Outline View*, and *Slide Only View*.

Navigator View

This view shows the slides in your presentation as thumbnails (**Figure 2.5**). The currently selected slide is highlighted with a white background. Navigator View is good for getting an overall view of your presentation, and you can use it to move slides to different spots in your presentation, and also to group them (you'll find more about moving and grouping slides later in this chapter).

Outline View

The Outline View displays your presentation as text, with each slide displaying its bullet points as indented text (**Figure 2.6**). Any graphics on your slide do not appear in Outline View. Outline View is useful when you want to concentrate on the words in your presentation, without the distractions of the slide layout or graphics. In fact, I recommend that you create the main structure of your presentations in Outline View. You'll find more about that subject in the "Writing in the Outline" section later in this chapter.

Figure 2.5 The Slide Navigator View shows the slides in your presentation as thumbnails.

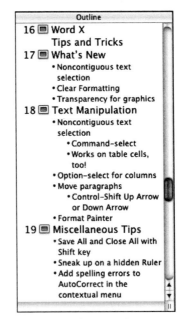

Figure 2.6 Outline View shows your slides as text, with indented bullet points.

Figure 2.7 The View pop-up menu in the toolbar allows you to change views.

Slide Only view

This view hides the Slide Navigator, displaying only the slide area (and the notes field, if that is turned on). Use this view when you want to concentrate on tweaking the appearance of a slide.

To change views:

◆ Select your choice of views from the View pop-up menu in the toolbar (**Figure 2.7**).

or

Choose View > Navigator, View > Outline, or View > Slide Only.

✔ Tip

■ You can move from one slide to the next in the Navigator and Outline Views by using the up arrow and down arrow keys. If you hold down the Shift key while using the arrow keys, you will select multiple slides.

CHANGING SLIDE NAVIGATOR VIEWS

Writing in the Outline

Every good presentation begins with a good outline, and Keynote's Outline View is the best and easiest way for you to make better presentations. Using the Outline View helps you keep the presentation logical and structured, because you can easily see the content of slides throughout your presentation. The benefit of working in Outline View is that it lets you create and edit the content of your presentation without focusing on the presentation's appearance, as always seems to happen when you add text directly on the slide. And after all, isn't the content of your presentation its most important aspect?

Another benefit of writing your presentation in the outline is that it is considerably faster than entering text directly on the slides. You can type your text entry in the outline without using the mouse, and any time that you can rely on the keyboard, work tends to get done quicker.

Consider sharing your outline with coworkers, and make changes based on their feedback. When the words are right, that's the time to spice them up with visuals. But first, get the words right.

Figure 2.8 Pressing the Tab key in the outline indents text and turns it into bulleted text.

To write your presentation in the outline:

1. If necessary, create a new Keynote document, and choose a theme.

2. Choose View > Outline.

3. Ignore the slide's entreaty to "Double-click to edit" and enter your text in the outline.

4. If you're working on a master slide that has a subtitle or bulleted text, press Return between lines and press Tab to indent the text (**Figure 2.8**).

5. When you're done with a set of bulleted text, press Return, then click New on the toolbar.

or

Choose Slide > New Slide.

6. Continue creating slides in this fashion until you are done.

✔ Tips

■ You can't style text in the outline. If you want to make text bold or italic, or make other style changes, you must do it on the slide. This appears to be a bug in Keynote; if you select text in the outline and choose Bold or Italic from Format > Font, or use the keyboard equivalents, the menu choices are checked as if the styles are applied, but the text in the outline doesn't change, and neither does the slide's text.

■ When you're working in the Outline View, use the size handle at the bottom of the scroll bar on the right side of the outline pane to make the Outline View as wide as possible. I often make the outline so wide that it crowds out the slide; I don't mind because I want to concentrate on the text, and not be distracted by the styled text and graphics on the slide.

WRITING IN THE OUTLINE

It's All About the Words

The most important part of your presentation is your message. All of Keynote's beautiful themes, slick graphics, and fancy transitions won't save your presentation if you don't have anything compelling to say. The presentation is *you*, not your visual aids.

Think of it this way: when you give a presentation, you're telling your audience a story. You know about stories; you've seen and heard thousands of them over the years, from movies, television, and real life. So you already know the most important thing about stories: they have to be interesting. If your story isn't, you'll lose your audience. And good stories begin with good, clear writing.

A good story has a conflict between characters or situations. In the course of the story, the conflict is resolved and the story ends. Good presentations hook audiences with a problem, then shows the audience how to deal with the problem. When the problem is resolved, the presentation is done.

Outlines are terrific for building stories. I know that you were probably turned off to outlines in some high school English class, but hear me out. Outlines make it easy to see the "bones" of your story. You can see the overall structure of the presentation, and easily see how each slide builds to your conclusion. In an outline, it's a snap to move points around if you see they could be in a better place.

Here's one good way to write (and give) your presentation:

- **Begin at the end**. Odd though it sounds, the first thing that you should write is your conclusion. Why? Because it's lots easier to take a journey when you know where you're going. That works when you're writing the presentation, and also when you're giving the talk; when you begin with your key message, the audience knows where you're going. This is where you lay out the problem that the rest of your story resolves.

- **Give the background**. You need to give your audience the reasons that your key message is true. So this is where you add the history, research, and other information that lays the groundwork for your story.

- **Make your argument**. Describe how your product or proposed action solves the problem. Share research that bolsters your points. Give examples, and quote sources. Tell stories that show your knowledge of the topic. Convince your audience of the power of your argument. At the end of this portion, give a quick summary, which leads you naturally to...

- **Finish where you started**. Repeat your main point. Then wrap it up and sit down; you've done the job.

One of the most common mistakes people make when writing and giving a presentation is to put the whole presentation on the slides, and then just read the slides aloud. All you're doing is turning the presentation into your speaker's notes, and it tends to put an audience right to sleep. Instead, use your slides to underscore what you're saying.

Spend the bulk of your time in the writing of your presentation, making sure that the message is strong and that what you're saying tells a compelling story. Then, and only then, you can start working on the look of your presentation.

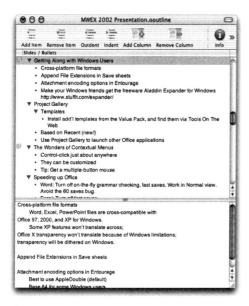

Figure 2.9 OmniOutliner's outline format, with its topics and subtopics, maps well to Keynote's titles and bulleted text. The contents of the Notes field at the bottom of the OmniOutliner window become speaker notes in Keynote.

Using OmniOutliner

Keynote's Outline View is adequate for many slide shows, but when you have a large presentation, it's a good idea to turn to a program that's designed to handle big outlines. The Omni Group's OmniOutliner is perfect for the task (**Figure 2.9**). It's got all the power you need to write an outline that you can move to Keynote to turn into a great presentation. The program's topics and subtopics correspond to slide titles and bullet points, and OmniOutliner has a Notes pane that translates neatly into Keynote's speaker notes.

The benefit of using OmniOutliner, however, is that it has many features for organizing ideas that Keynote's outliner lacks. For example, OmniOutliner allows you to sort topics, and lets you move topics around with more freedom than Keynote allows.

Beginning with version 2.2, OmniOutliner can import Keynote files to create outlines, and export its outlines as Keynote presentations.

Best of all, if you've bought a Mac recently, you may already have OmniOutliner. It has been bundled with the G4 tower machines and PowerBooks for some time. If you have the 2.0 version or later, you can download the free updater that gives OmniOutliner Keynote compatibility from www.omnigroup.com. If you don't have the program, you can download a free trial, and purchase it online for $29.95.

It's beyond the scope of this chapter to show how to create and work with outlines in OmniOutliner, but I'll show you how to get information back and forth between the program and Keynote.

Exporting outlines to Keynote

After you've created an outline in OmniOutliner, you'll need to check one setting before you export. By default, OmniOutliner exports to the 1024 × 768 version of Keynote's built-in Blackboard theme. If that's not the theme you want, you can change it in OmniOutliner's preferences. If you're happy with using the Blackboard theme, or if you'll just change the theme once you get the outline into Keynote, start with step 7, below.

To export an outline to Keynote:

1. In OmniOutliner, open the outline you wish to export.

2. Choose OmniOutliner > Preferences.
   The Preferences window appears (**Figure 2.10**).

3. Click the Keynote Export icon in the toolbar.

4. To change the theme that OmniOutliner will use for its export, choose from the Keynote Theme pop-up menu.

5. Choose the presentation size and the master slides you want to use from the pop-up menus.

6. Close the Preferences window.

7. Choose File > Export.
   The Export sheet appears (**Figure 2.11**).

8. From the File Format pop-up menu, make sure that Apple Keynote is selected.

9. Navigate to where you want to save the new Keynote presentation, then click Save.
   OmniOutliner exports the file.

Figure 2.10 Set the theme that you want for the new Keynote presentation in OmniOutliner's preferences.

Figure 2.11 Navigate to where you want to put the exported outline.

Importing Keynote presentations

It's a snap to import Keynote presentations into OmniOutliner. Since OmniOutliner understands how to read Keynote files, you just open the presentation in OmniOutliner.

To import a presentation:

1. In OmniOutliner, choose File > Open.

2. Navigate to the Keynote file you want to import.

3. Click Open.

   The Keynote file is imported, and opens as an outline.

✔ Tip

- With the current version of OmniOutliner (2.2.1 at press time), you can't go back and forth between Keynote and OmniOutliner. If you do, you will lose all the styles that you have applied in Keynote. It's best to use OmniOutliner to write the text of your presentation, and once you've exported it to Keynote, make further changes in Keynote.

Adding Speaker Notes

Speaker notes help guide you while you're giving the presentation. You can also print notes along with your slides, for use as audience handouts. Keynote's Notes field is completely free form, so you can enter text as you wish. The Notes field is just for text; you can't add graphics or charts to notes.

To add speaker notes:

1. Choose View > Show Notes.

   or

   Choose Show Notes from the View pop-up menu in the toolbar.

   The Notes field appears (**Figure 2.12**).

2. In the Slide Navigator, select the slide to which you want to add notes.

3. Enter your notes in the Notes field.

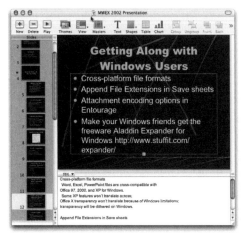

Figure 2.12 Speaker notes won't show on-screen during the presentation.

Figure 2.13 Once you've indented a slide, the slide above it shows a disclosure triangle, allowing you to hide or show the indented slides.

Grouping Slides

When you're in the Navigation View, Keynote allows you to organize your presentation by indenting related slides. Indenting slides in the Slide Navigator doesn't change the final presentation. It's a tool that helps you organize large sets of slides.

Once you have grouped related slides together, you can show or hide groups to make it easier for you to work with and organize the presentation.

To group slides:

1. Make sure that you are in Navigator View by choosing View > Navigator.

2. Select a slide that you wish to indent.

3. Press Tab.

   or

   Drag the slide to the right.

   The slide is indented, and a disclosure triangle appears next to the slide above the indented slide (**Figure 2.13**).

4. Repeat as necessary until you have indented all the slides that you want.

To hide and show slide groups:

◆ Double-click on the first slide in the group (the one that has the disclosure triangle) to hide a group of slides, as shown in **Figure 2.14**. Double-click the slide again to show the slides in the group.

✔ Tips

■ If you click next to a slide in the Slide Navigator, and then drag, you can select multiple slides. You can also select multiple slides by clicking on the first slide that you wish to select, holding down the Shift key, and clicking the last slide in the selection. And while you're at it, you can select discontiguous slides by selecting the first slide, holding down the Command key, and then selecting subsequent slides.

■ When multiple slides are selected, pressing the Tab key indents all the slides at once.

■ You can outdent slides (i.e., move slides to the left) by selecting the slides in the Slide Navigator and pressing (Shift)(Tab). Of course, you can also select a slide and drag it to the left.

Figure 2.14 You can see by the slide numbers that many slides are hidden here (slides 5 through 15, in fact).

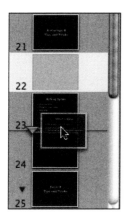

Figure 2.15 The blue line with the triangle shows you where slides that you move will end up.

Changing the Slide Order

The Slide Navigator also allows you to rearrange the slides in your presentation, by dragging the slide's thumbnail up or down in the Slide Navigator.

To rearrange slides:

1. Select the slide that you wish to move.

2. Drag it up or down in the Slide Navigator. A blue line with a triangle appears, indicating where the slide will go when you release the mouse button (**Figure 2.15**).

To move slide groups:

◆ Select the first slide in the group and drag the group up or down in the Slide Navigator. A blue line with a triangle appears in the Slide Navigator to show where the slides will be placed.

Copying Slides

There are two ways to duplicate slides in Keynote. Why might you want to duplicate a slide? The most common reason is that you have added some custom elements to a slide—such as a graphic or a custom text box—that you want to appear on a few slides, but that isn't worth saving as a new master slide.

You can duplicate slides in either the Navigator or Outline View. The two methods are copying and pasting, or by dragging.

To copy and paste slides:

1. Select the slide that you want to copy.

2. Choose Edit > Copy.

   or

   Press ⌘C.

   or

   Control-click on the slide (or if you have a multiple-button mouse, right-click) to bring up the contextual menu, then choose Copy.

3. Select the slide where you want to move the copied slide.

4. Choose Edit > Paste, or press ⌘V, or Control-click and choose Paste from the contextual menu.

   The new slide appears after the slide that you selected in step 3. You can now add text or graphics to the new slide.

To duplicate slides by dragging:

1. Select the slide that you want to copy.

2. Hold down the Option key, click on the slide, and drag the slide to another location in the navigator or Outline Views.

   A blue line will appear to show you where the slide will end up.

3. Release the mouse button.

   The new slide appears in the list.

✔ **Tip**

■ You can also cut slides, rather than copy them, to move slides around in your presentation.

Previewing the Presentation

When you're done writing your presentation, it's often useful to run it through as a slideshow once or twice. This helps you get a feel for the flow of the presentation and almost always shows you places where the presentation could use tightening or better explanation.

After you run the slideshow, you can return to Outline View to tweak the text, or you can begin adding graphics, tables, and charts to your presentation.

To run your presentation:

1. In outline or navigation views, click to select the first slide in the presentation.

2. Click Play in the toolbar.

   or

   Choose View > Play Slideshow.

   or

   Press ⌘ Option P.

   The slideshow begins. Click the mouse button, or use the right arrow key to advance through your slides.

3. To end the slide show, press Esc, or ⌘ .

Mastering
Slide Masters

3

The entire look of your presentation is dependent on the master slides, which are part of the presentation's theme. Master slides are templates for each of the different kinds of slides in your presentation. Master slides define slide attributes such as the title and body text box layouts and default font styles; the slide background; the default bullet styles; styles for charts and tables; and the type of slide transitions.

When you create a new slide, Keynote copies one of the master slides, and the objects (text boxes, pictures, tables, or charts) from the master slide are placed on the new slide. Then all you need to do is put content into the text boxes or graphic boxes.

Most of the time you'll use master slides without modification, but Keynote allows you to customize master slides within your presentation, to account for your presentation's special needs.

In this chapter, you'll learn about the different master slide types, as well as how to apply master slides to your presentation's slides and change master slides.

Master Slide Types

Keynote themes can contain any number of master slides, but in most themes, you'll find at least eleven master slides, because that's how many master slides are included in the twelve built-in Keynote themes. Themes aren't required to have eleven master slides; the lower limit is just one master slide, and I've seen themes that had 32 master slides from which to choose.

Most of the themes that you'll be working with will, however, contain the basic set of eleven master slides, as shown in **Table 3.1**. This set contains the master slides that you will use most often, so you should become familiar with them.

Table 3.1

Master Slide Types		
TYPE	ICON	DESCRIPTION
Title & Subtitle		Often the first slide in the presentation.
Title & Bullets		Includes two text boxes. Top text box uses large type to serve as the slide title; bottom text box uses smaller, bulleted text for body material.
Bullets		Includes one text box with bulleted text for body material. Usually contains up to five levels of bulleted indentation.
Blank		Contains only the slide background. Use this for really large or complex graphics.
Title – Top		Alternate title slide. Includes one text box with large type, justified to the top of the slide.
Title – Center		Alternate title slide. Includes one text box with large type, centered on the slide.
Photo – Horizontal		Contains one large photo cutout, oriented horizontally, with a large text box below to serve as a photo title.
Photo – Vertical		Contains one large photo cutout, oriented vertically, with a large text box to the left to serve as a photo title, and a second text box for bulleted text. Good for photos that need captions.
Title, Bullets & Photo		Contains a title box at the top of the slide, a text box for bulleted text below and to the left, and a photo cutout below and to the right.
Title & Bullets – Left		Same as Title, Bullets & Photo, but without the photo cutout. You should place graphics in the blank area.
Title & Bullets – Right		Same as Title & Bullets – Left, except body text box and blank area are reversed. Place graphics in the blank area.

Figure 3.1 The Master Slides Organizer allows you to work with the master slides.

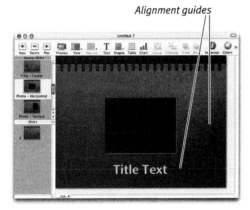

Alignment guides

Figure 3.2 Selecting a master slide in the Master Slides Organizer allows you to edit the master slide. This particular master slide has alignment guides showing the centers of the photo cutout and Title text box.

Viewing Master Slides

You can see the master slides contained within the theme you are using for your presentation in the Master Slides Organizer, which is a pane in the Slide Navigator.

To view master slides:

1. Open or create a Keynote document.

2. Choose View > Show Master Slides.

   or

   From the View pop-up menu in the Toolbar, choose Show Master Slides.

   or

   At the top of the scroll bar separating the Slide Navigator from the slide area, there is a handle that can be dragged up-and-down. Drag the handle down to expose the Master Slides Organizer (**Figure 3.1**).

3. Click on a master slide in the Master Slides Organizer to display the master slide in the slide area (**Figure 3.2**).

   With the master slide displayed, you can then edit the master slide's layout. Changes that you make to a master slide layout will be applied to all slides that use that layout. You'll find more about changing master slide layouts in the "Modifying Slide Layouts" section later in this chapter, and in Chapter 13, " Creating Custom Master Slides."

VIEWING MASTER SLIDES

Applying Master Slides

Every slide that you create in your presentation must have an associated master slide. When you first create a presentation, Keynote creates an initial slide based on the first master slide in the theme file. The slide is usually a Title slide of some sort.

When you create a second slide in your presentation, Keynote automatically switches the slide master to the second master slide in the theme file. This is usually the Title & Bullets master. Subsequently, each new slide you create takes on the master slide layout of the slide that was selected when you choose Slide > New Slide, or click the New button in the Toolbar. You can change the master slide associated with any slide in your presentation.

To apply a master to a slide:

1. In the Slide Navigator, select the slide for which you want to change its master slide.

2. From the Masters pop-up menu in the Toolbar, choose the new master slide (**Figure 3.3**).

   The slide changes to reflect the defaults associated with the new master slide.

✔ Tip

■ If you have already entered text or graphics on the slide, you might need to adjust them a bit to fit in the new format imposed by the new master slide.

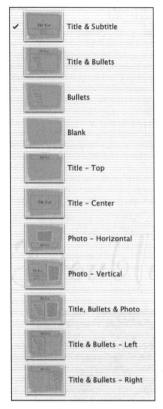

Figure 3.3 Apply a new master slide with the Masters pop-up menu in the toolbar.

APPLYING MASTER SLIDES

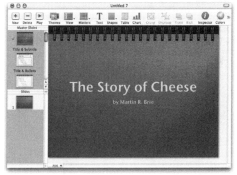

Figure 3.4 A bit of overzealous experimentation led to an overwrought slide (top). Reapplying the master slide resulted in a more dignified presentation (bottom).

Reapplying master slides

Sometimes you'll modify a slide, for instance by moving a graphic or text box, and then decide that your changes aren't quite what you want. Keynote allows you to reapply the format from the master slide to your current slide. When you do this, objects on your slide that you moved will return to their positions as defined in the master slide. Similarly, if you changed the text style or other attributes of the text boxes on the slide, they will return to their defaults from the master slide.

To reapply a master slide:

1. In the Slide Navigator, select the slide to which you wish to reapply the master slide styles.

2. Choose Format > Reapply Master to Slide. The slide and all its objects return to the master slide's formats (**Figure 3.4**).

✔ Tip

■ If any of the objects on the slide are selected, the menu choice in step 2 will read "Reapply Master to Selection." This is very useful when you want to reapply the master styles to just one part of the slide, without affecting any other changed elements.

APPLYING MASTER SLIDES

Modifying Master Slides

Most of the time, you'll probably be happy with the styles and layouts in the master slides from the theme that you are using. But each presentation is different, and sometimes you want to change one or more of the slide masters to better fit the content of your presentation. You'll do this by making changes to one or more of the master slides in your presentation.

It's important to understand that modifying a master slide changes it only for the presentation file you are currently working in; it doesn't modify the copy of the master slide that is in the theme file, and your changes also don't modify master slides of the same name in other themes. If you apply a new theme to your presentation, your customizations will be overwritten by the new theme, unless you select the "Retain changes to theme defaults" check box in the "Choose a theme" sheet (**Figure 3.5**).

You'll find much more information about modifying master slides in Chapter 13, "Creating Custom Master Slides."

To modify a master slide:

1. Choose View > Show Master Slides to display the Master Slides Organizer.

2. Click the Inspector button in the Toolbar to display the Inspector window.

3. Select the slide master that you wish to change.

   The Inspector window changes to the Master Slide Inspector (**Figure 3.6**).

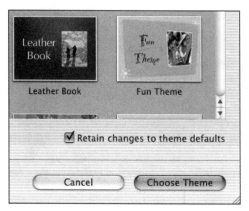

Figure 3.5 If you don't want your customizations to master slides to be wiped out when you change themes, make sure to select the "Retain changes to theme defaults" check box.

Figure 3.6 The Master Slide Inspector lets you hide or show the title, body, and slide number text boxes; change the background; set the slide transition (though that is usually done at the slide level, not the master slide level); and allow objects on the slide to layer with the master.

Number Those Slides!

You need to use the Master Slide Inspector to enable slide numbering in Keynote. In Keynote, all the slides are numbered sequentially from the first slide in the presentation to the last. When you select the "Show Slide #" check box in the Inspector, a number box appears on the slide master, and slides using that master will display the slide number (**Figure 3.7**). Note that you must turn slide numbering on for each master slide that you use in your presentation where you want the number to appear. You probably won't want slide numbering turned on for all master slides; for example, most presentations don't use slide numbers on the first slide.

You can change the font and style of the slide numbering text box, but you can't control the numbering format. So if you have that urge to use Roman numbers for your slide numbers, you'll have to place them in your slide manually.

Slide number

Figure 3.7 Once you turn on slide numbering in the Master Slide Inspector, the numbers appear on your slides.

4. Select elements on the master slide and modify them, or add new elements.

   See Chapter 4 for more information on modifying text boxes, and see Chapter 5 for more information on modifying graphics. If you want to change the slide background, see the next section in this chapter.

5. When you're done making changes to the master slide, select another master slide to modify, or click on one of the slides in the Slide Navigator to continue editing your presentation.

✔ Tips

- Keynote only allows you to have one Body text box per slide, which is the text box that has bulleted text. You can create other text boxes on your slides, but they can't contain bulleted text.

- Unfortunately, Keynote can't automatically display the date or time on your slides, as PowerPoint can. Keynote also lacks the ability to insert headers or footers throughout your presentation, another handy PowerPoint feature.

Changing Master Slide Backgrounds

The most common reason to change a master slide background is if you have a graphic or photo that doesn't work well with the theme's regular background. That's why, in fact, most themes have a Blank slide master, which you can use as an empty canvas for your content.

Another good reason to change a master slide's background is so that you can use that changed background for a group of related slides in your presentation. For example, let's say that you're doing a presentation about three different local sports teams, and you'll have several slides per team. For each team, you can use a different background, perhaps keyed to the team's colors. You could change the slide background for each individual slide, but that's more work than necessary. Just create a master slide with a different background for each team.

To change a master slide background:

1. Choose View > Show Master Slides to display the Master Slides Organizer.

2. Click the Inspector button in the Toolbar to display the Inspector window.

3. Select the master slide that you wish to change.

   The Inspector window changes to the Master Slide Inspector.

4. (Optional) If you want to work with a duplicate of the original master slide, rather than modify the original, choose Slide > New Master Slide.

   Keynote then duplicates the master slide, allowing you to modify the duplicate (**Figure 3.8**).

Figure 3.8 Rather than modifying one of your existing master slides, it's often more useful to duplicate the master slide, then make changes to the duplicate. Here, "Master #12" is the just-created duplicate.

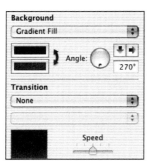

Figure 3.9 Use the Background section of the Master Slide Inspector to set your color, gradient, or image fill.

Layering with Master Slides

Objects in Keynote, whether they be text boxes or graphics, are layered. Each object has its own layer, and you can move each layer forward or backwards independently. So, for example, you can move a text box either in front of or behind a graphic, depending on the effect you are trying to produce.

Master slides can be set to either allow layering with objects in your presentation, or not, depending on whether the "Allow objects on slides to layer with master" option in the Layout section of the Master Slide Inspector is selected. If you want everything on your slide to sit on top of the master slide, turn this option off. Sometimes, you'll want this option on, though; that's how Keynote's photo cutout slides work. The cutout is a graphic with a transparent section. When you place a photo on the slide, then send it to the back, it goes behind the photo cutout layer, which frames the photo.

5. To change the background of the master slide, choose from the pop-up menu in the Background section of the Master Slide Inspector (**Figure 3.9**). You can choose between Color Fill (applies a solid color to the slide), Gradient Fill (applies a gradient pattern), Image Fill (uses a graphic image for the background), or None.

6. Add any other elements you wish to the background, including text, graphics, charts, or tables.

7. If desired, select the "Show Title," "Show Body," or "Show Slide #" checkboxes in the Master Slide Inspector.

✔ Tips

■ Once you have placed an element on the background, you can choose Arrange > Lock to keep it from accidentally being moved as you continue working.

■ You can rename a master slide by double-clicking its name in the Master Slides Organizer, then typing.

■ You can also layer a background, with, for example, a color or gradient fill in the back, overlaid with an image that doesn't take up the entire slide. See Chapter 5 for more information on using layers with graphics.

GETTING THE TYPE RIGHT

In Chapter 2, I strongly suggested that you write most of your presentation in either Keynote's Outline view, or in an external outline program, such as OmniOutliner. I'm not backing off from that advice; focusing on your presentation's text, rather than the text on your slides, will lead you to write better presentations.

But sooner or later, you will need to work with the text on your slides, and that's what this chapter is all about. For this chapter, at least, I'll assume that you'll be entering text directly onto slides.

Keynote showcases Mac OS X's superior text handling, layout, and display abilities (not surprising, since it is from Apple), and you've got a tremendous amount of control over the appearance and style of text within Keynote. Keynote's terrific text capabilities help set its presentations apart from presentations created in Microsoft PowerPoint.

In this chapter, you'll learn how to enter text on slides; style that text as you wish; change the alignment and spacing of text; work with indents and tabs on slides; save time when you're setting text styles; and avoid embarrassing spelling errors.

Adding Title and Body Text

The first slide in your presentation is almost always the title slide, which usually contains two pieces of information: the title of the presentation, and a subtitle, which is where you can put your name and company affiliation (**Figure 4.1**).

Figure 4.1 The Title slide starts off your presentation.

In Keynote, all text must be in *text boxes*. A text box defines the boundaries of the text. If you have more text than the text box can contain (which depends on the size of the text box and the size and style of the text within the box), text will be cut off, and Keynote will display a plus icon at the bottom of the text box to let you know that you are missing some text (**Figure 4.2**). Text automatically wraps inside text boxes.

Most of the time, you'll use the text boxes provided on the master slide that you have chosen for your slide, but you can also add your own text boxes to a particular slide, as discussed in the next section.

Figure 4.2
The plus icon at the bottom of the text box lets you know that you have cut off some text.

More text icon

To add title and body text:

1. Open a new presentation file, and apply a theme from the "Choose a theme" sheet.

   Keynote creates a new slide based on the first master slide in the theme file, which is usually (and is always in the built-in themes) the Title & Subtitle master slide. The new slide will contain placeholder text for its text boxes, which say, "Double-click to edit" as shown in **Figure 4.3**.

Figure 4.3 Text boxes in Keynote have placeholder text, until you add your own.

2. Double-click in the title box, which usually contains larger sized text than the subtitle.

An insertion point will begin blinking in the title box.

3. Type in your title.

4. When you're done entering the title, click outside of the title box to deselect it, or double-click in the subtitle box to begin entering your subtitle.

You'll know you're ready to enter text in the subtitle box when you see the insertion point blinking in that box.

5. Type in your subtitle.

6. Click outside of the subtitle box to deselect it.

✔ Tips

■ It's natural to want to press the Return or Enter keys when you're done entering text in a Keynote text box. But if you do that, Keynote will insert another line in the text box.

■ Keynote lacks a handy feature that you may have become used to in PowerPoint: Keynote doesn't automatically resize text and reduce line spacing in order to fit too-long text within text boxes. Instead, you'll have to manage the fit of your text within text boxes manually.

■ If you like, you can place a graphic on your title slide; there's no law saying that it just has to include text. See Chapter 5 for more information about placing graphics on slides.

ADDING TITLE AND BODY TEXT

Entering Bulleted Text

On most slides, you'll have *bulleted text*, which you've seen in most presentations to denote the individual talking points on a slide (**Figure 4.4**). Bulleted text is just that, text preceded by a marker called a bullet. In Keynote, a bullet can be either a text character or a graphic.

The bulleted text on a slide can have multiple levels, which denote sub-points or sub-topics. For example, you could have text on a slide such as this:

Contemporary Folk Music

    Artists

        Kaplansky, Lucy

        Peacock, Alice

        Shindell, Richard

Each level of text is subordinate to the level above. On a slide, just as in the text above, that subordination will be shown as indented text. There will be a bullet at each level, preceding the text. In some themes, you'll see different bullets for each indented level (**Figure 4.5**).

When you enter text in a bulleted text box, Keynote automatically inserts the bullets whenever you begin a new line by pressing Return. Pressing Tab at the beginning of a new line indents that line one level.

Keynote allows one bulleted text box per slide (this is a limitation of Keynote compared to PowerPoint, which allows multiple bulleted text boxes on a slide). You can manually insert other text boxes, and they can even contain bulleted text, but only one text box per slide can have automatic bullets.

Figure 4.4 You'll use bulleted text to make your points.

Figure 4.5 Some themes use different colors or shapes of bullets for each bullet level.

To enter bulleted text:

1. Create a slide with a slide master containing a bulleted text box.

   Typical slide masters include Title & Bullets, Bullets, and Title, Bullets & Photo.

2. In the text box with the "Double-click to enter" placeholder, double click to place the insertion point.

3. Enter your text.

   If your entry is too large for the text box, it will wrap within the text box, with the default left text alignment (see **Figure 4.2**).

4. Press Return to begin a new line.

   Keynote automatically inserts a new bullet at the beginning of the line.

5. (Optional) To indent text one level, press Tab before you begin typing on a new line.

✔ Tips

■ Press (Shift)(Tab) with the insertion point placed anywhere in a line of text to remove one level of indenting.

■ You can't indent the first bullet in the list.

ENTERING BULLETED TEXT

Adding Text Boxes

Besides the bulleted text boxes found on many master slides, you can also add your own text boxes to slides. These "free" text boxes can be used wherever you need extra text on a slide. For example, you can use a free text box as a picture caption (**Figure 4.6**).

To add a free text box:

1. On the slide where you want to add the text box, click the Text button on the toolbar.

   or

   Choose Edit > Place > Text.

   The text box appears in the middle of the slide, with the placeholder text "Text" (**Figure 4.7**).

2. Drag the text box to where you want to position it on the slide.

   As you drag the text box, Keynote will show you alignment guides (shown as yellow lines on the slide) to help you line the text up easily.

3. Double-click in the text box to get an insertion point, then enter your text.

✔ Tips

- Free text boxes only have two selection handles, at the right and left edges of the box. Free text boxes automatically grow or shrink vertically to handle the length of your text. They can't be made taller by dragging.

- If you don't see the alignment guides as you move objects on the slide, they are probably turned off in the Keynote Preferences.

Figure 4.6 You can use free text boxes as picture captions, among other things.

Figure 4.7 The new text box (with the placeholder text "Text") appears in the center of the slide.

Figure 4.8 The text behind the snowboarder was created, rotated, then sent behind the snowboarder and behind the picture cutout for added effect.

Figure 4.9 This text box was brought in front of the graphic on this slide.

Layering Text

Once text has been created in text boxes on a slide, the text box can be treated, in many ways, as if it were a graphic object. You can move text boxes around and rotate them, apply drop shadows and graphic fills, and change the opacity of the text. For more about those topics, see Chapter 5, and remember that the same tools can be applied equally to graphics and text boxes.

There's another useful text manipulation you can do, and that is to layer text boxes with the other elements on the slide. Imagine that each element—text, graphics, movies, shapes, etc.—on the slide is in its own layer on the slide, with the master slide making up the layer that's in the back. You can move each element forward or back in the stack. It's possible to get some interesting results by layering, as shown in **Figure 4.8**.

To layer text boxes:

1. Create the text boxes on the slide that you want to layer.

   These boxes can include the Title and Body text boxes.

2. Select a text box.

3. To move the text box backward in the layer order, click the Back button in the toolbar.

   or

   To move the text box forward in the layer order, click the Forward button in the toolbar.

   The selected item moves as you command (**Figure 4.9**).

Changing and Styling Fonts

Keynote does a great job of showing off the excellent font capabilities in Mac OS X. The operating system comes with a wide selection of razor-sharp fonts, and Keynote lets you display them to best effect. You can scale text with no loss of quality, so your presentations will remain readable (unless you make the text too small for people in the back row!).

The main tool you'll use to work with fonts is the Fonts window. The one in Keynote is the standard used by many of Apple's other programs, such as iChat and Mail. But because great-looking text is so vital to a good presentation, I'll be discussing the Fonts window in depth. Chances are you'll learn that it can do things you never knew.

Working with the Fonts window

At first glance, the Fonts window doesn't look very impressive. It's just a basic window that allows you to select the font family, the typeface, and the size of the text. But you can expand and customize it to make it considerably more useful.

The Fonts window's basic view (**Figure 4.10**) allows you to choose the *font family* (the name of the font, such as Arial or Palatino), *typeface* (the style of the font, such as Regular or Italic), and font size. In the expanded view (**Figure 4.11**), you can see there's a preview area and a column for *font collections*, which allows you to group fonts into useful categories, and even set fonts as favorites, so you can store and retrieve frequently used font settings. There's also a new way to select font sizes.

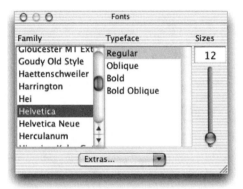

Figure 4.10 The Fonts window first shows up with basic font tools.

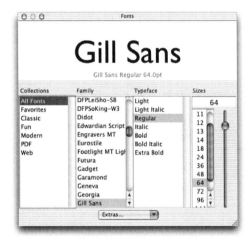

Figure 4.11 The expanded view lets you preview your type, and gives you more options for changing font sizes.

Figure 4.12 If you're short on screen real estate, you can minimize the Fonts window to be much smaller.

Figure 4.13 When you drag the Fonts window wider, the Collections column appears.

To show the Fonts window:

◆ Click the Fonts button in the toolbar.
or
Press ⌘T.
or
Choose Format > Font > Show Fonts.
Do any of these actions again to hide the Fonts window, or use the window's close button.

✔ Tips

■ If you get an error message when you attempt to open the Fonts window, you probably have a corrupted font, most likely in your Classic System Folder (Mac OS X shares the Mac OS 9 fonts in that folder). Unfortunately, there's no built-in way in Mac OS X to check fonts for corruption. One way to track down the offending font is to take fonts out of the Fonts folder one at a time, relaunching Keynote between each font you remove to see if the problem goes away. This is a long and tedious process. You might consider downloading the demo version of Insider Software's FontAgentPro (www.insidersoftware.com), which is a comprehensive font manager that can also identify problem fonts.

■ If the Fonts window takes up a bit too much screen real estate for your liking, resize the window so that the window's controls become a series of pop-up menus (**Figure 4.12**).

To show font collections:

◆ Font collections are always available, but they're initially hidden with the default Fonts window. To show them, simply resize the Fonts window so that it is wider (**Figure 4.13**).

CHANGING AND STYLING FONTS

To edit font collections:

1. If necessary, open the Fonts window by clicking the Fonts button on the toolbar.

   Make sure the Collections column is showing. Resize the Fonts window if necessary.

2. From the Extras pop-up menu at the bottom of the Fonts window, choose Edit Collections.

   The Fonts window changes to show the Collections editing window (**Figure 4.14**).

   Click an item in the Collections column to see the font families in that collection.

3. To move a font family into a collection, select the collection you want, find the font family that you want to move into that collection in the All Families list, then click the left pointing arrows button to move the font family.

   or

   To remove a font family from a collection, select the collection, select the font family you want to remove in the Family column, then click the right pointing arrows button to move the font family.

4. (Optional) To add a new collection, click the plus button at the bottom of the window.

   A new collection (named New) will appear in the Collections column. Type a name for the new collection, then add or subtract font families by using the arrow buttons.

Figure 4.14 Add or subtract fonts from collections in the Collections editing window.

Figure 4.15 The Favorites collection shows you miniature previews of your favorite fonts in the Favorites column.

More about Collections

Font collections can be very useful when you're specifying the type for a presentation. Collections organize fonts into groups, and you can use those groups for different sorts of presentations, or for particular presentation needs. For example, let's say that you design presentations for several corporate clients. Each client has settled on a set of fonts for their presentations. You could create a collection for each client, with their selected font set. But mostly, collections will save you from having to scroll through the huge list of fonts that come with Mac OS X to find the fonts you use the most.

Collections are flexible; you can have the same fonts in as many collections as you need, and you can make as many collections as you need. Apple starts you out with six collections: All Fonts, Classic, Fun, Modern, PDF, and Web. You can add to Apple's font collections, or create your own.

5. (Optional) To remove a collection, select a collection's name, then click the minus button at the bottom of the window.

   Removing a collection doesn't remove the fonts in that collection from the Fonts window.

6. (Optional) To rename a collection, select a collection, then click the Rename button at the bottom of the window. The name of the collection will become highlighted; enter the new collection name.

7. When you've finished editing collections, click Done.

To set fonts as favorites:

1. Set the Family, Typeface and Size for a font.

2. From the Extras pop-up menu at the bottom of the Fonts window, choose Add to Favorites.

   The font is added to a new collection called Favorites (**Figure 4.15**). The Favorites collection will be created if it does not already exist. The Fonts window changes, replacing the Family and Typeface columns with a Favorites column.

To remove a favorite font:

1. In the Fonts window, click to select the Favorites collection.

2. Select the font you wish to remove.

3. From the Extras pop-up menu at the bottom of the Fonts window, choose Remove from Favorites.

CHANGING AND STYLING FONTS

To enable the preview area:

1. From the Extras pop-up menu at the bottom of the Fonts window, choose Show Preview.

   The preview area appears at the top of the Fonts window (**Figure 4.16**). It contains a large sample of the font you have selected, plus a smaller label for the font family's name and typeface.

2. If you position the mouse pointer at the bottom of the preview area, the cursor will turn into a double-headed arrow. Click and drag up or down to resize the preview area.

✔ Tip

■ The preview area is live, so you can click in it to set an insertion point, select the text and press delete to eliminate the font name that appears by default, then enter your own text to see what it looks like in the selected font. When you select different font families, typefaces, or sizes, the text you entered changes, too. When you're pleased with the look of your type, select it in the preview area, copy it, and paste it into a text box on your slide.

To enable font size controls:

1. From the Extras pop-up menu at the bottom of the Fonts window, choose Edit Sizes.

   The Fonts window changes to show the Sizes editing window.

2. Select one of the buttons under "Display Font Sizes as:" to get different combinations of font size controls (**Figure 4.17**).

3. Click Done.

Figure 4.16 You can view and test type in the Preview area of the Fonts window.

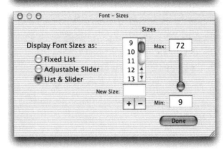

Figure 4.17 When you choose to edit sizes, you have three possibilities for displaying font sizes, shown top to bottom.

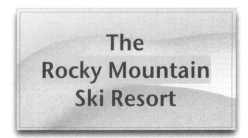

Figure 4.18 Only the selected text will change fonts.

Figure 4.19 The changed text.

Changing fonts

After you have mastered the Fonts window, actually changing fonts on your slides is easy. You can control fonts for an entire text box or for selected text within a text box.

To change fonts for a text box:

1. Click within a text box to select it.

   or

   If you only want to change some of the text within a text box, select the text first (**Figure 4.18**).

2. If it is not already opened, click the Fonts button in the toolbar to open the Fonts window.

3. Click the family and typeface that you want in the Fonts window.

   The slide text changes to reflect your choice (**Figure 4.19**).

Changing font sizes

Like changing fonts, changing font sizes is just a matter of selecting text boxes or text and making your choice from the Fonts window.

To change the size of type:

1. Click within a text box to select it.

   or

   If you only want to change some of the text within a text box, select the text first.

2. Use the size controls in the Fonts window to adjust the font size.

   Depending on the font controls that you have enabled, you can pick from the list of font sizes, use the slider to grow or shrink the font size dynamically, or type a font size in the Sizes field.

✔ **Tip**

■ Unfortunately, there's no keyboard command to change font sizes one point size at a time, as there is in PowerPoint. You must use the size controls in the Fonts window.

Setting, copying and pasting font styles

Many fonts have bold and italic versions, and you can apply these either in the Fonts window or using Keynote's Format menu. If a font does not show a bold or italic version in the Fonts window, the formatting commands in the Format menu will be dimmed. You can also underline text using the Format menu.

To set font styles:

1. In a text box, select the text that you want to make bold or italic.

2. Click on the style that you want in the Typeface column of the Fonts window.

   or

   Choose Format > Font > Bold, or press ⌘ B.

   or

   Choose Format > Font > Italic, or press ⌘ I.

   or

   Choose Format > Font > Underline, or press ⌘ U.

✔ Tip

- Some fonts use the term Oblique instead of Italic. There may be a difference to true font geeks, but for the purposes of your presentations you can treat them as identical.

Color well

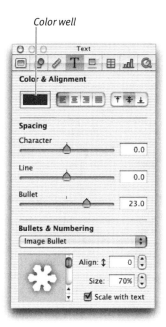

Figure 4.20 You'll use the Text Inspector to set many aspects of your text formatting.

Color well

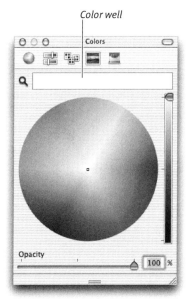

Figure 4.21 The Colors window allows you to set the color of type.

Modifying Text Color

You'll use both the Text Inspector and the Colors window to apply colors to text.

To change the color of text:

1. If necessary, open an Inspector window by clicking the Inspector button on the toolbar.

   The Inspector window appears.

2. Click the Text button in the Inspector window's toolbar.

   The window changes to the Text Inspector (**Figure 4.20**).

3. Select the text whose color you wish to change.

4. Click the color well in the Color & Alignment section of the Text Inspector.

   The Colors window appears (**Figure 4.21**).

5. Use the controls in the Colors window to select the color you want.

   The text will change color.

Changing Text Alignment

Keynote has two ways to control text alignment. You can set horizontal alignment in the four standard ways: Left, Center, Right, and Justified (**Figure 4.22**). You can also set vertical alignment, which controls where the text is placed (Top, Center, Bottom) within its text box (**Figure 4.23**). Once again, you'll use the Text Inspector to do the job.

Figure 4.22 Horizontal text alignment within a text box, showing (from top to bottom) Left, Center, Right, and Justified text alignments.

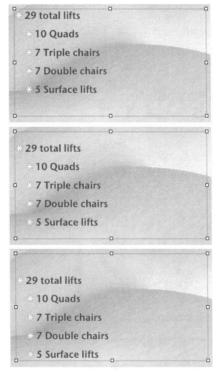

Figure 4.23 Vertical text alignment within a text box. From top to bottom: Top, Center, and Bottom alignments.

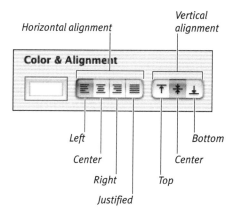

Horizontal alignment

Vertical alignment

Left

Center

Right

Justified

Bottom

Center

Top

Figure 4.24 Use the buttons in the Color & Alignment section of the Text Inspector to set horizontal and vertical alignment.

To set text alignment:

1. If necessary, open an Inspector window by clicking the Inspector button on the toolbar.

   The Inspector window appears.

2. Click the Text button in the Inspector window's toolbar.

   The window changes to the Text Inspector.

3. On your slide, select the text you wish to change alignment.

4. Use the appropriate alignment button in the Color & Alignment section of the Text Inspector (**Figure 4.24**).

   The text alignment changes.

✔ Tip

■ You can set horizontal spacing from the keyboard with the following keyboard equivalents:

   ◆ Left align: ⌘ [

   ◆ Center: ⌘ |

   ◆ Right align: ⌘ }

   There is no keyboard equivalent for Justify.

Adjusting Text Spacing

You have control over two attributes of the spacing of your text. *Character spacing* affects the amount of space that Keynote puts between the characters within a line. *Line spacing* is the amount of space between two or more lines of text.

A third adjustment, *bullet spacing*, is the spacing between bullet points on the slide. You can't set bullet spacing for a free text box.

To change character spacing:

1. Select the text that you wish to change.

2. In the Spacing section of the Text Inspector (**Figure 4.25**), move the Character slider, or type in a value in the field next to the slider.

   Moving the slider to the left decreases character spacing; moving it to the right increases the space between characters. The text changes (**Figure 4.26**).

To change line spacing:

1. Select the text that you wish to change.

2. In the Spacing section of the Text Inspector, move the Line slider, or type in a value in the field next to the slider.

   Moving the slider to the left decreases line spacing; moving it to the right increases the space between lines. The text changes (**Figure 4.27**).

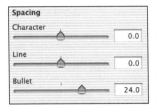

Figure 4.25 You'll use the Spacing section of the Text Inspector to set Character, Line, and Bullet spacing.

Figure 4.26 The effects of increasing character spacing.

Figure 4.27 This is what it looks like when you increase line spacing.

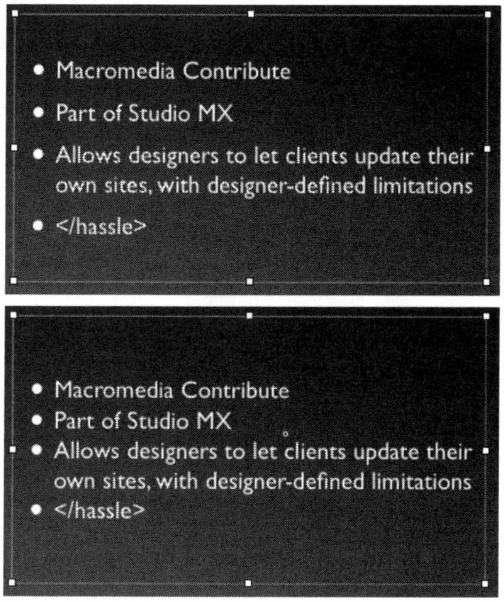

To change bullet spacing:

1. Select the text that you wish to change.

2. In the Spacing section of the Text Inspector, move the Bullet slider, or type in a value in the field next to the slider.

   Moving the slider to the left decreases bullet spacing; moving it to the right increases the space between bullets.

   The text changes (**Figure 4.28**).

✔ Tip

- Be aware of the differences when using line spacing and bullet spacing. You'll use line spacing most often when you want to move line spacing within a free text box. Bullet spacing is more often used when you want to compress the amount of vertical space a group of bullets takes up on the slide.

Figure 4.28 You can get more text on your slides by decreasing the Bullet spacing.

Copying and Pasting Font Styles

Another handy timesaving feature is Keynote's ability to copy and paste font styles, which includes most formatting that you have applied to text, including the font, font size, color, and character spacing, though not the line spacing or horizontal or vertical alignment. See **Table 4.1** for a list of which text attributes can and can't be copied.

To copy and paste font styles:

1. Select the text that has the formatting you want to copy.

2. Choose Format > Font > Copy Font, or press ⌘ Shift Option C.

3. Select the destination text.

4. Choose Format > Font > Paste Font, or press ⌘ Shift Option V.

Table 4.1

Text Attributes that can be Copied	
ATTRIBUTE	COPYABLE?
Font family	Yes
Font size	Yes
Font color	Yes
Bold, italic, underline	Yes
Character spacing	Yes
Line spacing	No
Horizontal alignment	No
Vertical alignment	No
Kerning	Yes
Baseline shift	Yes
Ligatures	Yes
Bullet or numbering style	No
Bullet spacing	No
Text shadows	No

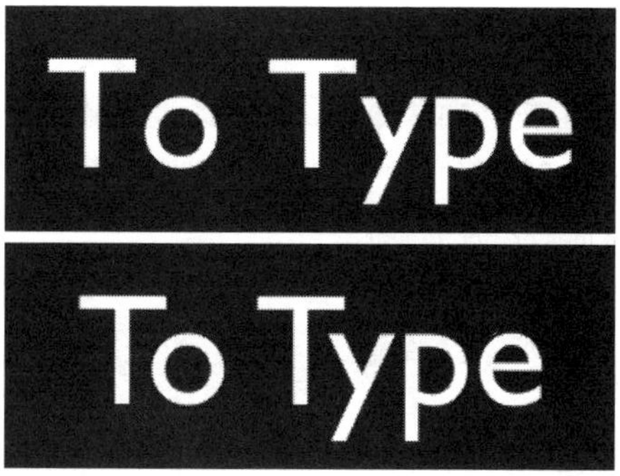

Figure 4.29 Text that is not kerned doesn't look as good as kerned text.

Kerning Text

Kerning is similar to character spacing, except that where character spacing controls the spacing between all the characters in a line (or a selection), kerning is concerned with making pairs of letters look good together. For example, certain pairs of letters appear to have gaps between them, because of their shape (**Figure 4.29**). Kerning these pairs of letters tightens up the space between the pair, making for a more pleasing look. If you really know your type, you can tighten or loosen kerning in Keynote to make precise changes.

Most of the time, the text in Keynote will be automatically kerned, and you can accept the default kerning. But if you want more control, you've got it.

To adjust text kerning:

1. Select the text you wish to kern.

2. Choose one of the following, depending on what you want to do:
   ◆ Format > Font > Kern > Use Default
   ◆ Format > Font > Kern > Use None
   ◆ Format > Font > Kern > Tighter
   ◆ Format > Font > Kern > Looser
   The text changes to match your adjustment.

Adjusting Text Baselines

The baseline of a font is the invisible line where characters rest. Some characters, such as the y and the g, have descenders that drop below the baseline (**Figure 4.30**).

You can adjust the baselines for individual letters, words or lines. Most of the time you'll want to shift the baseline of a single character, in order to make a superscript or a subscript.

To adjust a baseline for text:

1. Select the text that you want to change.

2. Choose one of the following, depending on what you want to do:
   ◆ Format > Font > Baseline > Use Default
   ◆ Format > Font > Baseline > Superscript
   ◆ Format > Font > Baseline > Subscript
   ◆ Format > Font > Baseline > Raise
   ◆ Format > Font > Baseline > Lower

   The text changes to match your adjustment (**Figure 4.31**).

✔ Tips

■ You'll see in **Figure 4.31** that Keynote doesn't create a true superscript or subscript when you do a baseline shift, because it doesn't automatically make the scripted characters smaller. You must do that as a separate, manual step (**Figure 4.32**).

■ Depending on the font you're using, once you shrink the scripted characters, you may have to use the superscript or subscript commands multiple times to get the characters where you want them.

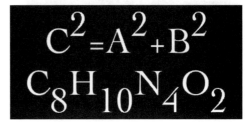

Figure 4.30 I've simulated the text baseline with one of Keynote's alignment guides. Normally, the text baselines do not appear.

$$C^2 = A^2 + B^2$$
$$C_8 H_{10} N_4 O_2$$

Figure 4.31 In the top line, the numbers are set to superscript, and in the bottom line, the numbers are set to subscript.

$$C^2 = A^2 + B^2$$
$$C_8 H_{10} N_4 O_2$$

Figure 4.32 When you manually change the superscript or subscript to a smaller font size, the effect is more pleasing. Time consuming, but more pleasing.

Using Equations in Keynote

If Keynote isn't especially helpful when creating superscripts and subscripts, its shortcomings in creating complex equations will make mathematicians, scientists, and engineers throw up their hands in horror. Keynote's built-in text tools just aren't made for specialized formatting of that complexity.

The solution is to use other applications to create an equation, save it as a graphic, then place the equation into your presentation. There are two candidates for equation creation that you should look at.

First, if you already own Microsoft Office v. X, there's the Microsoft Equation Editor. It's not part of the default installation of Office; you'll have to install it from the Value Pack on the Office CD. The Equation Editor does a decent job for light-duty equation wranglers. To use it, open Word, then choose Insert > Object, then choose Microsoft Equation from the resulting dialog. The Equation Editor will open, and you can type your equation into it, using the editor's tools to give it that equation-y goodness (**Figure 4.33**). Then select the equation, copy it to the Clipboard, and paste it into Keynote. You'll need to resize the graphic, but the result looks good (**Figure 4.34**). A similar equation editor comes with AppleWorks 6.

If you have hard-core equation needs, you'll want to turn to the LaTeX equation typesetting system. There are open source software implementations of LaTeX for Mac OS X, and there is also a program called Equation Service, which takes a snippet of LaTeX code and turns it into a PDF that you can then import into Keynote. You can find an excellent tutorial for using LaTeX and Equation Service with Keynote, written by David H. Clements, in the files section of the Keynote Users Group, at `http://groups.yahoo.com/group/applekeynote/files/`.

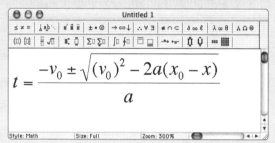

Figure 4.33 If you already own Microsoft Office v. X, the Microsoft Equation Editor is a handy way to get equations into Keynote.

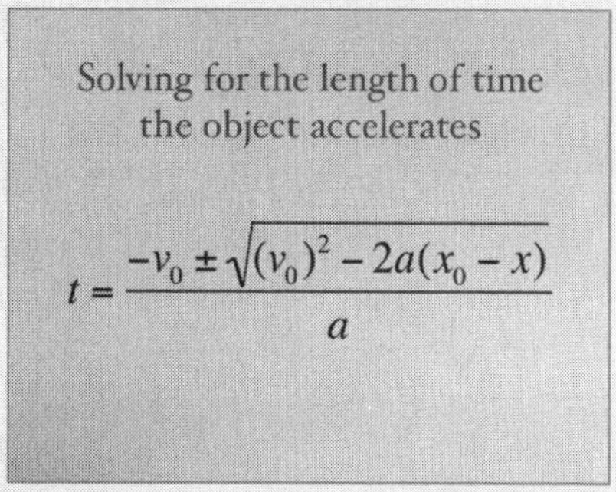

Solving for the length of time the object accelerates

$$t = \frac{-v_0 \pm \sqrt{(v_0)^2 - 2a(x_0 - x)}}{a}$$

Figure 4.34 This equation was created in the Microsoft Equation Editor, copied, and pasted into Keynote. After scaling the graphic up to a size where it will look good on a slide, the result is quite acceptable.

Setting Bullet and Number Styles

The bullets that appear at the beginning of lines of bulleted text can be customized. You can choose between the five types of bullet styles, and each type has its own characteristics, as shown in **Table 4.2**. You can mix different bullet styles within a group of bullets, as shown in **Figure 4.35**.

Most of the time, you'll probably use the bullet styles that are part of the theme for the presentation, because those styles have been designed to match the rest of the look of the theme. But it's sometimes useful to customize bullets for particular slides. For example, on a slide that discusses financial matters, you could change the usual image bullets into dollar signs to emphasize your point.

Table 4.2

Bullet and Numbering Styles		
CATEGORY	DESCRIPTION	OPTIONS
Text bullet	Any text character	Color Baseline shift Size Scale with text
Number	Automatic numbering	1. 2. 3. 4. I. II. III. IV. i. ii. iii. iv. A. B. C. D. a. b. c. d.
Custom image	Any graphic image	Baseline shift Size Scale with text
Image bullet	Keynote bullet images, presented in a scrollable list	Baseline shift Size Scale with text
None	No bullets	

```
1. Mercury
   • Freedom 7 - first suborbital flight
   • Friendship 7 - first orbital flight
2. Gemini
   A. Gemini IV - first space walk
   B. Gemini IX - first rendezvous and docking
3. Apollo
   • Apollo 8 - first lunar orbit
   • Apollo 11 - first moon landing
   • Apollo 13 - explosion and mission abort
```

Figure 4.35 You can mix-and-match different bullet types within the same text box. This example, however, takes the idea well into the Land of No Taste.

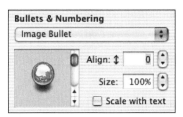

Bullets & Numbering
Image Bullet
Align: ↕ 0
Size: 100%
☐ Scale with text

Figure 4.36 When you are choosing an Image Bullet, you can scroll through a number of preset images.

African elephant population has dropped from 1.5 million in 1978 to 600,000 today
Poaching is the biggest threat

Figure 4.37 The Custom Image option allows you to make new, interesting bullets.

To set bullet and number styles:

1. To apply a bullet or number style to an entire bulleted text box, click once in the box to select it.

   or

   To apply a bullet or number style to multiple lines inside a bulleted text box, select the lines.

   or

   To apply a bullet or number style to a single line, click twice to set the insertion point in the line.

2. In the Bullets & Numbering section of the Text Inspector (**Figure 4.36**), choose the type of bullet or number style you want from the pop-up menu.

   The selection changes.

3. Use the additional controls in the Bullets & Numbering section to tweak the new style to your liking.

✔ Tip

- If you choose Custom Image from the pop-up menu, you will be prompted to find a graphic on your hard disk or network. You can use any image you like, and Keynote will scale it to fit (**Figure 4.37**).

Setting Text and Bullet Tabs

Keynote allows you to set tabs within bulleted text boxes and free text boxes in much the same way that you could set tabs in a word processor. As with word processors, you'll set tabs using rulers and tab markers.

When you show Keynote's rulers and set the insertion point into a text box, you'll see a variety of markers on the ruler showing you the tabs and indents for the text box (**Figure 4.38**). The markers are as follows:

◆ **Level indent markers** appear in text boxes that contain bulleted text. Moving these markers to the right or left moves all the bullet points at that level horizontally.

◆ **First-line indent marker** is useful mainly in free text boxes. It allows you to set a first-line indent. If you drag this marker to the left of the text indent marker, you'll create an outdent, where the first line hangs by itself to the left of the rest of the text.

◆ **Text indent marker** sets the left margin for the text within the text box. This marker is usually in the same position as the first-line indent marker.

◆ **Tab markers** allow you to set left, center, right, and decimal tabs.

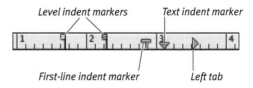

Figure 4.38 Use Keynote's rulers to set indents and tabs.

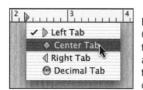

Figure 4.39
Control-clicking on a
tab marker brings up
a contextual menu
that allows you to
change the tab type.

To set and change text indents and tabs:

1. If they are not already visible, show Keynote's rulers by choosing View > Show Rulers, or by pressing ⌘R.

   The rulers appear.

2. Click to set the insertion point in a text box where you want to set or change tabs or indents.

   The indent and tab markers for that line appear on the ruler.

3. To add a new tab, click on the ruler.

   or

   To remove a tab from the ruler, drag it off the ruler.

   or

   To move tabs or indents, drag them left or right on the ruler.

   By default, Keynote puts a left tab on the ruler when you click.

4. (Optional) To change a tab on the ruler from one sort of tab to another, Control-click the tab marker to bring up a contextual menu (**Figure 4.39**), then choose from the menu.

Finding and Replacing Text

Keynote allows you to find and replace text on your slides, which is handy when Marketing tells you that they've decided to rename the SuperWidget to UltraWidget half an hour before your presentation.

To find text:

1. Choose Edit > Find > Find Panel, or press ⌘F.
   The Find panel appears (**Figure 4.40**).

2. In the Find field, enter the text you wish to find.

3. Click Next.
   Next is the default button for the Find panel, but if you press Return or Enter, the next instance of the text will be found and the Find panel will close.

4. To find the next instance of the text, choose Edit > Find > Find Next, or press ⌘G.
   or
   To find the previous instance of the text, choose Edit > Find > Find Previous, or press ⌘D.

✔ Tip

■ You can also find selected text by choosing Edit > Find > Use Selection for Find, or by pressing ⌘E.

Figure 4.40 You'll use the Find panel to find text in your presentation.

Figure 4.41 The Find panel is also useful for replacing text.

To find and replace text:

1. Choose Edit > Find > Find Panel, or press ⌘F.
   The Find panel appears.

2. In the Find field, enter the text you wish to find.

3. In the Replace field, enter the text you want to replace the found text (**Figure 4.41**).

4. In the Replace All Scope section of the Find panel, click either Entire File or Selection.

5. (Optional) In the Find Options section, choose either (or both) Ignore Case and Whole Words.

6. Click Replace to replace the first instance of the found text, Replace & Find to replace the first instance and find the next instance, or Replace All to replace the text throughout your presentation.

✔ Tips

- Keynote will find and replace text that is not only in your slides, but also in the speaker notes.

- If you make a mistake when replacing text, you can use Undo to fix the mistake.

- Unfortunately, in the Replace All Scope section of the Find panel, Selection means the current text selection on the displayed slide, not selected slides in the Slide Navigator, so there's no way to limit your search to just a portion of your presentation.

Checking Your Spelling

Keynote allows you check your spelling in two ways. You can have the program check spelling as you type, in which case misspellings will show up on your slides with red dotted underlines (**Figure 4.42**). Or you can check spelling manually.

To use dynamic spellchecking:

1. Choose Edit > Spelling > Check Spelling As You Type.

   or

   Choose Keynote > Preferences, then click the "Check spelling while you type" check box.

2. When Keynote flags a misspelling, Control-click the underlined word to bring up a contextual menu with suggestions.

3. If one of the suggestions is the correct word, choose it from the contextual menu.

   In the contextual menu, you can also choose Ignore Spelling (if the spelling is correct and you just want Keynote to ignore it), or Learn Spelling to add the word to the spellchecker's dictionary.

To check spelling manually:

1. Choose Edit > Spelling > Spelling, or press ⌘:.

   The Spelling window appears (**Figure 4.43**).

2. Use the controls in the Spelling window to check your text.

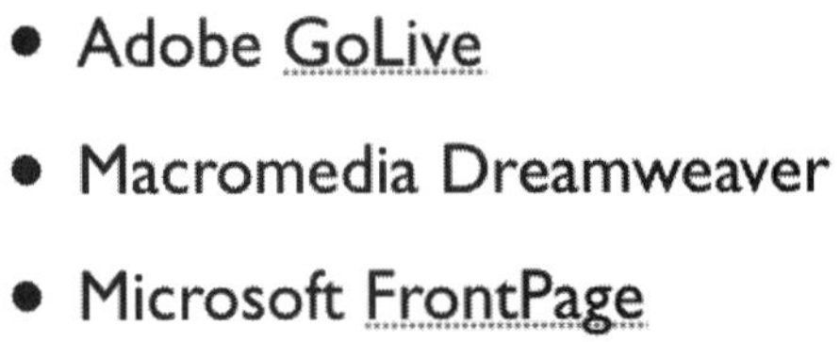

• Adobe GoLive
• Macromedia Dreamweaver
• Microsoft FrontPage

Figure 4.42 When dynamic spellchecking is turned on, Keynote flags suspect text with a dotted red underline.

Spelling
Guess
glove
oLive
Go-Live
Ignore
Guess
Find Next
GoLive
Correct
Dictionary
English
Forget
Learn

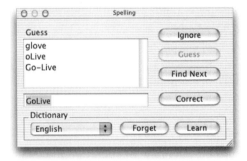

Figure 4.43 Use the controls in the Spelling window to check your spelling manually, and to add new words to the spelling dictionary.

WORKING WITH GRAPHICS

The text on your slides will usually carry the weight of your presentation, but the content can be greatly enhanced by the look of your slideshow. Much of that look is provided by the theme you select for your presentation. Graphics on the slide can add zing to a professional-looking presentation, and often they contribute a significant part of the content of the presentation, as well.

In this chapter, you'll learn how to use Keynote, with the help of other graphics programs, to add and enhance graphics for your slides.

Placing Graphics and Shapes

The graphics on your slides will be one of two types: *imported graphics*, which include photographs and drawings from other graphic programs; and *shapes*, which are simple vector graphics that you can create within Keynote. Keynote's shapes can be scaled and manipulated with no loss of resolution.

Because Keynote's repertoire of shapes is very limited (there are only six: line, rectangle, oval, triangle, right triangle, and an arrow), you'll probably be relying more on other graphics programs to provide slide graphics.

To place graphics:

1. In the Slide Navigator, click to select the slide you want to put the graphic on.

2. Choose Edit > Place > Choose, or press ⌘ Shift V.

   The Open dialog appears (**Figure 5.1**).

3. Navigate to the graphic file you want, then click Place.

   The imported graphic appears on the slide (**Figure 5.2**).

✔ Tips

■ You can also drag and drop graphic files into a Keynote slide from the Finder, and sometimes even from other applications. The latter doesn't always work correctly, so try it and see if it works.

■ Keynote can import a wide range of graphic file formats, including TIFF, JPEG, GIF, PDF, PNG, PSD (Adobe Photoshop files), PICT, BMP (Windows bitmapped image format), and more. See **Table 6.1**, in Chapter 6, for more details.

Figure 5.1 Use the Open dialog to find the graphic file that you want to place.

Figure 5.2 The picture of Pixel, my cat, is placed on the presentation slide, and will eventually be set into a photo cutout (partially visible behind the image).

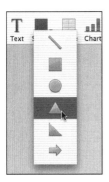

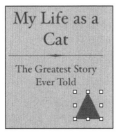

Figure 5.3 Use the Shapes menu from the toolbar to add simple drawing objects to your slides.

Figure 5.4 Once a shape is selected on your slide, you can modify it in many ways, including resizing it, changing its fill color, rotating it, and so on.

Using OmniGraffle

There's a darned good drawing program that works great with Keynote, and it may already be on your Mac. It's called OmniGraffle, from Omni Development (www.omnigroup.com). OmniGraffle is great for creating diagrams, flowcharts, and shapes that Keynote can't make, and it's an excellent tool for drawing custom bullets.

Graphics created in OmniGraffle can be exported as PDF. They retain their transparency, so they scale well and play well with other slide elements. You can draw shapes in OmniGraffle, fill them with images, and then export them to Keynote.

The reason you may already have OmniGraffle is that Apple has bundled it with their professional-level machines (Power Mac G4 and PowerBooks). Check in your Applications folder. If you don't have the program, it's only $70, with a Professional version that includes more features for $120.

- One format that you cannot import into Keynote is EPS (Encapsulated PostScript). Save the EPS file as a PDF, and the image will import just fine.

- If you want to import a Photoshop file with layers, the file can't contain adjustment layers or compositing layers, only normal layers. You can also save the file from Photoshop as a layered TIFF.

- You can almost always copy a graphic in another application, switch to Keynote, and paste the graphic into the slide.

To place shapes:

1. In the Slide Navigator, click to select the slide you want to put the shape on.

2. From the Shapes pop-up menu in the toolbar, choose the shape that you want (**Figure 5.3**).

    or

    Choose Edit > Place, then choose the shape you want from the menu (your choices are Line, Rectangle, Oval, Triangle, Right Triangle, or Arrow).

    The shape appears on the slide (**Figure 5.4**). It is selected, so you can modify it.

✔ Tip

- Once you place a shape, you cannot change it to a different kind of shape. For example, you can't convert a rectangle into a circle.

To delete graphics or shapes:

- To delete a shape or imported graphic, select it and press Delete, or choose Edit > Delete.

Using the Image Library

The Image Library is the generous name that Apple has given one of the folders that is installed along with Keynote. The folder is located at harddrive/Library/Application Support/Keynote/, and unless you save other Keynote files in it, it contains four Keynote presentation files with images:

◆ **Chart Colors.key** contains samples of all the chart colors and textures used in the twelve Apple themes (**Figure 5.5**). These samples are sometimes called color chips, and you are not limited to using these attractive colors and textures in charts; you can use them to fill other graphic objects in Keynote.

◆ **Flags.key** is a Keynote file that has nine slides, each with a large graphic of a flag (**Figure 5.6**). The countries and organizations represented are the United States, the United Kingdom, Canada, France, Germany, Italy, Japan, the Russian Federation, and the European Union. You can copy and paste these flag graphics into your own slides, and they are also scalable, so you can make them as large or as small as you want.

◆ **Objects.key** contains almost three dozen drawings and photographs of common objects, such as road signs, money, chess pieces, and clocks. There are also photographs such as the earth from space, a microscope, a handshake, and a pair of dice (**Figure 5.7**). You can use these pictures to dress up your slides.

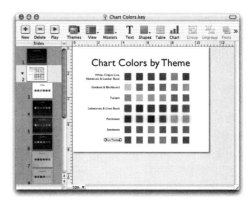

Figure 5.5 You'll find samples of all the chart colors used in the built-in Apple themes in the Chart Colors.key file.

Figure 5.6 The Flags.key file contains drawings of flags of eight countries, plus the European Union.

Figure 5.7 You'll find many useful images in the Objects.key file in the Image Library.

Figure 5.8 The Pictures.key file has a small selection of photographs that you can use in your presentations.

Figure 5.9 Keynote opens the Image Library folder so you can double-click on a file to open it.

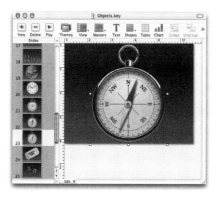

Figure 5.10 Select an image in one of the Image Library files, then copy and paste it into your presentation slide.

♦ **Pictures.key** has ten slides with photographs such as a city skyline, a road receding into the distance, and the façade of the New York Stock Exchange (**Figure 5.8**).

✔ Tip

■ Create additional slides in the four files in the Image Library, and add your own images, so that they will be easily accessible. Or create your own files, and save them in the Image Library folder.

To use the Image Library:

1. In Keynote, use the Slide Navigator to switch to the slide where you want to put an image from the Image Library.

2. Choose File > Open Image Library.
   Keynote switches to the Finder, and opens the Image Library folder (**Figure 5.9**).

3. Double-click the file that you want in the Image Library folder to open it.
   The file opens in Keynote.

4. Use the Slide Navigator in the file that you just opened to find and select the slide with the image that you want to use.

5. Click the image to select it (**Figure 5.10**).

6. Choose Edit > Copy, or press ⌘Ⓒ.

7. Switch back to your presentation file.

8. Choose Edit > Paste, or press ⌘Ⓥ.
   The copied graphic appears on the slide in your presentation file.

USING THE IMAGE LIBRARY

81

Using Clipart Packages

If you're looking for inexpensive ways to improve the graphics on your slides, there are many packages of clipart that are available. These usually come on a series of CD-ROMs (or sometimes on DVD-ROMs, which hold much more data), and are usually licensed as royalty-free, which means that you can use them as you want in your presentations, with no further payments needed to the photographers or artists that created the images. Clipart packages can consist of photographs, vector artwork, bitmapped artwork, or sometimes even fonts.

For example, many of the photographic images in this book were taken from the Hemera Photo-Objects 50,000 packages, Volumes 1 and 2 (www.hemera.com). These programs offer a browser program that lets you enter keywords to find the photos that you need (**Figure 5.11**), then you can export them in a variety of formats (for Keynote, TIFF with Transparency works best). Besides the photographs, Photo-Objects also offers PhotoFonts, which is a utility that fills text with photographic images, then lets you export it to other programs, including Keynote (**Figure 5.12**).

There are many other places to find goodclip art, such as Nova Development's Art Explosion series (www.novadevelopment.com), which come in versions that have from 125,000 to 750,000 images, including background images, animations, and fonts. Another worthy package is the Digital Juice for PowerPoint package, from Digital Juice (www.digitaljuice.com). This package, which can be used with Keynote, contains thousands of images, video clips, animations, textures, and backgrounds.

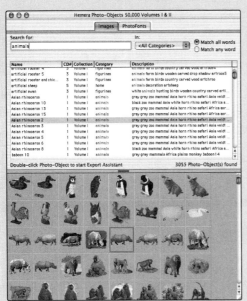

Figure 5.11 The Hemera Photo-Objects packages come with a browser that allows you to find images by keyword and category.

Figure 5.12 Hemera's PhotoFonts utility lets you put a photographic background into text.

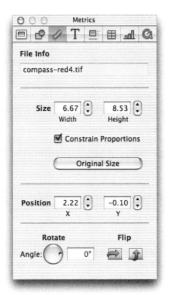

Figure 5.13
You'll use
the Metrics
Inspector to
change the
size and
position of
your images.

Figure 5.14 Drag the selection handles at the edges of an image to resize it.

Resizing Graphics

Once you have placed your image into Keynote, you will usually have to resize it in some way. That can mean scaling it (making it bigger or smaller) or cropping it (trimming the image to only the part you want). You can scale images in Keynote, but you'll have to use another program to crop images, since Keynote doesn't have that feature.

Scaling graphics

You can scale graphics in one of two ways: you can drag the graphic object's selection handles, or you can use the Metrics Inspector (**Figure 5.13**). The Inspector gives you more precise control, plus it gives you the ability to return the image to its original size with just one click if you made a mistake and want to try again.

To resize objects using selection handles:

1. Select the image on your slide.

   Selection handles appear around the image (**Figure 5.14**).

2. Click and drag one of the handles to resize the object.

3. After you resize the object to your liking, it will probably not be in the correct position on the slide. Drag it to a position more to your liking.

✔ Tip

■ If you want to change the proportions of the object as you drag the handles, uncheck the "Constrain Proportions" checkbox in the Metrics Inspector.

To resize objects with the Metrics Inspector:

1. Select the image on your slide.

2. Use the controls in the Size portion of the Metrics Inspector to enter a new size (**Figure 5.15**).

   You can type a figure into the Width and Height boxes, or you can use the arrow buttons to make small changes.

3. (Optional) If you are unhappy with the resized graphic, click the Original Size button to undo your changes.

✔ Tips

- It's not uncommon to import a graphic into Keynote, then forget its original name. This is frustrating, especially if you want to further modify the original file. You'll find the file's name, which can be copied, in the File Info field in the Metrics Inspector. You can then paste the name into the Finder's Find dialog to locate the file on your hard disk.

- You can also use the Position section of the Metrics Inspector to precisely position an object on the slide.

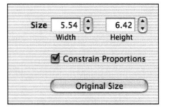

Figure 5.15 You can also use the Metrics Inspector to resize objects in more precise increments than you can do by dragging selection handles.

RESIZING GRAPHICS

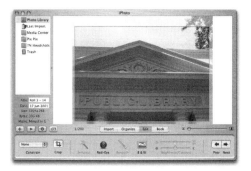

Figure 5.16 To begin the cropping process, select part of an image in iPhoto.

Cropping graphics

Unfortunately, there's no Crop tool in Keynote, so you'll have to do your photo cropping in another program, such as iPhoto, Adobe Photoshop Elements, or Adobe Photoshop, then bring the photo into Keynote. There are lots of ways to do this cropping process, but here's one that works fine for me, and uses software that comes for free with Mac OS X, namely iPhoto and Mail. If you're already using iPhoto to organize your digital photographs, this technique (sans the cropping part) also works fine to get your photos from iPhoto into Keynote. Perhaps a future version of iPhoto will be able to save a slideshow as a Keynote file, which you could then further dress up in Keynote.

To crop pictures with iPhoto:

1. If the image is already in iPhoto, find the image, or if it is not in iPhoto, drag the image file to iPhoto to open it.

2. Click the Edit button.

3. Drag to select the area you wish to crop.
   The area of the photo outside of the selection is dimmed (**Figure 5.16**).

4. Click the Crop button.
   The cropped image appears.

5. Click the Organize button.
   One way to get a photo out of iPhoto is to send it to Apple's Mail program. You could use iPhoto's File > Export command, but that would require you to save the cropped photo as a file on your hard disk. If you won't need the file again, why not skip that step? Another benefit: when you send the photo to Mail, you can reduce it to a size better suited for a Keynote slide.

continues on next page

continues on next page

RESIZING GRAPHICS

6. Make sure that the image you cropped is selected in Organize View, then click the Email button in iPhoto's toolbar.

The Mail Photo dialog appears (**Figure 5.17**).

7. From the Size pop-up menu, choose the size for the exported photo.

For most Keynote slides, the Small (or rarely, the Medium) choice is best.

8. Click Compose.

The Mail program launches and opens a new message with the photo in the body of the message (**Figure 5.18**).

9. Drag the photo from the email window into your Keynote presentation (**Figure 5.19**).

✔ Tips

- You can also cut and paste the photo from Mail to Keynote, but I found it worked more reliably when I used drag and drop.

- After you drag the photo from Mail to Keynote, you don't need the mail message anymore; you can close it without sending or saving it.

- If you do not want to choose the size of your photos, you can drag and drop the cropped image from the iPhoto window into Keynote. This works with JPEG files in iPhoto and all versions of Keynote, but with versions of Keynote earlier than 1.1, drag and drop didn't work with TIFFs. Once you have dropped the photo into Keynote, you can resize it in the usual fashion.

Figure 5.17 Use the iPhoto Mail Photo feature to send a copy of the photo to the Mail program.

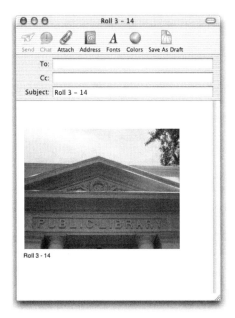

Figure 5.18 The new Mail message has the photo in the body of the message.

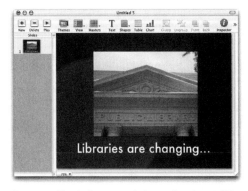

Figure 5.19 Here's the cropped photo, placed on a slide.

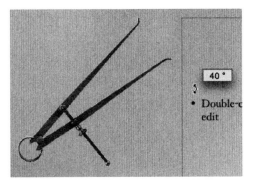

Figure 5.20 The angle tag tells you at what angle you have rotated your graphic.

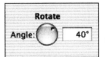

Figure 5.21 You can also use the angle wheel in the Metrics Inspector to rotate objects.

Rotating and Flipping Graphic Objects

Keynote allows you to rotate objects on the Slide Canvas. You can rotate objects by dragging the object's selection handles (this is called *free rotation*), or by using the Metrics Inspector. You can also flip objects around their horizontal or vertical axes.

To free rotate objects:

1. Select the object you want to rotate.
   The object's selection handles appear.

2. Hold down the Command key, and click and drag one of the object's selection handles.
   The cursor changes to a short curved line with arrows at both ends. As you rotate the object, an angle tag appears to show you the new angle for the object (**Figure 5.20**).

3. Release the mouse button.

To rotate using the Metrics Inspector:

1. Select the object you want to rotate.

2. In the Rotate section of the Metrics Inspector (**Figure 5.21**), click and drag the angle wheel.
   or
   Type a value into the angle field and press the Tab key.
   The object rotates.

✔ Tip

- When you need to make small or precise changes, you can often get better results by typing a value into the angle field, rather than using the angle wheel.

To flip objects:

1. Select the object you want to flip.

2. In the Flip section of the Metrics Inspector (**Figure 5.22**), click the button with the right-pointing arrow to flip the object vertically.

   or

   Click the button with the arrow pointing up to flip the object around its horizontal axis.

   or

   Choose Arrange > Flip Horizontally.

   or

   Choose Arrange > Flip Vertically.

   The object flips as you command.

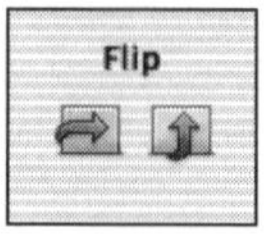

Figure 5.22 Use the Flip buttons to Flip images horizontally or vertically.

Table 5.1

Alignment Options	
OPTION	RESULT
Left	
Center	
Right	
Top	
Middle	
Bottom	

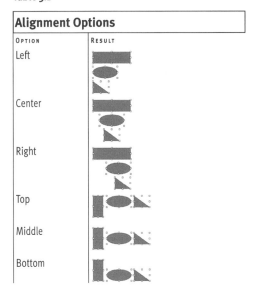

Table 5.2

Distribution Options		
OPTION	BEFORE COMMAND	RESULT
Horizontally		
Vertically		

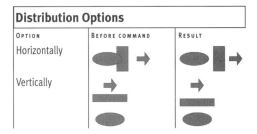

Aligning and Distributing Objects

Keynote provides commands that make it easy to arrange multiple objects so that they all line up with their edges or centers along the same line. You can also distribute objects so that they are arranged, either horizontally or vertically, with equal space between them.

To align objects:

1. Select the objects that you want to align.

2. Choose Arrange > Align Objects, then choose the kind of alignment you want from the hierarchical menu. Your choices are Left, Center, Right, Top, Middle, and Bottom.

   See **Table 5.1** to see how the different alignments work.

To distribute objects:

1. Select the objects that you wish to distribute.

2. Choose Arrange > Distribute Objects, then choose the kind of distribution you want from the hierarchical menu. Your choices are Horizontally or Vertically.

   See **Table 5.2** to see how the different distributions work.

Grouping and Locking Objects

If you have several graphic objects, you might find it easier to work with them as a group. You can move the group on the slide or copy and paste it between slides, which is much easier than selecting multiple objects. Grouping objects also preserves their positions relative to one another.

Once you have objects precisely where you want them on the Slide Canvas, it's annoying to accidentally select and move them when you're trying to move another object. Prevent that problem by *locking* the object, which makes the object immovable. You can still select a locked object, but the only thing that you can do to it is unlock it; you can't move it or change any of its properties until it is unlocked.

To group objects:

1. Select the objects you want to group (**Figure 5.23**).

2. Choose Arrange > Group, or press ⌘ Shift G.

   or

   Click the Group button on the toolbar.

   The objects group, and there is now one set of selection handles for the group. The selection handles are now gray, instead of white, to denote that it is a grouped object (**Figure 5.24**).

✔ Tip

- You can't free rotate grouped objects, but you can still rotate and flip them with the Metrics Inspector.

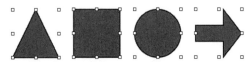

Figure 5.23 These four objects are all selected; you can tell because all of their selection handles are visible.

Figure 5.24 The selection handles for the grouped object are gray.

Figure 5.25 This fire hydrant picture is locked; you can tell because each selection handle has turned into an x.

To ungroup objects:

1. Select the group.

2. Choose Arrange > Ungroup, or press ⌘ Option G.

   or

   Click the Ungroup button on the toolbar.

   The objects ungroup.

To lock objects:

1. Select the object or objects you want to lock.

2. Choose Arrange > Lock, or press ⌘ L.

   The object's selection handles change to show they are locked (**Figure 5.25**).

To unlock objects:

1. Select the object or objects you want to unlock.

2. Choose Arrange > Unlock, or press ⌘ Option L.

   The object's selection handles change to standard selection handles.

GROUPING AND LOCKING OBJECTS

Using Rulers and Alignment Guides

In order to precisely place objects on the Slide Canvas, Keynote provides two tools: rulers and alignment guides. Rulers appear at the top and left edges of the Slide Canvas, and you can put guides anywhere on the slide.

Unlike the alignment guides on master slides, which appear only whenever the center or edge of an object you are moving aligns with the center or edge of another object, alignment guides that you place on a presentation slide are always visible (though they do not appear when you play the presentation).

To toggle rulers on and off:

1. Choose View > Show Rulers, or press ⌘R.

   The rulers appear in the Slide Canvas (**Figure 5.26**).

2. Press ⌘R again to hide the rulers.

To set the ruler units:

1. Choose Keynote > Preferences.

   The Preferences window appears.

2. In the Ruler Units section of the window (**Figure 5.27**), choose a unit from the pop-up menu.

   Your choices are pixels, centimeters, inches, or percentage.

3. (Optional) Check "Place origin at center of ruler" if you want the zero point at the ruler's center, rather than at the upper-left corner of the slide (**Figure 5.28**).

   This can make it easier to place objects equal distances from the horizontal or vertical centers of the slide, especially in conjunction with alignment guides.

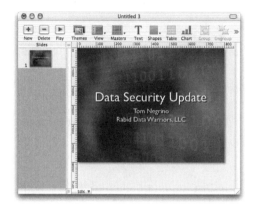

Figure 5.26 Rulers appear at the top and left edges of the Slide Canvas.

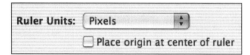

Figure 5.27 You can set the units that rulers use in Keynote's Preferences window.

Figure 5.28 This is what the horizontal ruler looks like when you set its origin point to be the center of the ruler.

Figure 5.29 When you click inside a ruler, the pointer turns into the alignment guide cursor.

Figure 5.30 As you drag an alignment guide onto the Slide Canvas, a position tag accompanies the guide.

To place alignment guides on a slide:

1. Choose View > Show Rulers, or press ⌘R.

   The rulers appear in the Slide Canvas.

2. In the Slide Navigator, select the slide for which you want to set alignment guides.

3. To create a horizontal alignment guide, click in the ruler at the top of the Slide Canvas.

   The pointer turns into the alignment guide cursor (**Figure 5.29**).

4. Drag down into the Slide Canvas.

   A yellow alignment guide, the width of the slide, appears.

5. Continue dragging, and drag the guide to where you want it on the Slide Canvas.

   As you drag, a position tag appears with the guide to help you precisely place the guide (**Figure 5.30**).

6. To create a vertical alignment guide, click in the ruler at the left side of the Slide Canvas.

   The pointer turns into the alignment guide cursor.

7. Drag to the right, into the Slide Canvas.

   A yellow alignment guide, the height of the slide, appears.

8. Drag the guide to where you want it on the Slide Canvas.

   The position tag will appear as you drag the guide.

✔ Tip

■ You can place as many alignment guides on the Slide Canvas as you want.

Layering Graphics

When you place objects on slides, you can think of each object as being in its own layer on the slide. For example, if you have five objects on a slide, you have six layers: one layer for each object, plus the slide background, which is defined in the master slide. You can move each of these layers forward and back. The exception is the slide background, the layer furthest back, which can't be brought forward. The only way that you can layer slide objects with the background is if you select the "Allow objects on slide to layer with master" checkbox for the slide's master slide in the Master Slide Inspector (see Chapter 13 for more details); then you can move slide objects behind a layer on the background. This is how Keynote's photo cutouts work.

Any text boxes that are part of the master slide, such as the title box and the body box (with or without bulleted text), are part of the background layer, but you can still layer other objects behind these text boxes, whether or not the "Allow objects on slide to layer with master" option is set for that master slide. Free text boxes that you create on presentation slides can be layered like any other object. Free text boxes placed on master slides are treated like graphic objects and can't be layered with objects on presentation slides.

To layer slide objects:

1. Select a slide object that you want to move forward or backwards in the slide layers (**Figure 5.31**).

2. To move the object back in the layers, choose Arrange > Send Backward, or press ⌘─ (minus). This moves the object one layer back.

   or

Figure 5.31 The picture of the hapless couple is in front of the title text and the image of the television.

Figure 5.32 After sending the image backwards, the benighted couch potatoes appear to be trapped inside the television.

Figure 5.33 This slide contains only a title and a large photo cutout.

Figure 5.34 Use the Open sheet to find the photo that you want to place on the slide.

To move the object forward in the layers, choose Arrange > Bring Forward, or press ⌘= (equals). This moves the object one layer forward.

or

To send the object to the back of the layers, choose Arrange > Send to Back, or press ⌘Option− (minus), or click the Back button on the toolbar.

or

To bring the object to the front, choose Arrange > Bring to Front, or press ⌘Option= (equals), or click the Front button on the toolbar.

The object moves as you command.

3. Drag the still-selected object to position it as you want with the other layers (**Figure 5.32**).

You can also resize the object to get a more pleasing effect.

To place photos on slides with photo cutouts:

1. Click New in the toolbar to create a new slide.

2. From the Masters pop-up menu in the toolbar, choose a master with a photo cutout.

The master slide is applied to the slide (**Figure 5.33**).

3. Choose Edit > Place > Choose.

An Open sheet slides down from the top of the window (**Figure 5.34**).

continues on next page

LAYERING GRAPHICS

4. Navigate to the picture that you want, then click Place.

The picture appears on the slide (**Figure 5.35**).

5. If necessary, resize the picture so that it will fit the photo cutout better.

6. Drag to position the picture over the photo cutout.

7. Click the Back button on the toolbar.

or

Choose Arrange > Send to Back, or press ⌘ Option – (minus).

The picture is sent behind the photo cutout.

8. If necessary, drag the image so that it appears in a pleasing fashion behind the photo cutout (**Figure 5.36**).

✔ Tip

■ You don't have to use photo cutouts just for photos. Try placing diagrams, charts, or even free text boxes in the cutout for greater emphasis.

Figure 5.35 The picture appears on the slide, but you'll probably have to resize it and reposition it, as this picture needed.

Figure 5.36 Sending the image to the back makes it appear within the photo cutout. Notice that the image is still selected (you can still see its selection handles), so you can further reposition it so that it looks best within the photo cutout.

LAYERING GRAPHICS

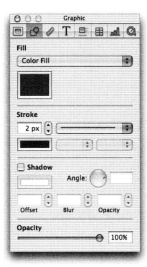

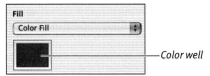

Figure 5.37 The Graphic Inspector lets you apply the different kinds of fills to objects.

Figure 5.38 A color fill fills an object with a solid color.

Color well

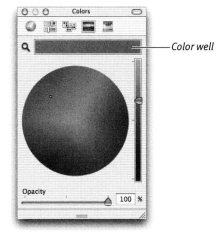

Color well

Figure 5.39 Select a color in the Colors window for the color fill.

Using Color and Gradient Fills

You can fill shapes created in Keynote with solid colors, color gradients, or an image (see the next section for image fills). A *color fill* replaces the interior of the object with a solid color, picked from the Colors window. A *gradient fill* creates a smooth blend from one color that you set to a second color. You can fill any of the drawing objects created in Keynote's Shapes menu, and you can also fill the shapes (bars, columns, pie slices, and so on) in Keynote's charts. You use the Graphic Inspector to apply fills to shapes (**Figure 5.37**).

To fill a shape with a color:

1. Display the Graphic Inspector.

2. Display the Colors window.

3. Select the shape you want to fill.

4. In the Fill section of the Graphic Inspector, choose Color Fill from the pop-up menu (**Figure 5.38**).

5. Click the color well in the Fill section of the Graphic Inspector to select it.

6. In the Colors window (**Figure 5.39**), select the color that you want to use for the fill.

   The color will appear in the color well in the Graphic Inspector, and will fill the selected shape.

✔ Tip

■ If the Fill section in the Graphic Inspector is inactive, you accidentally deselected the shape that you want to fill. Click the shape to select it again.

To fill a shape with a gradient:

1. Display the Graphic Inspector.

2. Display the Colors window.

3. Select the shape you want to fill.

4. In the Fill section of the Graphic Inspector, choose Gradient Fill from the pop-up menu (**Figure 5.40**).

   The Gradient Fill section has two color wells, for the beginning and end colors of the gradient, plus controls that allow you to swap the two colors and change the angle of the gradient.

5. In the Colors window, select the color that you want to use for the fill.

   The color will appear in the color well at the top of the Colors window.

6. Click in the color well in the Colors window, and drag the color to the first color well in the Gradient Fill section of the Graphic Inspector.

7. Repeat steps 5 and 6, but drag the color to the second color well in the Graphic Inspector.

   The shape is filled with the gradient (**Figure 5.41**).

8. (Optional) To swap the two gradient colors, click the swap arrow in the Gradient Fill section of the Graphic Inspector.

9. To change the gradient angle, use the angle controls.

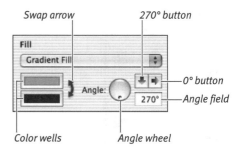

Figure 5.40 When you choose Gradient Fill, you'll need to set two colors and the angle of the gradient.

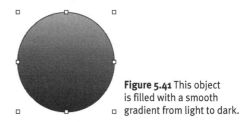

Figure 5.41 This object is filled with a smooth gradient from light to dark.

✔ Tip

■ You can adjust the transparency of just a color fill (or just the stroke; see "Modifying Image Borders," below) by using the Opacity slider in the Colors window. It's a cool trick that let's you change the transparency of the fill while leaving the stroke solid. Instead of using the Opacity slider in the Graphic Inspector, you use the slider on the Colors window and the opacity setting affects the color fill or stroke, not the entire object.

USING COLOR AND GRADIENT FILLS

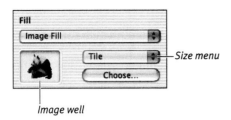

Size menu

Image well

Figure 5.42 When you choose Image Fill, you can see a preview of the image in the image well.

Figure 5.43 The image of the tiger fits neatly into the shape, because the Scale to Fill option was chosen from the Size pop-up menu.

Placing Images Within Objects

In a similar manner to color and gradient fills, you can fill shapes in Keynote with images. You can use any kind of image that Keynote can import.

To fill a shape with an image:

1. Display the Graphic Inspector.

2. Select the shape you want to fill.

3. In the Fill section of the Graphic Inspector, choose Image Fill from the pop-up menu (**Figure 5.42**).

   By default, the shape will be filled with one of the Keynote file's chart patterns.

4. To pick an image for the fill, do one of the following:

   ▲ Click the Choose button.

   An Open dialog appears; navigate to the image you want and click Open.

   ▲ Drag an image from the Finder into the image well in the Fill section of the Graphic Inspector.

   The image fills the shape (**Figure 5.43**).

5. Choose from the Size pop-up menu to set the way the image fills the shape.

   See the "Image Fill Options" sidebar for more information.

Image Fill Options

You can use the Size pop-up menu in the Fill section of the Graphic Inspector to change the way that the image appears inside the shape. There are five options:

◆ **Scale to Fit** makes the image bigger or smaller to fit into the shape as well as possible (**Figure 5.44**).

◆ **Scale to Fill** makes the image fill the shape, leaving no space around the edges (**Figure 5.45**).

◆ **Stretch** distorts the image, if necessary, to make it fill the shape (**Figure 5.46**).

◆ **Original Size** puts the image in the shape with no change in its dimensions (**Figure 5.47**). If the image is larger than the shape, part of the image will be cut off. If the image is smaller, there will be blank space around the image.

◆ **Tile** repeats the image inside the object. If the image is smaller than the shape, you will see multiple copies of the image inside the shape (**Figure 5.48**). If the image is larger, you will only see part of the image.

Figure 5.44 The Scale to Fit option scaled the panda to fit within the rectangle.

Figure 5.45 Scale to Fill made the panda image fill up as much of the rectangle as possible, but cut off part of the image.

Figure 5.46 The Stretch option also fills the rectangle, but distorts the image.

Figure 5.47 The Original Size option cuts off part of the panda image in this case, because the original size of the image is larger than the containing rectangle.

Figure 5.48 Because the panda is not as wide as the rectangle, the Tile option repeats the panda inside the rectangle.

Figure 5.49 You can control the stroke width, line style, and line color for any object.

Figure 5.50 The Line Style pop-up menu gives you four choices of line styles, or you can choose no line at all.

Figure 5.51 The two endpoint pop-up menus contain identical options to add graphics to each end of a line.

Figure 5.52 This image uses a dashed, fairly thick stroke.

Modifying Image Borders

The borders of a shape or image are delineated in Keynote by the *stroke*, which is the line around the object. Keynote allows you to set the line style, line thickness, and line color for shapes. If you prefer, you can have no stroke around an object. For the line shape, you can also set a graphic (such as an arrowhead, or a circle) for the line's endpoints.

To set the stroke for an object:

1. Open the Graphic Inspector.

2. Select the object for which you want to set the stroke.

3. In the Stroke section of the Graphic Inspector (**Figure 5.49**), set the following:

   ▲ Type an entry, in pixels, into the thickness field, or use the arrow buttons next to the field.

   ▲ Choose a line style from the pop-up menu (**Figure 5.50**).

   ▲ Click the color well to open the Colors window, then set a line color by clicking it in that window.

   ▲ If the shape you are working with is a Line, select a graphic for the endpoints from the two endpoint pop-up menus (**Figure 5.51**).

The shape's stroke changes as you command (**Figure 5.52**).

Using Drop Shadows

Shadows are vital tools in Keynote because they give objects on your slides an appearance of depth. You can use the Graphic Inspector to add a drop shadow to objects and to control the shadow's color, angle, how far it is offset from the object, how blurry the shadow is, and the shadow's opacity.

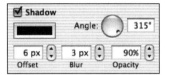

Figure 5.53 Apply drop shadows with the Shadow section in the Graphic Inspector.

To apply a shadow to an object:

1. Select the object to which you want to add the shadow.

2. Click the Shadow checkbox in the Shadow section of the Graphic Inspector (**Figure 5.53**).

   The shadow appears under the object.

3. (Optional) Click the color well in the Shadow section to open the Colors window, then select a color in that window to change the shadow color from the default black.

4. Use the Angle wheel to set the angle for the shadow.

   or

   Type a value for the shadow angle in the Angle field.

   Changing the shadow angle changes the apparent light source for the shadow.

5. Set the shadow offset (the distance in pixels the shadow is from the object) by typing a number in the Offset field, or by using the field's arrow buttons.

   Higher values will cause the shadow to appear more separated from the object (**Figure 5.54**). The maximum shadow offset value is 50 pixels.

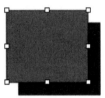

Figure 5.54 The drop shadow for this image uses the maximum 50 pixel shadow offset.

Figure 5.55 The Blur and Opacity settings have been applied so that this drop shadow looks more natural.

6. Adjust the shadow's blur by typing a number in the Blur field, or by using the field's arrow buttons.

Higher blur values will make the shadow appear more dispersed.

7. Set the shadow's opacity by typing a number in the Opacity field, or by using the field's arrow buttons (**Figure 5.55**).

You can set the shadow's opacity separately from the object's opacity; see the "Adjusting Object Opacity" section next in this chapter.

✔ Tips

- If you have more than one object with drop shadows, it's usually a good idea to give all the objects the same shadow values.

- You can copy and paste shadow settings from one object to another by selecting the first object, choosing Format > Copy Style, selecting the second object, and choosing Format > Paste Style. Be aware that this will also copy and paste the stroke, fill, and opacity of the object.

USING DROP SHADOWS

Adjusting Object Opacity

One of the things that gives Keynote its unique graphic look is its ability to control the opacity of objects. By making some objects partially transparent, you can achieve some terrific-looking effects. For example, you can use translucent shapes to create tables that look better than you can achieve using Keynote's regular table tools (you'll find the details of this technique in Chapter 7). Once again, you'll use the Graphic Inspector to change an object's opacity.

To modify the opacity of an object:

1. Select the object.

2. Drag the slider in the Opacity section of the Graphic Inspector (**Figure 5.56**) to make the object more or less transparent.

   or

   Type a value into the Opacity field.

   The object changes opacity (**Figure 5.57**).

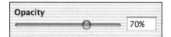

Figure 5.56 Use the Opacity slider in the Graphic Inspector to change the transparency of an object, or type a value in the Opacity field.

Figure 5.57 The picture of the older car in the background is at 30% opacity; you can see the background texture through the image. The newer car in the front is at 100% opacity.

ADDING RICH MEDIA

6

Rich media is the omnibus term for sounds, music, animations, and video files that you can add to your slides to enhance your presentation. You might want to include a Flash animation on a slide to show a dynamic process, or insert a video clip to illustrate one of your points.

Background music, sound effects, and narration can add interest to your presentation, especially if you plan to export the presentation as a QuickTime movie for use on the Web. Sounds and music are less useful when you're giving the presentation live, because people generally want to hear you, not a fancy production.

In this chapter, you'll learn how to add music and sounds to slides; use QuickTime movies in your presentation; and add Flash animations to your slideshows.

Adding iTunes Music

The good news about adding music to your presentation is that you can easily add music to any slide. The not-so-good news is that in the current version of Keynote, you can only add music to a slide, but not to an entire presentation. So when you change slides, any music you've added to the slide will stop. If you've added music to the next slide, that music will start.

This limitation is a major drawback of the current version of Keynote when compared to Microsoft PowerPoint, which allows you to easily lay down a soundtrack for an entire presentation. There is a workaround for the problem, but it involves exporting your Keynote presentation to a QuickTime movie, then editing the QuickTime movie with an application like iMovie to add an audio track that would then play for the length of your presentation. You then use the edited QuickTime file to show your presentation with the QuickTime Player. Obviously, this isn't terribly convenient, but it is doable. If music is integral to your presentation, you'll need to do this. See Chapter 11 for more information about exporting Keynote files to QuickTime movies.

On most people's systems, the most convenient repository of music will be their iTunes music library. The best way to use files from iTunes is to use iTunes to find the file you want, then drag that file into Keynote.

Figure 6.1 You can use the contextual menu in the iTunes track list to show your song file.

Figure 6.2 Using iTunes to display your file is faster than digging through several layers of folders in your iTunes music library.

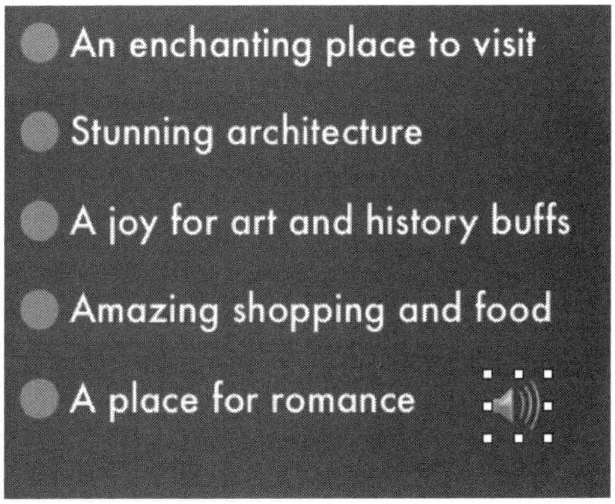

An enchanting place to visit

Stunning architecture

A joy for art and history buffs

Amazing shopping and food

A place for romance

Figure 6.3 The music file appears on the Keynote slide as a small speaker icon.

To add music to a slide:

1. In Keynote, go to the slide where you want to add music.

2. Launch iTunes, if it isn't already running.

3. In iTunes, find the track that you want to add to the slide.

4. Click the track name to select it.

5. Control-click (or right-click if you have a multiple button mouse) on the track name.

   A contextual menu will appear (**Figure 6.1**).

6. From the contextual menu, choose Show Song File.

   The song file is revealed and selected in the Finder (**Figure 6.2**).

7. Drag the song file onto the Keynote slide.

   A sound icon appears on the Slide Canvas (**Figure 6.3**). This icon will not be visible when you play the presentation.

Playing music

Sound files that you put onto slides will begin playing immediately when you run the slideshow and switch to the slide. Keynote doesn't have controls that allow you to directly set a delay in playing media files. There is a workaround to get a delay before your media file begins playing, however. You can move the sound icon onto your slide using an object build. This allows you to delay playing the sound until you click the mouse, and then gives you up to a four second delay before the sound begins. See "Creating Object Builds" in Chapter 9 for more information.

Thank you, QuickTime!

Keynote uses QuickTime, Mac OS X's media architecture, to read all types of media, from pictures, to sounds, to animations. As a result, you can import—and Keynote can use—any type of media that QuickTime can handle. A complete list is too extensive for this book, but for a list of the most common media types QuickTime handles that you might use in a presentation, see **Table 6.1**.

Table 6.1

QuickTime Media Types

Category	Format	Comments
Images	BMP	Windows bitmap images
	GIF	
	JPEG	Used for photographs; used by iPhoto
	PDF	Portable Document Format, AKA Adobe Acrobat file
	PICT	Old Mac vector graphics format
	PNG	Portable Network Graphics; native file format for Macromedia Fireworks
	PSD	Adobe Photoshop file, will import layers
	TIFF	
Sounds	AAC	Compressed music and sound format used by iTunes 4 and later
	AIFF	Audio CD format
	MIDI	
	MP3	Compressed music and sound format; used by iTunes
	WAV	Windows audio format
Video & Animations	AVI	Windows video format
	DV	Most DV camcorder formats
	Flash 5 (SWF)	Also earlier versions
	MPEG-1	
	MPEG-4	
	QuickTime Movie (MOV)	

Adding Slide Narration

You can add slide narration to any individual slide; as with music, Keynote doesn't allow you to create one narration track that can play throughout the entire slideshow. So you'll need to have separate audio narration files for each slide, then add each narration file separately to each slide.

Before you can add a narration file to the slide, you will of course have to record it. Recording isn't especially difficult, but it does take some preparation. You'll need a number of pieces of hardware and software to record narration, including:

◆ A Macintosh

◆ A microphone

◆ Audio recording software

Mac OS X has the ability to accept sound input from a variety of audio devices. Some Macs, such as the iMac and portables such as PowerBooks and iBooks, have microphones built-in, although these are not of very good quality and you will probably not want to use them for narration, except in a pinch. If your Mac has a Line In port (on some Macs this is labeled as the Microphone port), you can plug a microphone into it. Some Macs, notably most of the current Power Mac G4 tower machines, do not have Line In ports, and you will have to purchase a USB audio adapter, such as the Griffin Technologies iMic (`www.griffintechnology.com`).

Microphones vary widely in price and quality. There are a wide variety of headset microphones that will serve nicely for recording narration, at prices well under $100. Some of these microphones connect to computers via the USB port, so if you have a Mac that doesn't include a Line In port, you can purchase a USB microphone and save yourself the extra cost of the USB audio adapter.

You may already have audio recording software on your Mac, especially if you have a recent vintage iMac. Those iMacs come with a licensed version of Felt Tip Software's Sound Studio, an easy-to-use audio recording, editing, and effects program (**Figure 6.4**). If you don't already have Sound Studio, you can download a trial version from www.felttip.com. There are many other audio recording packages available, ranging from the simple and free (Audio In, which you can find on Version Tracker, www.versiontracker.com) to the complex and expensive (such as Emagic's Logic Platinum). For the explanation below, I've used Sound Studio as the audio recording application.

To record narration files:

1. Plug your microphone into your Macintosh.

2. Open System Preferences, then choose the Sound pane.
   The Sound pane appears (**Figure 6.5**).

3. Click the Input tab.
   The Input pane appears (**Figure 6.6**).

4. Select the input method used by your microphone.

5. Quit System Preferences.

6. Open your audio recording software.
   This example uses Sound Studio.

7. In the audio recording program, click the Record button, then speak your narration.
   Record the narration for one slide at a time, as each slide has to have its own narration file.

8. Click Stop to halt the recording (see **Figure 6.4**).

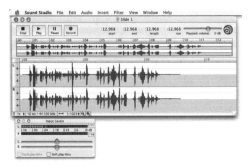

Figure 6.4 Sound Studio is an inexpensive audio recording and editing application that makes it easy to record audio narration for your slides.

Figure 6.5 You'll need to use the Sound pane in System Preferences to set up your audio input.

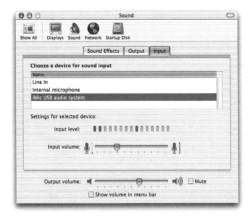

Figure 6.6 Select your sound input device in the Input tab of the Sound pane.

Figure 6.7 Save the narration file on your hard disk. If possible, use the MP3 format, but if not, use AIFF.

9. (Optional) If necessary, and if the software supports the function, use the recording software to edit the sound file. You might, for example, want to cut out extraneous noise, or trim the sound track to make it shorter.

10. Save the recording to disk by choosing File > Save.

The Save dialog appears (**Figure 6.7**).

11. If the Save dialog gives you a choice of audio formats to use for the saved file, choose MP3 if it is available, because it produces smaller files; otherwise, choose AIFF, which is the same format used by audio CDs.

12. Navigate to where you want to save the audio file, then click Save.

13. Repeat steps 7 through 12 for the narration for each slide.

At the end of the process, you'll have a group of narration files on your hard disk, ready to be imported into Keynote.

To add narration to your presentation:

1. In Keynote, go to the slide where you want to add narration.

2. In the Finder, find the narration file that corresponds to the slide you just displayed in Keynote.

3. Drag the narration file onto the Slide Canvas.

A sound icon appears on the Slide Canvas (see **Figure 6.3**). This icon will not be visible when you play the presentation.

✔ Tip

- You can use an object build to insert a delay before the narration begins. See Chapter 9 for more information about creating object builds.

✔ Tips

- Don't save the narration file until you're happy with it. Use the audio recording software to playback what you have recorded. If you're not happy with what you have recorded, don't be afraid to delete it and record again.

- When you are recording audio narration, speak and enunciate clearly, using a measured pace. On the other hand, don't use a plodding pace, either. You want to shoot for a pace that is slightly slower than normal conversation, but that isn't interpreted as you speaking deliberately slowly. Think back to the narration that you've heard in TV programs, and try to use that sort of pace.

- If you have object builds or animations that you want to occur on the slide before the narration starts, you can add as many seconds of silence as you need to the narration file using your audio recording software.

Inserting QuickTime Movies

Adding video files to your presentation can be a powerful tool that enhances your talk. Or it can be a needless bit of fluff that doesn't really help your presentation. Which is to say that you should give using video some serious thought before you put it in your slideshow.

You can add movies to slides in much the same way you add other media files. But the difference is that Keynote gives you some control over the movie with a Media pane in the Inspector window (**Figure 6.8**).

To add QuickTime movies to your presentation:

1. In Keynote, go to the slide where you want to add a QuickTime movie.

2. In the Finder, find the movie file that you want to put in the presentation.

3. Drag the movie file onto the Slide Canvas.

   The movie appears on the Slide Canvas, showing a preview frame, called the *poster frame* (**Figure 6.9**).

4. Drag the movie to position it where you want it on the slide.

   Once the movie is on the slide, you can use the Media Inspector to work with it.

Controlling QuickTime movies

You can use the Media Inspector to affect the behavior of movies you add to a slide. It has the following controls:

◆ **Poster Frame** uses a slider to choose a frame of the movie that will appear when the movie is not playing. The poster frame reminds you of the movie's content when you are working with your slides, and it will also briefly appear in your slideshow before your movie begins playing.

Figure 6.8 The Media Inspector gives you some control over the way your movie will be displayed on your slide.

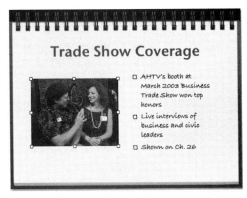

Figure 6.9 The poster frame for the movie is what you see when you drag the movie onto a slide.

Saving Media Files with your Presentation

Media files tend to be big. A QuickTime movie can easily take up tens or even hundreds of megabytes of disk space. By default, Keynote doesn't save media files, such as sound, QuickTime, or Flash animations, in the Keynote presentation file. Instead, Keynote stores aliases to the media files. If you copy your presentation file to another computer without also copying the external media files, the media files will be lost to the presentation. To avoid this, use Keynote's option to save media files into the presentation file. Choose File > Save As, then click the check box labeled "Copy movies into document." Then give the file a name and save it in the location where you want it, as usual.

◆ **Repeat** is a pop-up menu that lets you choose how the movie will repeat when playing on the slide. Your choices are None, Loop (the movie will repeat until you change slides), and Loop Back and Forth (the movie will play forwards, then backwards, until you change slides).

◆ **Volume** uses a slider to control the volume of the movie's soundtrack.

◆ **Controls** has CD-style controls that allow you to play the movie while you are working with the movie on the Slide Canvas. These controls do not affect the movie when it is playing in your presentation.

✔ Tips

■ Movie files can be resized just like any other graphic in Keynote. Just click the movie on the slide to select it, and drag the resize handles that appear. Be aware that if you scale the movie up more than a little bit, the video quality will degrade.

■ Slower machines sometimes have problems playing full-screen movies within Keynote (that is, movies that take up the entire area of the slide). Video tends to stutter and not run smoothly. You should, as always, be sure to play your presentation through before you give your talk.

■ If you double-click a movie on the Slide Canvas, it will start playing.

■ You can add more than one movie to a slide.

■ The pixels in a DV movie (such as one made in iMovie or Final Cut Express) are not the same shape as movies made for your computer screen. You can use the Metrics Inspector to unlock the proportions of your movie and change its size from 720×480 to 640×480 to fix this problem. You can then scale the movie up or down proportionally on the Slide Canvas by holding down the Shift key while you resize the movie.

INSERTING QUICKTIME MOVIES

113

Using QuickTime Pro

QuickTime is built into Mac OS X, and it provides the basic features you need to import and play movies. Keynote relies on QuickTime for all of its graphic, sound, and video capabilities.

You'll probably want to use the QuickTime Player application to view movies before you place them on slides. With QuickTime Player, you can review movies, checking to see if they start and end at appropriate times for your slide, and you can also use the program to review music and narration clips.

If you will be spending any significant amount of time working with media files in your presentations, I suggest that you invest $30 at the online Apple Store to upgrade the free QuickTime Player to QuickTime Player Pro. The Pro version gives you many extra capabilities, too numerous to go into in detail here. But the main extra feature that matters the most to Keynote users is that it allows you to edit QuickTime movies. Of course, QuickTime Player Pro isn't a full editing program like iMovie or Final Cut Pro, but it is perfect for trimming excess video from the front or back of a movie clip; cutting and pasting video and sound to rearrange it in the clip; and even applying special effects, like a grainy film look, or turning your video sepia tone.

Though it is certainly possible to accomplish these editing tasks in iMovie or Final Cut Pro, it takes much longer. QuickTime Player Pro is the most efficient way to make quick changes to video and sound clips, so you can get on with building your presentation.

Another worthy feature of QuickTime Player Pro is that it allows you to "present" movies, that is, to play them full screen. This is especially useful when you export your Keynote file as a QuickTime movie. You can then play the movie as you would a slideshow, taking up the entire screen. The other good thing about exporting your presentation to a QuickTime movie is that the presentation will then be playable on all platforms that support QuickTime, including Windows and some Unix systems.

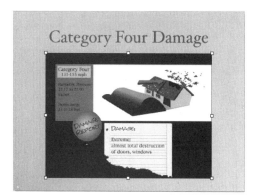

Figure 6.10 After you drag a Flash animation onto your slide, you can choose a poster frame—the frame which will show while you're working with the slides—using the slider in the Media Inspector.

Adding Flash Animations

Macromedia Flash movies are the most popular animation format, used for most animations you see on the Web. Flash is great for creating animated logos, animations that describe a process, or even cool animated charts for use in your presentations. Because Flash animations are usually vector graphics, you can scale the Flash movie on your slide with no loss of quality.

Keynote handles Flash movies in much the same way that it handles QuickTime movies. The Media Inspector works the same way for a Flash movie as it does for QuickTime.

To add a Flash movie to a slide:

1. In Keynote, go to the slide where you want to add a Flash movie.

2. In the Finder, find the Flash file that you want to put in the presentation.

3. Drag the Flash file onto the Slide Canvas. The Flash movie appears on the Slide Canvas, showing the poster frame (**Figure 6.10**).

✔ Tips

- You can place as many Flash movies as you wish on a slide.

- You can use the Poster Frame slider in the Media Inspector to set the poster frame for the movie, which can be any frame of the Flash movie.

- You can use animated GIFs on your slides. Place them on the slide in the same way that you would add a Flash movie. You can then use the Media Inspector to control the animated GIF.

ADDING FLASH ANIMATIONS

Compositing Images and Movies

Because Keynote treats a media file as just another object on the Slide Canvas, you can layer and composite QuickTime and Flash movies with other graphics on your slide to get visually interesting effects. In the example below, I've taken a photograph of a television, modified it a bit in Macromedia Fireworks MX, brought it into Keynote and scaled it, and then placed a movie file behind the television so that the movie appears to be playing on the TV.

To composite images and movie files:

1. Obtain a photograph that you want to use as a layer in Keynote (**Figure 6.11**).

   This photograph came from Hemera Photo-Objects 50,000 Volume II, a royalty-free collection of images. The photograph looks good, but it isn't ready for use in Keynote yet. The area of the TV screen needs to be made transparent.

   The photograph will also work better if it is in TIFF format, rather than JPEG. If you have a choice of formats, use TIFF with transparency.

2. Open the photograph in an image editor that supports transparency (**Figure 6.12**).

   I used Macromedia Fireworks MX, but Adobe Photoshop would also be a good choice.

3. Use the image editor's tools to select the area of the photograph that you want to make transparent.

   In Fireworks, I used the Magic Wand, and added to the selection using the Shift key until the entire TV screen was selected.

Figure 6.11 This picture of a television will make a fine cutout for our QuickTime movie.

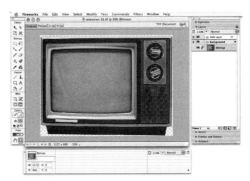

Figure 6.12 Fireworks makes it easy to select parts of an image and make them transparent.

Figure 6.13 The areas of this image that are shown with a checkerboard pattern are transparent.

Figure 6.14 This image will need a bit of further scaling within Keynote to fit properly on the slide.

Figure 6.15 When you drag a movie file onto the slide, it appears on top of the image that you previously added to the slide.

4. Make the selection transparent.

In Fireworks, I pressed Delete, and the selection was removed, leaving the area transparent (**Figure 6.13**).

If necessary, do some additional cleanup of the selection so that all of the area you want to be transparent is clear.

5. (Optional) Scale the image so that it is closer to the size of your slide.

In the case of my photograph, it was 1172 × 866 in size, so I wanted to scale it down a bit. I could have done the scaling in Keynote, but sometimes you'll get a better result by scaling in your image editor.

6. In the image editor, save the modified image as a new file, in TIFF format.

Fireworks requires that you use the Export command to save images as TIFFs.

7. Switch to Keynote, and display the slide to which you want to add the photograph and movie.

8. Drag the modified photograph from the Finder onto the slide (**Figure 6.14**).

9. If necessary, scale the image a bit further in Keynote so that it fits the slide better.

10. Drag the movie file from the Finder onto the slide (**Figure 6.15**).

Because you added the movie file after the photograph, the movie file ends up on top of the photograph.

11. Adjust the scale of the image to more closely match the movie.

12. Position the image, the movie, or both so that the movie fits over the cutout in the image.

continues on next page

COMPOSITING IMAGES AND MOVIES

13. Select the movie, then click Back on the toolbar.

The movie moves behind the image.

14. Adjust the movie or image position to get the final effect you want (**Figure 6.16**).

✔ Tips

■ You can add additional layers over the moving video if you like. For example, a text line that slides over the video as it is playing can be a neat effect.

■ You can set the opacity of movies in the Graphic Inspector. This allows you to use a movie as a moving background behind the other elements on your slide.

■ Because QuickTime movies don't scale well, it's better to scale the image to match the movie, rather than the reverse. Flash movies are generally quite scaleable, so you can shrink or grow them as needed.

■ Don't group the movie and image files. If you do, the movie won't play on your slide.

Figure 6.16 The final composition shows the movie file apparently on the television screen.

WORKING WITH TABLES

In presentations, you'll often find it useful to present data in tables. A table's rows and columns make it easy to present complex information in a simple way. Examples of such data would be quarterly financial results, a performance comparison of two or more products, or even a simple list.

Keynote provides an excellent set of tools for creating and formatting tables and their contents. These tools allow you to make even dry financial data visually interesting. Using object builds, you can also make parts of your table animate onto the screen, allowing you to build your points one step at a time. You'll find more information about using animation in tables in Chapter 9.

In this chapter, you'll learn how to use Keynote to create and modify a table, and ensure that tables and their content look the way you intend.

Creating a Table

Tables consist of rows and columns. *Rows* are the horizontal divisions of the table; *columns* are the vertical divisions. A row and a column intersect to form a *cell*, which is where the content of the table goes. You can put either text or a graphic (or both) into a cell.

When you add a table to a slide, Keynote automatically creates a table with three rows and three columns. After the table is added, you can modify the table and its contents by changing the number of rows and columns, formatting the text, modifying table and cell borders, and changing the size of the table.

You're probably familiar with using tables in word processors, such as Microsoft Word or AppleWorks. Using tables in Keynote is similar, with one important caveat: tables in presentations should be simpler than tables that you would use in a printed document. Too much information in a table can overwhelm the viewer (**Figure 7.1**).

To create a table:

1. In the Slide Navigator, select the slide on which you wish to create a table, or create a new slide by clicking New in the toolbar.

2. If you created a new slide, choose an appropriate slide master using the Masters pop-up menu in the toolbar.

   Because you want to leave enough room on the slide for the table, you'll probably want to choose a slide master such as Blank or Title - Top. Keynote attempts to place tables so that they will fit properly on the slide, so, for example, if you choose the Title & Bullets - Left master, adding a table will create a small table in the open area on the slide. If there isn't enough free space on a slide, such as with a master like Title & Bullets, Keynote simply drops a full-size table onto the slide, and lets you sort things out.

Sales Results (millions)

Division	Q1	Q2	Q3	Q4	Goal %
North	$162	$141	$148	$152	-5%
East	$120	$117	$117	$121	-7%
West	$152	$149	$144	$146	-2%
South	$110	$112	$111	$112	+1%
Pac. Rim	$14	$14	$15	$15	+12%
Asia	$9	$11	$14	$13	+10%
India	$1	$2	$1.5	$2	n/a
Europe	$91	$94	$93	$92	+2%
Canada	$26	$28	$30	$34	+11%

AHTV Funding Sources

Gov't	Private	Membership
Annual city grant	Telethon	Membership dues
Sonoma County stipend	Annual sponsors	Production fees

Figure 7.1 Too much information in a table will make the table too hard for your audience to read (top). It's best to keep tables for presentations simple (bottom).

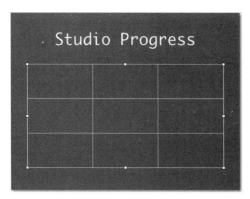

Figure 7.2 By default, Keynote tables have three rows and three columns.

Table Inspector button

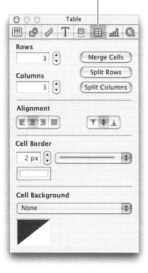

Figure 7.3 The Table Inspector allows you to set the number of rows and columns for a table, set alignment for items in the table, and specify the cell borders and backgrounds.

3. Click the Table button in the toolbar.

or

Choose Edit > Place > Table.

The table appears on the slide (**Figure 7.2**). The table will have three rows and three columns. To increase the number of rows and/or columns, see "Inserting Rows and Columns," later in this chapter.

✔ Tip

■ If you have an Inspector window open, when you insert a table the Inspector window switches to the Table Inspector (**Figure 7.3**). We'll explore the Table Inspector more later in this chapter.

Selecting table elements

To work effectively with a table, you'll need to know how to select its elements. You can select an entire table; one or more rows and columns; an individual cell or multiple cells; and nonadjacent cells, rows, or columns.

To select the entire table:

◆ Click once anywhere in the table.

Selection handles will appear at the edges of the table, which you can use to resize the table (**Figure 7.4**).

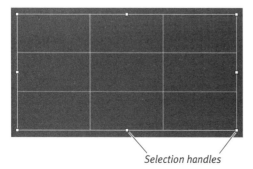

Selection handles

Figure 7.4 Use the selection handles to resize the table.

To select a single cell:

◆ With no part of the table selected, double-click in the cell that you wish to select. If any part of the table is selected, click once outside the table to deselect, then double-click on the cell you want.

The border of the selected cell is highlighted in yellow (**Figure 7.5**). This indicates that you have entered *text edit mode*. In this mode, any text that you type will replace any text that already appears in the cell. You can move between cells in the table by pressing the arrow keys on your keyboard.

To place a text insertion point in a cell:

◆ Double-click to select a cell, then click in that cell again. A text insertion point will appear inside the cell (**Figure 7.6**).

When the insertion point appears in a table cell, you can move the cursor between table cells by pressing Tab.

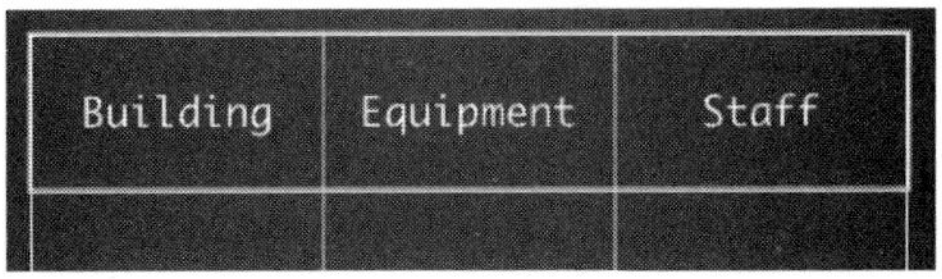

To select a contiguous group of cells:

◆ Double-click the first cell, hold down the Shift key, then click the last cell.

The selected cells will be highlighted in yellow (**Figure 7.7**). You can use this technique to select any rectangular group of cells, be it a row, column, or any other area of the table.

To select nonadjacent cells:

◆ Double-click the first cell, hold down the Command key, then select additional cells.

The selected cells will be highlighted in yellow (**Figure 7.8**).

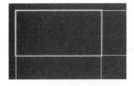

Figure 7.5 It's hard to see in black-and-white, but this cell is highlighted in yellow.

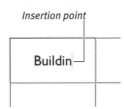

Figure 7.6 When you click three times in a cell, the text insertion point appears.

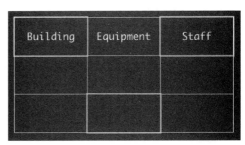

Figure 7.7 The three cells at the top of the table are all selected.

Figure 7.8 Keynote allows you to select noncontiguous cells in a table. Here I selected the cells that contain the words "Building" and "Staff," and the cell in the center of the bottom row.

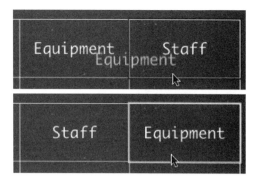

Figure 7.9 When you drag the contents of one cell to another you get a ghost image (top). When you release the mouse button, the contents of the two cells are switched (bottom).

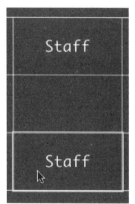

Figure 7.10 When you Option-drag the contents of a cell, you make a copy of those contents in the destination cell.

To switch the contents of two cells:

1. Select a single cell and drag it to another cell.

   As you drag, you'll see a ghost image of the contents of the cell that you are dragging, and a destination cell will be highlighted in blue (**Figure 7.9**).

2. Release the mouse button.

   The contents of the two cells will switch places.

To copy the contents of one cell into another:

1. Select a single cell, hold down the Option key, and drag it to another cell.

   As you drag, you'll see a ghost image of the contents of the cell that you are dragging, and the destination cell will be highlighted in blue.

2. When you have reached the destination cell, release the mouse button.

   The contents of the first cell will be copied into the second cell (**Figure 7.10**).

✔ Tips

- If there is content already in the destination cell, it will be replaced when you Option-drag the new content to the cell. Be careful and avoid accidentally deleting content you want to keep.

- If you select multiple cells (like a row or a column) before you Option-drag, the contents of all the cells will be copied into the destination cells.

CREATING A TABLE

To select a cell border:

1. Click once outside the table to make sure that no table element is selected, then click once in the table to select it.

2. Click a border within the table to select the entire row or column border (**Figure 7.11**).

   Click the border again to select a single border segment (i.e. the border of just one cell).

✔ Tip

■ If you hold down the Shift key when clicking on border segments, you will select nonadjacent border segments.

Resizing table elements

You can resize tables horizontally or vertically, and also make columns wider and rows taller.

To resize an entire table:

1. Click anywhere in a table to select it.

   The selection handles will appear at the edges of the table.

2. Drag one of the selection handles. To widen the table, drag the handle on the right edge of the table; to make the table taller, drag the handle on the bottom edge of the table; and to make the table grow in both directions simultaneously, drag the handle at the bottom-right corner of the table.

To resize a row or column:

1. Click once outside the table to make sure that no table element is selected, then click once in the table to select it.

2. Click a border within the table to select the entire row or column border.

   As you hover your cursor over the border, it will turn into a double-headed arrow (**Figure 7.12**).

3. Drag the border to resize the row or column.

Figure 7.11 Click a border of the table to select it.

Building	Staff	Equipment

Figure 7.12 When the cursor turns into a double-headed arrow, you can drag it to move a row or column border.

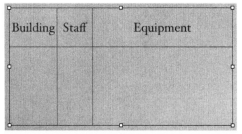

Figure 7.13 If you have moved columns so that they are not evenly distributed (top), you can fix it (bottom).

To distribute row heights or column widths evenly:

1. Select a table that has some rows taller than others, or some columns wider than others.

2. Depending on which you want to do, choose Format > Table > Distribute Rows Evenly or Format > Table > Distribute Columns Evenly.

   Keynote will even out the space between rows or columns, depending on which you chose (**Figure 7.13**).

✔ Tip

■ You can also Control-click (or right-click if you have a multiple-button mouse) and choose Distribute Rows Evenly or Distribute Columns Evenly from the resulting contextual menu.

Deleting table elements

Keynote makes it easy to remove tables, cell contents, rows, or columns.

To delete a table:

1. Click anywhere in a table to select it.

2. Press Delete, or choose Edit > Delete.

To delete the contents of cells:

1. Select one or more cells.

2. Press Delete, or choose Edit > Delete.

To delete rows:

1. Select one or more rows.

2. Choose Format > Table > Delete Row.

To delete columns:

1. Select one or more columns.

2. Choose Format > Table > Delete Column.

Inserting Rows and Columns

Keynote allows you to add rows or columns to your table, either by adding rows or columns to the overall table, or by inserting rows or columns at a selected spot in the table.

To add rows or columns to a table:

1. If you have no Inspector window open, click the Inspector button on the Toolbar. The Inspector window opens.

2. Click the Table button on the Inspector window's toolbar to switch to the Table Inspector.

3. Click anywhere in a table to select it.

4. Using the arrow buttons in the Table Inspector, click to set the number of rows or columns you want in your table (**Figure 7.14**).

   or

   Type a number in the Rows or Columns field in the Table Inspector.

   Keynote increases the number of rows or columns in the table.

✔ Tip

■ Note that increasing the number of rows or columns within a table does not change the size of the table; to do that you'll need to use the table's selection handles.

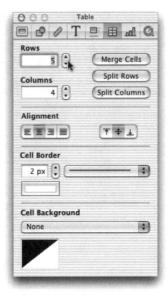

Figure 7.14 Use the Table Inspector to set the number of rows and columns that you want.

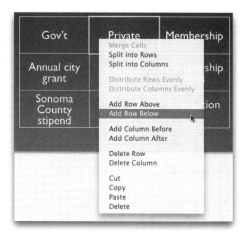

Figure 7.15 Using contextual menus in Keynote can be a real timesaver, especially if you have a mouse with more than one button.

To insert rows in a table:

1. Double-click a cell to select it.

The cell will be outlined in yellow.

2. Choose Format > Table > Add Row Above, or choose Format > Table > Add Row Below.

Keynote inserts an empty row above or below your selection, depending on which menu choice you used. This will also increase the height of the table.

✔ Tip

■ You can also Control-click (or right-click if you have a multiple-button mouse) the selected cell and choose Add Row Above or Add Row Below from the resulting contextual menu (**Figure 7.15**).

To insert columns in a table:

1. Double-click a cell to select it.

The cell will be outlined in yellow.

2. Choose Format > Table > Add Column Before, or choose Format > Table > Add Column After.

Keynote inserts an empty column before or after your selection, depending on which menu choice you used. This will increase the table's width.

✔ Tip

■ As with rows, you can also Control-click (or right-click if you have a multiple-button mouse) the selected cell and choose Add Column Before or Add Column After from the resulting contextual menu (**Figure 7.15**).

Merging and Splitting Cells

Keynote lets you *merge cells*, which is combining two or more adjacent cells into one larger cell, or split a single cell into two or more cells, either vertically or horizontally.

To merge cells:

1. Select the cells you want to merge.

2. In the Table Inspector, click Merge Cells.
   or
   Choose Format > Table > Merge Cells.
   or
   Control-click or right-click the selection and choose Merge Cells from the contextual menu.
   The cells merge (**Figure 7.16**).

✔ Tip

■ You can merge an entire row or column into one cell. The contents, if any, of the row or column will be incorporated into the new cell, and if necessary, text will wrap to fit in the new cell.

To split cells:

1. Click outside the table to make sure that nothing in the table is selected, then double-click in the cell that you want to split.

2. In the Table Inspector, click Split Rows or Split Columns.
   or
   Choose Format > Table > Split into Rows or choose Format > Table > Split into Columns.
   or
   Control-click or right-click the selection and choose Split into Rows or Split into Columns from the contextual menu.
   The cell splits as you command (**Figure 7.17**).

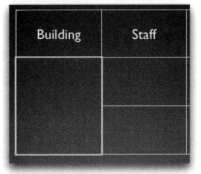

Figure 7.16 First there were two cells (top), then there was one (bottom).

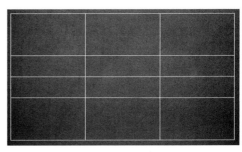

Figure 7.17 The middle row of this table has been split into two.

✔ Tip

■ If you select more than one cell, Keynote will split all of them evenly. This works even if the selected cells are not adjacent.

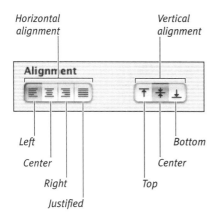

Horizontal alignment

Vertical alignment

Left

Center

Right

Justified

Bottom

Center

Top

Figure 7.18 Use the alignment controls in the Table Inspector for both horizontal and vertical alignment of text and graphics.

Formatting Tables and Cell Contents

Once you have the layout of your table set to your liking, you can begin working on the formatting of the text and graphics within the table. You can also control the thickness and color of the table and cell borders. You'll use the Table Inspector for most of this work. Working with cell backgrounds, another table attribute, will be covered in "Adding Cell Backgrounds," later in this chapter.

When you select the entire table, and then use the controls in the Table Inspector, the changes are applied to the entire table, including the contents of all the cells in the table. You can set alignment for the contents of all of the cells, and there are separate controls for horizontal and vertical alignment (**Figure 7.18**). The alignment controls work for either text or graphics within the cell.

If you want to apply alignment to the contents of a single cell, or group of cells, you must select the cell or cells first. In addition to text alignment, you also have the same control over the text in tables that you do with any text in Keynote, including character and line spacing, and the use of rulers and tabs. See Chapter 4 for more information about text handling in Keynote.

To set alignment in cells:

1. If you want to apply the same text alignment to all the cells in a table at once, click once outside the table to make sure that nothing is selected, then click once anywhere in the table to select it.

   or

   If you want to apply text alignment to individual cells, select those cells.

2. Use the alignment tools in the Table Inspector to set your desired text alignment. You can set horizontal alignment (**Figure 7.19**) and vertical alignment (**Figure 7.20**) separately.

✔ Tip

- You can also use the alignment tools in the Color & Alignment section of the Text Inspector.

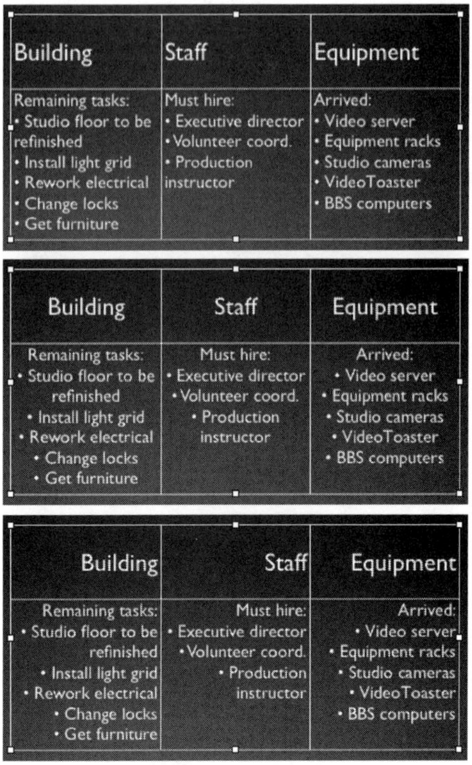

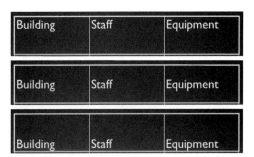

Figure 7.19 Horizontal text alignment within table cells. From top to bottom: Left, Center, and Right text alignment.

Figure 7.20 Vertical text alignment within table cells. From top to bottom: Top, Center, and Bottom alignment.

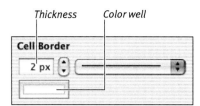

Thickness   *Color well*

Figure 7.21 Use the Cell Border controls to set the line thickness and color for borders.

Saving Tables for Later Use

It can take a considerable amount of effort to format a table that's just the way you want, and there's no reason why you can't reuse that same format again and again. For this and other reasons, it's a good idea to create a Keynote file that you can use as a library for objects that you want to save.

To create a library file, create a new Keynote file, using one of the neutral themes such as Gradient. Create one or more slides based on the Blank slide master, then copy the objects that you want to save from your presentation file, switch to the library file, and paste them in. Then save the library file. If you save it in *harddisk*/Library/Application Support/Keynote/Image Library/, then you'll be able to access your library file easily by choosing File > Open Image Library from within Keynote.

To apply and change cell borders:

1. Select the table, or if you only wish to make changes to a particular border segment, select that segment.

2. In the Cell Border section of the Table Inspector (**Figure 7.21**), do one or more of the following:

   ◆ To change the border thickness, use the arrow buttons to increase or decrease the thickness (in pixels), or type your desired thickness in the field.

   ◆ From the pop-up menu, choose a line style for the cell borders, or choose None.

   ◆ To change the border color, click the color well to select it and open the Colors window, then choose a color (see Chapter 4 for more information on using the Colors window).

Adding Cell Backgrounds and Graphics

Filling cells with a background image is an excellent way to help give your table a slick, professional look. Keynote gives you three choices for cell backgrounds:

- ◆ **Color Fill** puts a solid color in the cell background.

- ◆ **Gradient Fill** puts a smooth color blend in the cell background.

- ◆ **Image Fill** puts an image in the cell background. You'll also use this option for images you wish to place in a cell.

The benefit of using one of the fills available in the Cell Background section of the Table Inspector is that they will move with the table and adjust their positions within cells when you resize the table, which can save you a tremendous amount of time. Alternatively, you can place a graphic on the slide and position it so that it appears to be in a table cell, but it will not really be part of the table. You should think of the table and its contents as being one layer on the slide; image fills in cells of the table will be part of the table layer, whereas graphics placed on the slide will not, and will move and resize independently. That's useful sometimes; see the "Using shapes as backgrounds" section later in this chapter. Keynote handles fills in tables in the same way it does anywhere else on slides, such as in graphic shapes and backgrounds. See Chapter 5 for more information on how to add and modify color, gradient, and image fills.

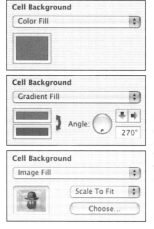

Figure 7.22 You can choose three kinds of background fills for tables, each with its own set of controls: Color Fill (top), Gradient Fill (middle), or Image Fill (bottom).

Figure 7.23 With image fills, Keynote scales the images to fit the cells, though you can use other scaling options.

To fill cells with a color, gradient, or image:

1. Select the cell or cells you wish to fill.

2. In the Cell Background section of the Table Inspector, choose the type of fill—Color, Gradient, or Image—from the pop-up menu.

   Depending on your choice, your options will change (**Figure 7.22**).

3. Set the appropriate options for the type of fill you've chosen.

   The table cell or cells are filled (**Figure 7.23**).

✔ Tips

- When adding cell fills, always keep in mind that the most important information in a table is the text in it, not the cell backgrounds. You don't want to add cell backgrounds that will detract from the readability of the text in the table cells. That goes for the pattern, as well as the color, of the cell background. Remember that the data in the table needs to be easily read by the people in the back row of the auditorium.

- Make sure that the cell backgrounds complement, rather than clash, with the rest of the slide. Again, you should evaluate patterns, as well as the colors.

- Keynote does a good job of scaling images that are used as cell backgrounds, as you can see in **Figure 7.23**, but you'll also notice that the image presses right up against the cell borders. To get a bit of breathing room around the figures, you'll need to build that into the image when you are preparing your images for import, using an image editor like Adobe Photoshop.

ADDING CELL BACKGROUNDS AND GRAPHICS

133

Using shapes as backgrounds

Keynote's built-in fills are useful, but if you're willing to take a bit more time, there's a technique that can give you a lot more flexibility in the look of your table backgrounds. You can use Keynote's drawing shapes to create cell backgrounds, and layer them with the table to create different effects. For example, you can create a table like the one in **Figure 7.24**. This table uses rectangular shapes with an image fill from Keynote's Chart Colors file. Each of the product columns has its own, different background color, and the color has different opacities for the header row and the body of the table. Because you can't adjust the opacity of a table cell fill, using shapes gives you more options for cell backgrounds. You can adapt this technique for any number of looks for your tables.

To use shapes as cell backgrounds:

1. Add a table to a slide.

   It's best to add some text to the table; it will help you gauge the effects you get later.

2. From the Shapes pop-up menu in the toolbar, add a square shape.

3. Position and resize the shape so that it covers up one of the cells in the header row of the table.

4. Choose File > Open Image Library.

   The Image Library window will open in the Finder (**Figure 7.25**).

5. Double-click the Chart Colors.key file to open it.

6. In the Chart Colors file, select the color chip that you want (**Figure 7.26**).

   You don't have to choose a color chip from the theme that you are using; any color chip that strikes your fancy will do.

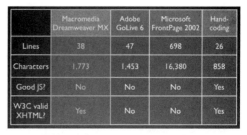

Figure 7.24 Using shapes as background fills, layered with tables, can get you excellent, colorful results (though it's hard to tell in this black-and-white example).

Figure 7.25 Open the Chart Colors.key file in the Image Library folder to access color chips.

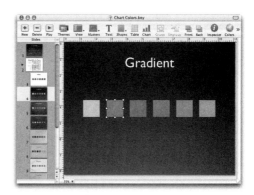

Figure 7.26 Select and copy the style of one of the color chips in the Chart Colors.key file.

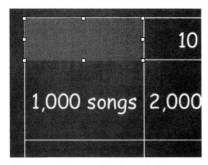

Figure 7.27 After pasting the style from one of the color chips, the shape is opaque. But not for long.

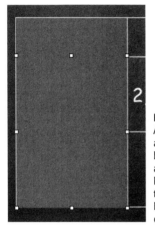

Figure 7.28 After you create a shape for the body cells (shown as the selection here), you'll need to copy it for the body cells in the other columns.

Figure 7.29 When you're done creating all of the shapes for the body cells, set their opacity to a lower number than the opacity for the header row.

7. In the Chart Colors file, choose Format > Copy Style.

8. Switch back to your presentation file, and select the square shape.

9. Choose Format > Paste Style.

   The shape takes on an image fill of the color chip (**Figure 7.27**).

10. Option-drag the shape to create a copy of the shape, then resize and position it over the body cells in the same column (**Figure 7.28**).

11. Option-drag the first shape you created, and position it over the next cell in the header row.

    If you want the new shape to have a different color, repeat steps 6 through 9.

12. Repeat step 11 for the rest of the cells in the header row of the table.

13. Option-drag the shape you created in step 10 for the body cells, and position the resulting new shape over the next column of body cells.

    If you want the new shape to have a different color, repeat the procedure in steps 6 through 9.

14. Repeat step 13 for the rest of the columns in the body of the table.

15. Select the shapes that are now covering the cells in the header row of the table.

16. In the Graphic Inspector, set the opacity of the header shapes to 80% (**Figure 7.29**).

continues on next page

17. Select the shapes that are now covering the cells in the body of the table.

18. In the Graphic Inspector, set the opacity of the body shapes to 40% (**Figure 7.30**).

19. Select all of the shapes that you have created.

20. Click the Back button on the toolbar to send the shapes behind the table and you've completed your slide (**Figure 7.31**).

✔ Tips

■ If you want the same color for all of the header row's cells, just make one large shape to cover all of those cells in step 10; no need to make copies of the rectangular shape. Do the same for the shapes over the body cells.

■ You can create interesting effects by using images as the backgrounds, instead of the color chips. See the "Working with Images as Backgrounds" sidebar.

■ In many cases, using a higher opacity setting for the header rows (or columns) of a table is a good way to set off the information. But you could also use this highlighting-by-opacity technique to highlight a single cell, or group of cells in the middle of a table. For example, you could put a shape, colored red, behind table cells that showed negative financial results. Or you could use different colors in each row of a table to highlight the performance of the different divisions of your company.

■ It's a good idea to set the Stroke of the shapes to None in the Graphic Inspector. This eliminates lines at the borders of the shapes.

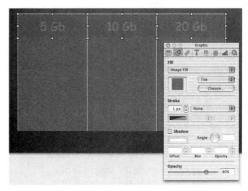

Figure 7.30 Use the Graphic Inspector to reduce the opacity of the shapes that you have overlaid on the table.

Figure 7.31 After you send the shapes behind the table, your table is complete.

Working with Images as Backgrounds

When you use images as backgrounds, you'll almost always want to use them as an image fill in a shape, then reduce the image's opacity. That allows you the control you need, because images placed directly into a table will often overwhelm the table's content. For example, in **Figure 7.32**, the same image has been used as an image fill. In the left example, the picture of the ship was used as an image fill in the table itself; in the right example, I created a rectangular shape, used the ship picture as the image fill, reduced the shape's opacity, and sent it behind the table. The example on the left shows the drawback of placing image fills directly in tables; you can't read some of the information in the table.

Figure 7.32 Placing an image directly in a table can obscure the table's message (left). The example on the right reduces the image's opacity, allowing the image to add visual interest, rather than detract from the message.

CREATING CHARTS

Charts can help viewers of your presentation better understand quantitative information without overwhelming the viewer with an avalanche of numbers. Using a chart, you can present complex data that can be understood at a glance. Charts illustrate the relationships between different sets of data, and they are also good for showing trends over time.

Keynote provides you with a wide variety of chart types, and you can manipulate those charts in many different ways to get your point across. You should have no problems tailoring your charts to suit your taste and the needs of your presentation.

You can also animate the parts of a chart to have them appear on your slide one at a time. To create these chart builds, see Chapter 9.

In this chapter, you'll learn about the different chart types; how to use Keynote to create charts; and how to manipulate those charts so that they look the way you want.

About Chart Types

Keynote can create eight different types of charts, as shown in **Table 8.1**. Each type of chart is useful for displaying a particular kind of data.

It's not always easy to decide on which kind of chart to use. Sometimes the data that you're trying to present will practically beg for a particular chart type; for example, when you're trying to show values as percentages that add up to 100%, a pie chart is almost always the right approach. But in other instances, several chart types might fit your data and do a good job of presenting it. Here are a few tips to help you choose the right chart for the job.

◆ Evaluate the data that you are trying to present, particularly the aspect of the data that you want to highlight. Data where the totals are more important than the individual values are good candidates for area charts, stacked bar and stacked column chart types.

◆ If you have many data series to present, use a chart type like bar or column, which show many data points well.

◆ Choose the chart type that produces the simplest chart for your data. If necessary, switch between the different types in Keynote to see the visual effect of each type on the data. Because your viewers don't have control of how long your slide is on screen, it will help if you give them charts they can grasp quickly.

◆ Pie charts shouldn't be used to represent data with more than 5 to 8 data series. Each series will appear as a slice of the pie, and too-small pieces will not have a good visual impact.

Table 8.1

Chart Types		
ICON	CHART TYPE	DESCRIPTION
	Column Chart	Column charts show unique values. They are useful when comparing values, such as sales, over different time periods.
	Stacked Column Chart	Stacked column charts, like area charts, display both individual values and the sum of several values for a given item.
	Bar Chart	Bar charts, like column charts, show individual items and their relationship to one another.
	Stacked Bar Chart	This variation of the bar chart is similar to the stacked column chart.
	Line Chart	Line charts show data trends over time or other intervals. They are useful for showing variations in values, such as stock prices.
	Area Chart	Area charts show the magnitude of change over time.
	Stacked Area Chart	Stacked area charts show the magnitude of change over time, and they display both individual values and the sum of all values in the chart.
	Pie Chart	Pie charts show proportional relationships between several values and a whole, often expressed as percentages.

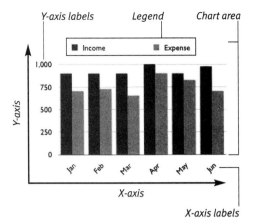

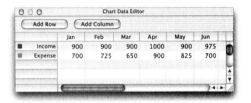

Figure 8.1 The parts of a column chart.

Figure 8.2 The Chart Data Editor resembles a spreadsheet, but it doesn't do any calculations.

Figure 8.3 The Chart Inspector gives you the controls you'll use to customize your charts.

Chart anatomy

Before you begin creating charts, you'll need to know a little about the terminology Keynote uses to refer to the different parts of a chart, and the different tools that Keynote gives you to manipulate charts. The column chart in **Figure 8.1** labels the main parts that appear on a slide. Keynote provides the Chart Data Editor, which is a spreadsheet-like window where you enter the information that makes up the chart (**Figure 8.2**), and the Chart Inspector, which gives you many controls that allow you to customize the chart (**Figure 8.3**).

The data for the chart appears in the *chart area*, which contains the bars, columns, lines, etc. All chart types (except for pie charts) have two axes, the horizontal *X-axis* and the vertical *Y-axis*. One of these will be the *value axis*, which is where you read the values you are charting. For example, in Figure 8.1, the value axis is the Y-axis. In column charts, area charts, and line charts, the Y-axis is the value axis. For bar charts, the X-axis is the value axis. Pie charts don't have a value axis.

Charts show the relationship between two types of data (for example, financial performance over a time period such as months or years). These two data types are called the *data series* and *data sets*. In Figure 8.2, each row in the Chart Data Editor represents a data series, and each column represents a data set. The *legend* is the label or labels on the chart that explain what the different data series represent.

Adding Charts

You'll want to add a chart to a slide that has plenty of room for the chart, though you can add a chart to any slide. Of the built-in master slides, the ones that are most appropriate for charts are Title - Top, Title & Bullets - Left, Title & Bullets - Right, and of course Blank, which is a good master slide to use for charts that need to be as large as possible.

To add a chart to a slide:

1. Display the slide where you want to add a chart.

2. Click the Chart button on the toolbar, or choose Edit > Place > Chart.

   A sample chart appears on the slide (**Figure 8.4**) and the Chart Data Editor and the Chart Inspector open.

3. In the Chart Inspector, choose the chart type that you want from the pop-up menu (**Figure 8.5**).

4. Enter your data into the Chart Data Editor.

   For more information about using the Chart Data Editor, see the next section.

✔ Tips

- If you Option-click the Chart button in the toolbar, the pointer turns into a crosshair, which you can then drag on the Slide Canvas to create a chart any size that you want (**Figure 8.6**). Size tags will appear as you drag to let you know how large the chart is.

- You can add as many charts as you want to a slide, subject only to how many will fit on the slide, and to your sense of good taste.

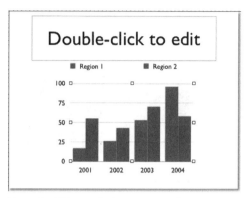

Figure 8.4 This sample chart appears whenever you add a chart to a slide.

Figure 8.5 Use the pop-up menu in the Chart Inspector to change between the eight chart types.

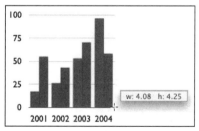

Figure 8.6 After you Option-click the Chart button in the toolbar, you can draw a chart any size you want on the slide.

ADDING CHARTS

Charting Alternatives

Keynote's charting abilities are decent, but they are hardly complete. For example, Keynote doesn't provide 3-D charts, and lacks many chart types found in other charting programs. Keynote also lacks the ability to create combination charts, which contain more than one chart type. If you need more charting power than Keynote can provide, you'll need to turn to other applications that can create charts.

Microsoft Excel has many chart types that Keynote lacks, including 3-D, surface, stock, radar, scatter, bubble, and doughnut charts. Excel gives you control over the transparency of chart objects, which allows you to create some nice effects (**Figure 8.7**). Because Excel's charting abilities are coupled with a powerful spreadsheet, you can do all of your calculations in Excel, chart your results, dress-up the chart using Excel's advanced tools, and paste the finished chart into Keynote.

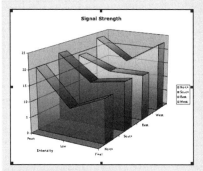

Figure 8.7 Microsoft Excel can create these nifty 3-D area charts with transparency that Keynote can't match.

Chartsmith, from Blacksmith (`www.blacksmith.com`), is a standalone charting application for Mac OS X (**Figure 8.8**). It creates all of the Keynote chart types, plus many more, such as base-error, histogram, XY, and intensity scatter charts. As a nice bonus, you can export Chartsmith documents in Keynote format, making it especially easy to get charts into your presentations. You can even select a particular Keynote theme, and Chartsmith will use that theme when it exports.

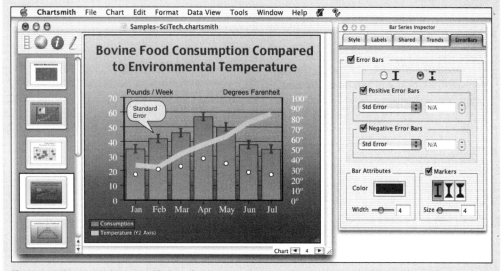

Figure 8.8 Chartsmith does a terrific job of creating combination charts with error bars and a trend line. This chart can then be exported as a Keynote file.

Using the Chart Data Editor

When you create a new chart in Keynote, the Chart Data Editor is filled by default with two rows and four columns of sample data. Chances are this won't be the data that you want, so the first thing you'll need to do is get rid of the sample data so that you don't accidentally mistake it for your own data. Next, you'll need to change the row and column labels so that they match your chart's data. After that, you can enter your data in the Chart Data Editor's spreadsheet cells.

Once your data is in place, you can rearrange it by dragging rows or columns around on the spreadsheet, or you can see more of your data on-screen by resizing the spreadsheet's column width.

To delete all data in the Chart Data Editor:

1. Click and drag over the sample data in the Chart Data Editor to highlight it (**Figure 8.9**).

2. Choose Edit > Delete.

   The values in the selected cells are replaced by zeros. You can't clear the cells entirely; the best you can do is put zero values in the cells.

✔ Tip

- Oddly, pressing the Delete key in step 2 does nothing; you must choose Delete from the Edit menu. Similarly, you cannot use the contextual menu to delete the contents of the cells.

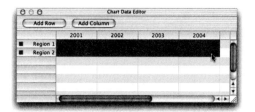

Figure 8.9 You'll need to highlight the sample data in the Chart Data Editor before you can delete it.

Table 8.2

Chart Data Entry Shortcuts	
KEY	**WHAT IT DOES**
Tab	Completes a cell entry and moves the selection to the right
Shift-Tab	Completes a cell entry and moves the selection to the left
Return	Completes a cell entry and moves the selection down
Shift-Return	Completes a cell entry and moves the selection up
Enter	Completes a cell entry and selects the cell contents
Home	Moves the selection to the beginning of the row
End	Moves the selection to the last non-blank cell in the current row

	2001			2001
■ Region 1	17		■ North Bay	17
■ Region 2	55		■ Region 2	55

Figure 8.10 First you highlight one of the labels in the Chart Data Editor (left), and then you type in the new label (right).

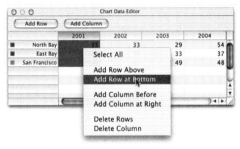

Figure 8.11 The contextual menu is often faster to use than the Format menu or the Chart Inspector.

To change row or column labels:

1. In the Chart Data Editor, double-click the name of the row or column that you want to change.

The name is highlighted (**Figure 8.10**).

2. Type the new name.

The new name replaces the old.

3. Click outside the label to accept the change.

To enter data in the Chart Data Editor:

1. Click a cell in the Chart Data Editor, then type.

2. Press the Tab key to complete the entry and move the selection to the right.

See **Table 8.2** for more ways to enter data and move the selection in the Chart Data Editor.

3. (Optional) If you need another row or another column, click the Add Row or Add Column button in the Chart Data Editor.

or

Select a row or column, then Control-Click (or right-click if you have a multiple-button mouse) to bring up the contextual menu, then choose Add Row Above, Add Row at Bottom, Add Column Before, or Add Column at Right (**Figure 8.11**).

✔ Tip

■ You can also copy and paste data from a spreadsheet application, such as Microsoft Excel or AppleWorks, into the Chart Data Editor.

USING THE CHART DATA EDITOR

To move rows or columns:

1. In the Chart Data Editor, click and drag one of the row or column labels (**Figure 8.12**).

2. When the row or column is where you want it, release the mouse button.

   The row or column moves.

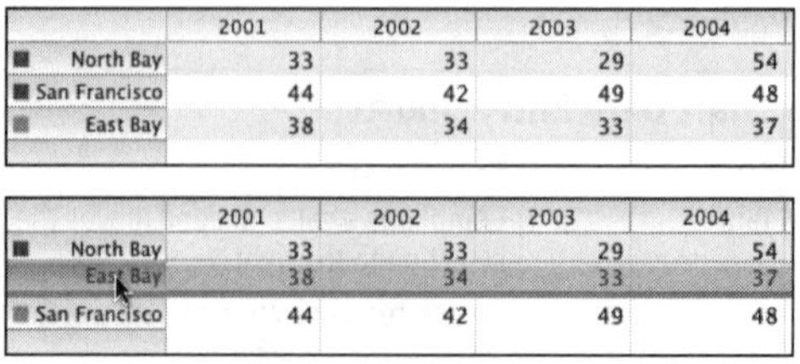

To resize columns in the Chart Data Editor:

1. Position the mouse pointer over the boundary between two of the column labels.

   The cursor will change into a double-headed arrow.

2. Click and drag right or left to increase or decrease the column's width.

To delete a row or column:

1. Click a row or column label to select an entire row or column.

2. Choose Edit > Delete.

   or

   Select a row or column label, then press Delete.

   or

   Move the mouse pointer over the selected data, then Control-click (or right-click if you have a multiple-button mouse) to bring up the contextual menu, then choose Delete Row or Delete Column.

   The row or column disappears.

	2001	2002	2003	2004
North Bay	33	33	29	54
San Francisco	44	42	49	48
East Bay	38	34	33	37

	2001	2002	2003	2004
North Bay	33	33	29	54
East Bay	38	34	33	37
San Francisco	44	42	49	48

Figure 8.12 Here, I'm dragging the East Bay line above the San Francisco line.

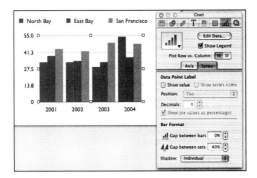

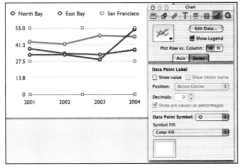

Figure 8.13 When you change the chart type from column (top) to line (bottom), the Chart Inspector reflects the change.

Changing Chart Types

You can change the chart type at any time in Keynote. All you need to do is select the chart and then choose from the chart type pop-up menu in the Chart Inspector.

To change the chart type:

1. Select a chart on the Slide Canvas.

2. In the Chart Inspector, choose a new chart type from the pop-up menu.

   or

   Choose Format > Chart > Chart Type >, then choose one of the chart types from the hierarchical menu.

   The chart changes (**Figure 8.13**). The Chart Inspector also changes, to show options appropriate to the new chart types.

Transposing Chart Plots

Sometimes you need to look at your data in a different way, and Keynote can transpose the way it plots the data series and data sets, to give you a different perspective on your data.

In the example in **Figure 8.14**, the rows (data series) in the Chart Data Editor show income and expense figures distributed across four months, which are expressed in the columns (data sets). The resulting graph (**Figure 8.15**) groups each month's financial results together. If we transpose the data series and data sets, we get a very different view of the same data (**Figure 8.16**). In this view, you can see how income and expenses change over the four months. The income figures and the expense figures for all months are grouped together, making it easier to see the trend for each group over time. Keynote changes the legend of the graph to reflect the new ordering of the data, and the labels in the Chart Data Editor also change to match.

The benefit of being able to transpose data series and data sets is that it allows you to change the presentation of the data in the Chart Data Editor without the need to retype your data.

To transpose data series and data sets:

1. Select a chart on a slide.

2. Click the Inspector button on the toolbar to open the Inspector window, if it isn't already open, then click the Chart button in the Inspector window.

3. Click the Plot Row vs. Column button in the Chart Inspector (**Figure 8.17**). The chart changes.

   The row button makes the rows in the Chart Data Editor the data series, and the column button makes the columns in the Chart Data Editor the data series.

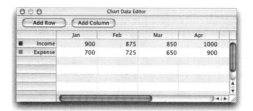

Figure 8.14 The rows in the Chart Data Editor represent the data series.

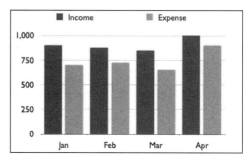

Figure 8.15 When charted, the data series group the financial data together by month.

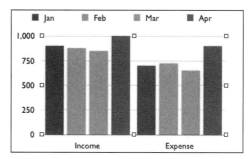

Figure 8.16 By transposing the data series and data sets, you see all the income and all the expense figures grouped together.

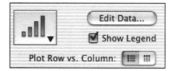

Figure 8.17 Use the Plot Row vs. Column button to transpose data sets.

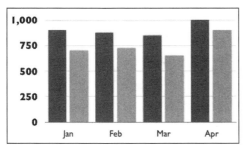

Figure 8.18 I used the Fonts window to increase the size of the labels on the Y-axis and make them boldface.

Modifying Chart Elements

You can format the different parts of a chart to serve your needs. You can change the chart's colors, fonts, gridlines, legend and axis labels and control the formatting of numbers in charts.

You'll use the Chart Inspector to make most of the formatting changes to your charts. If you prefer, you can use the Format > Chart hierarchical menu, but it's less convenient than using the Inspector.

Changing colors and fonts

There's not much difference between the text and graphics on a chart than any other text and graphic objects in Keynote. You select the item you wish to change, then use the same tools to make the modifications as you would any similar text or graphic.

You change chart colors as you would any graphic, and you can apply image, gradient, or color fills, change the opacity, add shadows, and change the line styles.

For more details about working with text, see Chapter 4; for more about working with graphics, see Chapter 5.

To change text in charts:

1. Select the text that you wish to change.

   You can select several text boxes in each chart: the legend, the data point labels (if they are visible), the X-axis label, and the Y-axis label.

2. Use the Fonts or Colors windows, or the Format > Font menu, to adjust the appearance of the text (**Figure 8.18**).

To change graphics in charts:

1. Select the graphic element that you wish to change.

   In bar and column charts, if you select one element in a series, all the elements in that series are selected (**Figure 8.19**). In a pie chart, you can select one or more wedges of the pie.

2. Use the Graphic Inspector to adjust the fill, stroke, shadow, or opacity of the selected object or objects (**Figure 8.20**).

✔ Tips

- The Apple themes, and many third-party themes, come with color chips that you can use as chart fills. These chips are image samples that you can use as image fills in chart objects, to give your charts a more appealing look. For more information about using image fills, see Chapter 5. You can find the Apple color chips by choosing File > Open Image Library, then opening the Chart Colors.key file.

- It's a good idea to put color chip files that come with third-party themes in the Image Library folder, which you'll find at *harddisk*/Library/Application Support/Keynote/Image Library.

- To easily copy a color chip, select it, and choose Format > Copy Style. Then select the destination graphic, and choose Format > Paste Style. The copied style will be applied to the selected graphic.

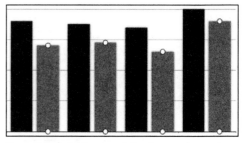

Figure 8.19 Selecting one of the elements in a series selects all of the elements of that series.

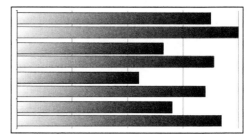

Figure 8.20 You can use the Graphic Inspector to add gradient fills and other effects to the parts of your chart.

Tick marks

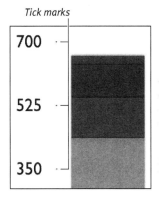

700

525

350

Figure 8.21 Tick marks help you visualize the divisions of the chart, but in Keynote, the tick marks are rather small, so gridlines tend to do a better job.

Figure 8.22 The Axis tab of the Chart Inspector lets you set options for labels, tick marks, and gridlines.

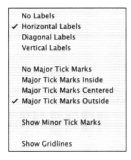

Figure 8.23 The X-Axis pop-up menu lets you select label styles, tick marks, and gridlines.

Figure 8.24 The Y-Axis pop-up menu lets you turn on labels and gridlines, set tick mark styles, and show or hide the minimum value for the axis.

Modifying axis elements

Axis elements include the labels and tick marks for the X-axis and Y-axis, gridlines, the range of values that are displayed along the value axis, and the number format of the values in the chart. (Tick marks are marks on one or both axes that help you visualize the divisions of the chart, as in **Figure 8.21**.) You can also adjust the borders of the chart. You'll find the controls for these settings in the Axis tab of the Chart Inspector (**Figure 8.22**).

To change axis labels, tick marks, and gridlines:

1. Select the chart.

2. In the Labels, Ticks, & Grids section of the Axis tab of the Chart Inspector, make one or more selections from the pop-up menu for the X-Axis (**Figure 8.23**).

3. Make one or more selections from the pop-up menu for the Y-Axis (**Figure 8.24**). As you make changes to the pop-up menus, the chart changes.

✔ Tip

■ Column and Stacked Column charts usually look better without gridlines in the X-axis, and with gridlines turned on in the Y-axis. The reverse is true for Bar and Stacked Bar charts. Line charts often look good with gridlines turned on for both axes.

To change the range of displayed values on the value axis:

1. Select the chart.

2. In the Axis tab of the Chart Inspector, type a number in the Minimum field under Value Axis Format.

   This number will be the value that will be shown at the *chart origin*, which is where the X-axis and Y-axis meet.

3. Enter a number in the Maximum field.

   This will be the highest number displayed on the Y-axis label. It must be as high as or higher than the highest value in your data set.

4. Enter a number in the Steps field.

   This will create marks in the Y-axis with values at equal intervals. The more steps that you specify, the more axis markings there will be.

✔ Tip

■ Choosing even numbers as your maximum and steps values will make for clean labels on the Y-axis. If the maximum value isn't easily divisible by the steps value, Keynote will display numbers with decimals.

To set the number format of chart values:

1. Select the chart.

2. In the Axis tab of the Chart Inspector, type text or a text symbol in the Prefix or Suffix field under Number Format.

   or

   Choose the dollar, euro, or pound symbols from the Prefix pop-up menu.

   or

   Choose a symbol from the six listed under the Suffix pop-up menu.

Figure 8.25 You can turn borders on and off with the Axes & Borders buttons.

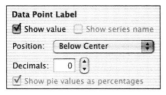

Figure 8.26 Clicking the Show value check box makes the numeric values in the Chart Data Editor appear in the chart.

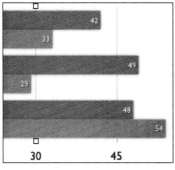

Figure 8.27 Value labels initially appear within bars or columns, but you can change that with the Position pop-up menu.

3. If you want commas in your numbers, choose the comma from the Separator pop-up menu.

✔ Tip

- In the Prefix and Suffix fields, you cannot use the characters 0 through 9, or the comma, period, or number sign (#).

To turn on chart borders:

◆ Use the four buttons in the Axes & Borders section of the Axis tab of the Chart Inspector to turn on or off the borders on the four sides of the chart (**Figure 8.25**).

Adjusting series elements

For data series, you can specify whether or not a series has labels showing the values of the data points, and you can also change the format of the bars and columns in the series. Line, area, and pie charts have different formatting options.

To format data point labels:

1. Select the chart.

2. In the Data Point Label section of the Series tab of the Chart Inspector, select the Show value check box (**Figure 8.26**). This turns on the value labels for each data point in the chart (**Figure 8.27**).

3. From the Position pop-up menu, choose where you want the data point label to appear.

4. If you want to show decimals in your data point values, type a number in the Decimals field.

✔ Tip

- You can change the font or style for data point labels in the same way you change other chart elements; select the data point labels, then make changes in the Fonts window.

To set the bar format:

1. Select the chart.

2. In the Bar Format section of the Series tab of the Chart Inspector (**Figure 8.28**), set the desired gap between bars.

3. Set the gap between data sets (**Figure 8.29**).

4. Specify whether or not you want shadows on the bars.

✔ Tip

■ It's a good idea to always make sure that the gap between bars is less than the gap between sets. Otherwise, it can be difficult for your viewers to differentiate between sets.

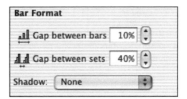

Figure 8.28 Use the Bar Format section of the Chart Inspector to set the gap between bars and data sets on your bar or column chart.

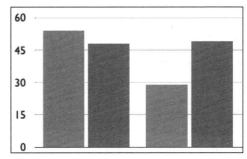

Figure 8.29 A gap between data sets helps the viewer differentiate between each set.

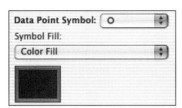

Figure 8.30 Line and area charts use data point symbols. Choose the one you want from the pop-up menu.

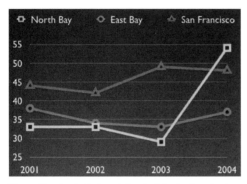

Figure 8.31 I selected each line in this chart and set a different data point symbol for each one.

Figure 8.32 Use the Show Legend check box to reveal or banish legends from your charts.

To set formats in line and area charts:

1. Select the chart.

2. In the Data Point Label section of the Series tab of the Chart Inspector, set the data point label formats as described above.

3. In the chart, click to select one of the lines or areas.

4. In the Data Point Symbol section of the Chart Inspector (**Figure 8.30**), choose a data point symbol from the pop-up menu, or choose None.

5. If you've chosen to use a data point symbol, pick the kind of fill you want for the symbol from the Symbol Fill pop-up menu.

6. Repeat steps 3 through 5 for each of the lines or areas in the chart.

   The chart changes as you complete each line or area's modifications (**Figure 8.31**).

✔ Tip

- If you use a fill for a data point symbol, be especially careful that the result doesn't look too visually busy, detracting from the message of your chart.

Editing chart legends

You can change the text that appears in a legend by editing the text of the data series in the Chart Data Editor (see **Figure 8.14**).

To hide or show the chart legend, select or clear the Show Legend checkbox in the Chart Inspector (**Figure 8.32**).

MODIFYING CHART ELEMENTS

Working with Pie Charts

Pie charts work a bit differently than the other charts in Keynote. Because a pie chart doesn't have an X-axis and a Y-axis, Keynote charts only the first data set in the Chart Data Editor. If the data series are in rows in the Chart Data Editor, only the first column will be charted. If the data series are in columns in the Chart Data Editor, only the first row will be charted. A single pie chart represents a single data set, and each wedge in the pie chart represents one element of that set. If there are other data sets in the Chart Data Editor, and you switch the chart type to a pie chart, the excess data sets will not disappear, but they will not be used, either.

Because pie charts are different, the Chart Inspector changes to reflect those differences. For example, because a pie chart does not have more than one axis, the Axis tab of the Chart Inspector is disabled, and different options appear in the Series tab of the Chart Inspector.

Keynote allows you to manipulate the individual wedges of a pie chart separately. You can select a wedge and manually drag it away from the main body of the pie chart for effect, or you can use a slider in the Chart Inspector to "explode" a wedge of the chart if you like, separating it from the rest of the chart by a specified percentage.

✔ Tip

- You can chart any data set that is in your Chart Data Editor by moving it to the first position in its row or column.

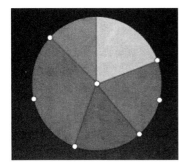

Figure 8.33 The selected wedges here are the wedges with dots at the center of their outside curves.

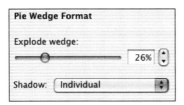

Figure 8.34 The Explode wedge slider lets you move the selected wedge away from the rest of the pie.

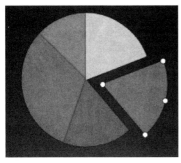

Figure 8.35 This pie chart has one wedge exploded away from the rest of it.

To select pie wedges:

1. Select the chart.

2. Click to select a single wedge.

   or

   Hold down the Command key and click to select multiple noncontiguous wedges (**Figure 8.33**).

   or

   Hold down the Shift key as you select the first and last wedges in a range. All wedges in between will be selected.

   or

   Press ⌘Ⓐ to select all of the wedges.

To explode a pie chart:

1. Select one or more pie wedges.

2. In the Pie Wedge Format section of the Series tab of the Chart Inspector, use the Explode wedge slider to move the selected wedge or wedges away from the rest of the pie (**Figure 8.34**).

   The selected wedges separate from the pie (**Figure 8.35**).

To show values in pie wedges:

1. Select the chart.

2. In the Data Point Label section of the Series tab of the Chart Inspector, select the Show value check box (**Figure 8.36**). This turns on the value labels for each data point in the chart (**Figure 8.37**).

3. From the Position pop-up menu, choose whether you want the data point label to appear inside the pie, or outside of it (**Figure 8.38**).

4. If desired, select the Show series name check box (**Figure 8.39**).

   The series name will appear inside or outside the pie.

5. If you want to show decimals in your data point values, type a number in the Decimals field.

6. If you want to (and with a pie chart you usually will), select the Show pie values as percentages check box.

7. Set the shadow effect on wedges with the Shadow pop-up menu (**Figure 8.40**).

   Your choices are None (no shadows), Group (allows you to use the Graphic Inspector to apply shadowing or opacity changes to the entire pie chart), or Individual (allows you to use the Graphic Inspector to apply shadowing or opacity changes to one or more wedges).

Figure 8.36 The Series tab of the Chart Inspector lets you turn on data point labels.

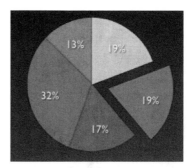

Figure 8.37 Using value labels inside the pie is a common way to show data in pie charts.

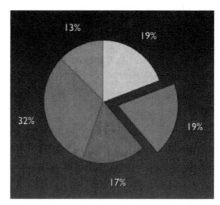

Figure 8.38 You also have the option of putting the value labels outside of the pie.

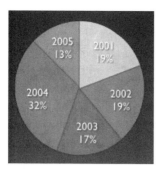

Figure 8.39 Showing the series name along with the value label will help your viewers understand your chart better.

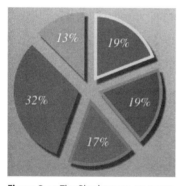

Figure 8.40 The Shadow pop-up menu lets you add a shadow effect to the wedges in your pie chart.

Figure 8.41 You can use the wedges of pie charts as photo cutouts by applying image fills to each wedge.

✔ Tips

■ You can select and set font styles for each data point label separately. This allows you to do things like increase the font size and change the color of the label inside an exploded wedge, further highlighting that wedge.

■ You can also set the shadow and opacity of data point labels in the Graphic Inspector.

■ Pie charts can make fun photo cutouts (**Figure 8.41**). Apply image fills to the individual wedges in the Graphic Inspector.

Resizing Charts

You resize any kind of chart as you would any other graphic object in Keynote.

To resize a chart:

1. Select the chart.

   Selection handles appear at the chart's edges.

2. Click and drag one of the selection handles.

   The chart resizes. Charts always resize proportionately, and size tags appear as the chart changes size (**Figure 8.42**).

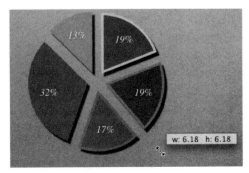

Figure 8.42 As you resize the chart, the size tags let you know how big the chart is getting.

USING SLIDE TRANSITIONS AND ANIMATIONS

Once you have written your presentation, pulled together all the text and graphics that will go into the presentation, and organized your slides the way you like them, you can finish off the presentation with slide transitions and animations on your slides that add motion and visual appeal to your slideshow.

Slide transitions are animated effects that occur when you switch from one slide to another. Transitions between slides can enhance the effect of your presentation and help your audience by clearly marking when you're done with a slide (and also, presumably letting them know that you're moving from one topic to the next). An *object build* is the generic name for an animation that occurs within the body of the slide. Most builds involve one or more elements of an object, and you can control how objects animate onto the slide and how they leave the slide. For example, you can have the parts of a graph appear on the screen one at a time (called a *chart build*), or make text boxes or graphics fly onto (or off of) the screen (I'm also referring to these builds as object builds). *Text builds* are used for animating the way that different lines of bulleted text appear on the slide. *Table builds* let you animate parts of a table onto the screen.

In this chapter, you'll learn how to apply slide transitions and create the different types of object builds.

Applying Slide Transitions

Slide transitions are a good way to add visual interest when you change slides. They also serve as a cue for the audience to reinforce the fact that you are changing slides; if someone isn't paying particularly close attention, that flash of motion will often help them refocus on your slideshow.

All slide transitions involve an animated effect where the first, old slide (which I will refer to in this chapter as Slide A) is replaced by the second, new slide (you guessed it, Slide B). Keynote provides fifteen built-in transition styles, plus None. Eleven of them are 2-D transitions, where one slide replaces another in the same plane. For example, Slide A can dissolve into Slide B. Four of the transitions are 3-D transitions, where Slide A is replaced by Slide B with an effect that appears to occur out of the plane of the slides. An example of this is the Flip effect, where the slide spins 180 degrees on its vertical or horizontal axis, revealing the next slide. All of the transitions are detailed in **Table 9.1**.

You apply transitions using the Slide Navigator and the Slide Inspector (**Figure 9.1**). You can set a transition between any two or more slides (they must be contiguous in the Slide Navigator, of course). Many transitions have options that you can set to adjust the look of the effect. For example, you can set a wipe transition to move from left to right, right to left, top to bottom, or bottom to top. You can also control (to a point) the speed of a transition.

To apply a slide transition:

1. If necessary, display the Slide Navigator by choosing View > Navigator.

   The Slide Navigator appears.

Table 9.1

Slide Transition Styles

TRANSITION TYPE	TRANSITION NAME	DESCRIPTION
3-D	Cube	Slides appear to be the sides of a rotating cube. Slide A turns off screen as Slide B turns onto the screen.
	Flip	Slide A spins on its vertical or horizontal axis, revealing Slide B on the "back" side.
	Mosaic Large	Like Flip, but built of many smaller tiles that flip over, revealing Slide B. The effect sweeps over the slide.
	Mosaic Small	A version of Mosaic Large, using smaller tiles.
2-D	Dissolve	A cross-dissolve to Slide B. Slide A fades out as Slice B fades in.
	Drop	Slide B drops in over Slide A, with a bounce effect.
	Fade through Black	The screen fades to black over Slide A, then comes up from black to show Slide B.
	Motion Dissolve	Slide A gets bigger, appearing to zoom off the screen and fade away, as Slide B zooms onto the screen and fades in.
	Move In	Slide B slides over to cover Slide A.
	Pivot	Slide B pivots from one of the slide's corners to cover Slide A.
	Push	Slide B enters and appears to push Slide A off of the screen.
	Reveal	Slide A slides off the screen, revealing Slide B underneath.
	Scale	Similar to Motion Dissolve, this transition zooms only one of the slides as it fades between the two.
	Twirl	Like the spinning newspaper effect in old movies. Slide A spins around its center and recedes into a black background, then is replaced by a spinning Slide B that zooms to fill the screen.
	Wipe	Slide B sweeps over Slide A, with a soft edge.
	None	The default choice; Slide A switches to Slide B with no intervening effect.

APPLYING SLIDE TRANSITIONS

Figure 9.1 The Slide Inspector is where you'll set transitions between slides.

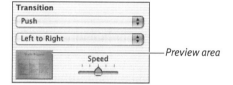

—*Preview area*

Figure 9.2 The Transition section of the Slide Navigator lets you set the type of transition, its direction, and its speed.

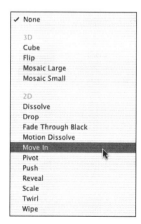

Figure 9.3 Choose the transition style you want from the Transition pop-up menu, which is split into 3-D and 2-D transitions.

2. If the Inspector window isn't open, click the Inspector button in the toolbar, then click the Slide button in the Inspector's button bar to display the Slide Inspector.

You'll be using the Transition section of the Slide Navigator (**Figure 9.2**).

3. Click a slide in the Slide Navigator to select it.

(Optional) If you want to apply the transition to more than one slide, after you click the first slide, hold down the Shift key and click the last slide. All of the selected slides will highlight in the Slide Navigator.

4. From the Transition pop-up menu in the Slide Inspector (**Figure 9.3**), choose the transition style you want.

After you choose a transition, Keynote displays a thumbnail preview of the transition in the Slide Inspector.

5. Some transitions can be set to move in a direction that you specify. If the transition you have selected allows you to do this, choose a direction from the Direction pop-up menu (**Figure 9.4**).

The directions listed in this pop-up menu will change, depending on the transition style you have selected. If the style doesn't support a direction, the menu will be inactive.

6. Drag the Speed slider to the right to make the transition occur faster or to the left to make it happen slower.

Slides with transitions appear in the Slide Navigator with a small blue triangle in the lower-right corner, as in **Figure 9.5**.

continues on next page

APPLYING SLIDE TRANSITIONS

✔ Tips

- You can use slide transitions to communicate different types of information or to denote sections in your presentation. For example, you can use a transition to signify that you're moving to an entirely different topic in your presentation. Let's say that you have a presentation with three distinct sections. You can use no transitions between the slides in each section, and use transitions only between slides at the end of one section and the beginning of the next.

- The Speed slider doesn't give you much control over the transition speed; you can vary the speed from about 1 to 3 seconds.

- Keynote through version 1.1 doesn't allow you to create your own transition styles. You are limited to the ones that come with the program. Perhaps future versions of Keynote will allow third-party developers to produce custom transitions, such as those developed for iMovie.

- Keynote version 1.1 added a new option to the Presentation Mode section of the Preferences window. "Shrink 3D transitions to avoid clipping" makes the 3D transitions, such as Cube and Flip, seem to pull back a bit on the screen before the slide rotation begins. The idea is that the entire slide remains on the screen during the rotation; in older versions of Keynote, parts of the slide would be clipped off by the edges of the screen.

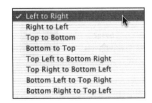

Figure 9.4 The Direction pop-up menu lets you choose which way the slide transition will move (for those transitions that support direction).

Figure 9.5 You can tell which slides have transitions in the Slide Navigator by the little blue triangle in the slide thumbnail's lower-right corner.

Less Really Is More

When it comes to slide transitions, restraint really should be the order of the day. Chances are you've seen presentations where presenters used way too many transitions and animated effects. Did you like them? No? That's what I thought.

Too-busy slide transitions and animations of objects on the slide can easily distract the audience from the content of your presentation. Make sure not to overdo them, or you might find your audience slipping out of the room before your talk is over—which is not the sign of a successful presentation. Too much swooping and spinning can even make some audience members nauseous!

Figure 9.6 The Build Inspector gives you all the controls you need for build animations.

Figure 9.7 This close-up of the Build In tab shows you the controls you'll use to create your builds.

Creating Text Builds

Object builds, as noted above, animate one or more objects on the slide. When you create a build, you can set the way the object "builds in" (appears on the slide) and "builds out" (leaves the slide). You control the build process with the Build Inspector (**Figure 9.6**). On that Inspector, the Build In and Build Out tabs set the build options.

Probably the most common sort of build you will be doing is with bulleted text, to make each bullet and its associated text appear when you click the mouse button during the presentation. These text builds can be set up with a number of options so that you can control how the text appears on the slide.

To apply bulleted text builds:

1. Switch to a slide with bulleted text.

2. Display the Build Inspector.

3. By default, the Build In tab is selected (**Figure 9.7**). If you want to create a Build Out, click that tab. Otherwise, continue on the Build In tab.

4. On your slide, select a bulleted text box.

5. By default, the "First build requires click" checkbox is selected. This means that you will need to click the mouse while giving your presentation in order for the build to start. If you want the build to begin automatically as soon as you switch to the slide, click to deselect this checkbox.

continues on next page

6. From the Build Style pop-up menu (**Figure 9.8**), choose the type of animation you want. You'll find a list of the build styles and their options in **Table 9.2**.

Whenever you make a change in the Build Inspector, you'll see a thumbnail preview of the build in the Inspector's preview area.

The Order pop-up menu is used to control the order of multiple object builds. See "Ordering object builds" later in this chapter for more information.

7. From the Direction pop-up menu, choose the direction from which you want bulleted text to move onto the slide.

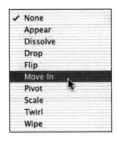

Figure 9.8 The nine build styles are common to every type of object build in Keynote.

Table 9.2

Bulleted Text Build Styles		
STYLE NAME	DIRECTION OPTIONS	DELIVERY OPTIONS
None	None	None
Appear	None	All at Once By Bullet By Bullet Group
Dissolve	None	All at Once By Bullet By Bullet Group
Drop	None	All at Once By Bullet By Bullet Group
Flip	Left to Right Right to Left	Top to Bottom Bottom to Top All at Once By Bullet By Bullet Group
Move In	Left to Right Right to Left Top to Bottom Bottom to Top Top Left to Bottom Right Top Right to Bottom Left Bottom Left to Top Right Bottom Right to Top Left	All at Once By Bullet By Bullet Group
Pivot	Top Left Top Right Bottom Left	All at Once By Bullet By Bullet Group
Scale	Up Down	All at Once By Bullet By Bullet Group
Twirl	None	All at Once By Bullet By Bullet Group
Wipe	Left to Right Right to Left Top to Bottom Bottom to Top	All at Once By Bullet By Bullet Group

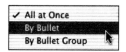

Figure 9.9 The Delivery pop-up menu changes, depending on what sort of object you are building. This is the Delivery menu for a bulleted text box.

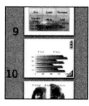

Figure 9.10 You can tell which slides have builds in the Slide Navigator by the little blue dots in the slide thumbnail's upper-right corner.

8. From the Delivery pop-up menu (**Figure 9.9**), choose one of the following:

- **All at Once** builds the entire contents of the bulleted text box onto or off of the slide.

- **By Bullet** builds each bullet point onto or off of the slide, one bullet point at a time. Second-level bullets animate separately.

- **By Bullet Group** also builds each bullet point onto or off of the slide, but second-level bullets animate with their parents.

Depending on the object you have selected, the context-sensitive Delivery menu may contain different items.

9. Drag the Speed slider to the right to make the build occur faster or to the left to make it happen slower.

Slides that have any kind of build on them appear in the Slide Navigator with three small blue dots in the upper-right corner (**Figure 9.10**).

10. If you want to create a Build Out, click the Build Out tab, then repeat steps 4 through 9.

CREATING TEXT BUILDS

Building Animated Tables

You can animate Keynote tables so that the parts of the table appear on the screen in sequence. This adds some visual flair to the table, and can even add a touch of drama. It's especially effective to have the contents of a table build in to your slide. With tables, you can control direction and delivery options as listed in **Table 9.3**.

To add a build to a table:

1. Switch to a slide with the table you want to animate.

2. Display the Build Inspector.

3. By default, the Build In tab is selected. If you want to create a Build Out, click that tab. Otherwise, continue on the Build In tab.

4. On your slide, select the table.

5. By default, the "First build requires click" checkbox is selected. If you want the build to begin automatically as soon as you switch to the slide, click to deselect this checkbox.

6. From the Build Style pop-up menu, choose the type of animation you want.

7. From the Direction pop-up menu, choose the direction from which you want the parts of the table to move onto the slide.

Table 9.3

Table Build Styles		
STYLE NAME	**DIRECTION OPTIONS**	**DELIVERY OPTIONS**
None	None	None
Appear	None	All at Once By Row By Column By Cell By Row Content By Column Content By Cell Content
Dissolve	None	All at Once By Row By Column By Cell By Row Content By Column Content By Cell Content
Drop	None	All at Once By Row By Column By Cell By Row Content By Column Content By Cell Content
Flip	Left to Right Right to Left Top to Bottom Bottom to Top	All at Once By Row By Column By Cell By Row Content By Column Content By Cell Content
Move In	Left to Right Right to Left Top to Bottom Bottom to Top Top Left to Bottom Right Top Right to Bottom Left Bottom Left to Top Right Bottom Right to Top Left	All at Once By Row By Column By Cell By Row Content By Column Content By Cell Content
Pivot	Top Left Top Right Bottom Left Bottom Right	All at Once By Row By Column By Cell By Row Content By Column Content By Cell Content
Scale	Up Down	All at Once By Row By Column By Cell By Row Content By Column Content By Cell Content

continues on next page

Table 9.3

Table Build Styles *(continued)*		
STYLE NAME	DIRECTION OPTIONS	DELIVERY OPTIONS
Twirl	None	All at Once By Row By Column By Cell By Row Content By Column Content By Cell Content
Wipe	Left to Right Right to Left Top to Bottom Bottom to Top	All at Once By Row By Column By Cell By Row Content By Column Content By Cell Content

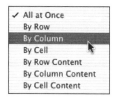

Figure 9.11 The Delivery pop-up menu for tables gives you fine-grained control over the animated appearance of table elements.

Figure 9.12 In the Preview pane of the Build Inspector, you can see the bottom row of the table sliding into place.

✔ Tip

■ Using the Wipe build style is especially nice for tables; the wipe has a soft edge that looks quite attractive.

8. From the Delivery pop-up menu (**Figure 9.11**), choose one of the following:

 ◆ **All at Once** builds the entire contents of the table onto or off of the slide.

 ◆ **By Row** builds each row of the table onto or off of the slide, one at a time. The rows begin with the top of the table and work down, regardless of the choice in the Direction pop-up menu.

 ◆ **By Column** builds each column of the table onto or off of the slide, one at a time. The columns begin with the leftmost column of the table and work to the right, regardless of the choice in the Direction pop-up menu.

 ◆ **By Cell** brings each cell onto or off of the slide, one at a time. The cells begin with the upper-leftmost cells, and work across, and then down.

 ◆ **By Row Content** first brings on the table background (the grid and any cell fills), then causes the contents of the table to appear, one row at a time.

 ◆ **By Column Content** first brings on the table background (the grid and any cell fills), then causes the contents of the table to appear, one column at a time.

 ◆ **By Cell Content** first brings on the table background (the grid and any cell fills), then causes the contents of the table to appear, one cell at a time.

 Whenever you make a change in the Build Inspector, you'll see a thumbnail preview of the build in the Inspector's preview area (**Figure 9.12**).

9. Drag the Speed slider to the right to make the animation occur faster, or to the left to make it happen slower.

10. If you want to create a Build Out, click the Build Out tab, then repeat steps 4 through 9.

Creating Chart Builds

Chart builds rank just behind bulleted text builds in usefulness. You can get some dramatic effects when you make the parts of a chart appear sequentially on the screen, as shown in **Figure 9.13**.

To animate a chart:

1. Switch to a slide with the chart you want to animate.

2. Display the Build Inspector.

3. By default, the Build In tab is selected. If you want to create a Build Out, click that tab. Otherwise, continue working with the Build In tab.

4. On your slide, select the chart.

5. By default, the "First build requires click" checkbox is selected. This means that you will need to click the mouse while giving your presentation in order for the build to start. If you want the build to begin automatically as soon as you switch to the slide, click to deselect this checkbox.

6. From the Build Style pop-up menu, choose the type of animation you want.

7. From the Direction pop-up menu, choose the direction from which you want the chart to move onto the slide.

   Some build styles will not allow a direction, and the pop-up menu will be inactive.

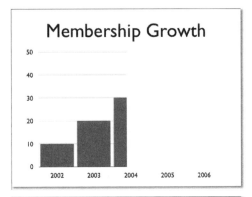

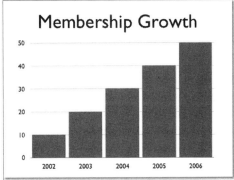

Figure 9.13 As the build wipes across the slide from left to right, it dramatically reveals the impressive growth in membership.

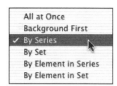

Figure 9.14 The Delivery pop-up menu for chart objects.

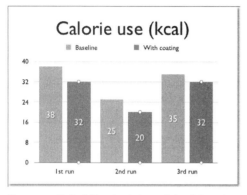

Figure 9.15 By building chart elements by data series, the columns marked "Baseline" appear before the columns marked "With coating."

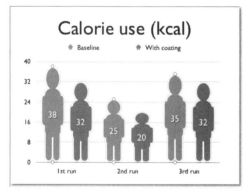

Figure 9.16 By replacing the columns in a chart with interesting shapes (these people shapes are graphics in PDF format), you can increase the impact of your graphs.

8. From the Delivery pop-up menu (**Figure 9.14**), choose one of the following:
   - **All at Once** builds the entire contents of the chart onto or off of the slide.
   - **Background First** builds the chart background first, followed by the other elements of the chart (bars, columns, or area shapes).
   - **By Series** builds each data series onto or off of the slide, one at a time.
   - **By Set** builds each data set onto the chart, one at a time.
   - **By Element in Series** builds each element in a data series, one at a time. For example, in a chart like the one in **Figure 9.15**, the columns marked "Baseline" appear first, followed by the columns marked "With coating."
   - **By Element in Set** builds each element in a data set, one at a time.

9. Drag the Speed slider to the right to make the build occur faster, or to the left to make it happen slower.

10. If you want to create a Build Out, click the Build Out tab, then repeat steps 4 through 9.

✔ Tips

- You can create more interesting chart builds by using the Graphic Inspector to replace the image fills for the chart elements with shapes, as in **Figure 9.16**. With builds like this, the Wipe build style, with the Direction set to Bottom to Top and Delivery set to By Set, is especially effective.

- The chart legend is treated as separate from the rest of the chart. You can apply a different build setting to it, or if you want it to move with the rest of the chart, select the chart and the legend, and group them by clicking the Group button in the toolbar before you apply any build styles.

CREATING CHART BUILDS

Creating Object Builds

General object builds work much the same way as the previous builds in this chapter. The only difference is that you will be working with any element that you can place on the Slide Canvas, including text boxes, shapes, graphics, or movies. Actually, to Keynote, anything on the Slide Canvas is an object, including bulleted text boxes, tables, and charts, so you can animate almost everything.

When you are animating multiple objects, you can control the order in which those objects appear, and each object can have its own build style, direction, and delivery options. So you can, for example, have a slide with bulleted text that moves in from the right side, a graphic that twirls in on the left side, and a title box that drops in from the top (**Figure 9.17**). Unfortunately, Keynote doesn't allow you to animate all of these different objects so that they move on to the slide with a single click while you are giving your presentation; you must click between each object to trigger its build.

You can animate more than one object at a time by grouping them. So, for example, you can move several graphic elements onto the slide by first grouping them, then applying a build style.

To animate several objects:

1. Switch to a slide you want to animate.

2. Display the Build Inspector.

3. Click the Build In tab.

4. Place the objects that you want to animate on your slide.

5. Select the first object you want to animate.

6. From the Build Style pop-up menu, choose the type of animation you want.

Figure 9.17 This slide has multiple object builds. The title box drops in from the top of the slide, the mission patch twirls onto the screen, and the bulleted text slides in from the left. Yes, that would be tasteless; it's only an example.

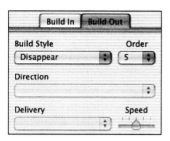

Figure 9.18 The Order pop-up menu on the Build In and Build Out tabs lets you set the build order for each object to which you have assigned a build style.

✔ Tips

■ Keynote can only animate one build at a time; you can't have two objects move simultaneously unless you group them, and then they will both use the same build effect. There's no way to get two objects to animate simultaneously with separate effects.

■ Choosing a number from the Order pop-up menu in the Build In tab can change the order of objects in the Build Out tab because there is only one list of the order of object builds, not two, and the two tabs share the list.

7.   From the Direction pop-up menu, choose the direction from which you want the object to move onto the slide.

8.   Choose the option you want from the Delivery pop-up menu.

9.   Drag the Speed slider to the right to make the animation occur faster, or to the left to make it happen slower.

10.   Select the next object you want to animate, and repeat steps 6 through 9.

11.   If you want to create a Build Out, click the Build Out tab, then repeat steps 4 through 10.

Ordering object builds

You can control the order in which objects build on or off the slide by selecting the object and choosing from the Order pop-up menu in the Build Inspector (**Figure 9.18**). Every time you create a different object build, Keynote adds a number to the Order pop-up menu. If you have both a Build In and a Build Out for a slide, the same object can have different Order numbers on the Build In and Build Out tabs. For example, let's say that you have the following graphics that fly onto the screen in this order during the Build In:

◆   Earth

◆   The Moon

◆   Mars

In the Build Out, the three graphics fly out in the reverse order. On the Build In tab, the graphic of the Moon would have an Order number of 2. On the Build Out tab, the Moon's Order number is 5. This is a simple example, but you can have objects exit the slide in any order by making selections in the Build Out tab. Keynote automatically prevents two objects from having the same Order number.

Previewing Your Work

The thumbnail preview panes in the Build and Slide Inspectors are useful, but they are no substitute for seeing how your build and transitions will look when you give your presentation. For that, you'll need to play the presentation through.

To preview your transitions and builds:

1. In the Slide Navigator, select the slide from which you want to begin the preview.

2. Click the Play button in the toolbar. Keynote begins playing the slideshow.

3. Click the mouse button, or press the right arrow key to advance through your slideshow.

4. Note any problems with transitions or builds as you watch the slideshow.

5. When you want to make a change to a transition or build, press the [Esc] key or ⌘[.] to end the slideshow, then make the needed changes in the Slide Inspector or the Build Inspector.

WORKING WITH POWERPOINT FILES 10

One of the great things about Keynote is that it does a very good job of reading and writing Microsoft PowerPoint files. For the most part, you should be able to take a PowerPoint file, open it in Keynote, and then modify it in Keynote or use it to give a presentation.

That's the theory, anyway. In the real world, you'll find that PowerPoint presentations opened in Keynote usually need a little tweaking before they are ready for prime time. In rare cases, you won't be able to open up a PowerPoint presentation in Keynote at all, at least until you modify the presentation a bit in PowerPoint.

In this chapter, you'll learn about the good and bad points of Keynote's PowerPoint compatibility, and you'll learn how to import PowerPoint files into Keynote and export Keynote files in PowerPoint format.

PowerPoint Issues

Keynote's ability to open PowerPoint files is one of its major benefits; in fact, if it were not PowerPoint-friendly, chances are that many people would not have given Keynote a second glance. Compatibility with Microsoft Office applications is essential for programs that want to inhabit the same market segment; that's why, for example, AppleWorks can read and write Microsoft Word and Microsoft Excel documents.

Keynote has taken some criticism for not being able to open every PowerPoint file that people have thrown at it, but in my experience, Keynote does a good job. As a test, I imported fifty PowerPoint files into Keynote. Some I had created myself, but the majority were files I downloaded at random from the Web. The files ranged in size from less than 100K (plain text, with only 12 slides) to 4 MB (this file contained many embedded photographs). Of the fifty files, Keynote was able to open all of them. That's a pretty good record.

On the other hand, once the files were open, it didn't take long to run across problems in the import process. The most common problem was that some slides had text boxes that were not big enough to display all of the text they contained (**Figure 10.1**). This text overflow is usually due to font differences between Mac OS X and Windows. Because of Mac OS X's advanced font-handling abilities, even fonts that exist on both platforms may not perform identically.

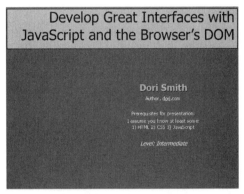

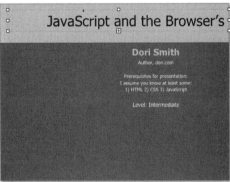

Figure 10.1 The Title box in this PowerPoint file (top) was too full to display all the text when it was imported into Keynote (bottom). The solution was to make the text box in Keynote a little bit bigger, both horizontally and vertically, then nudge the text box higher on the slide so that the text fits in the lighter-colored background.

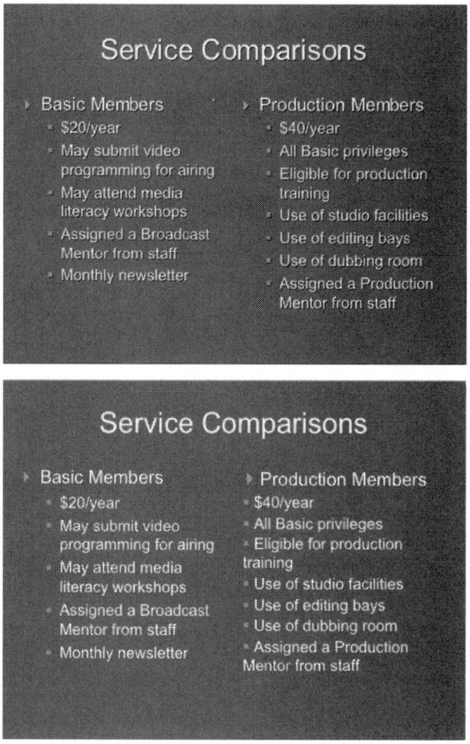

Figure 10.2 PowerPoint slides with multiple bulleted text boxes (top) import into Keynote with one of the text boxes maintaining automatic bullets, and the other importing as a free text box with the bullets and tabs awry (bottom). Note how the bullets in the right-hand box in the Keynote example are placed under the main triangle bullet, instead of being indented, and how the bullets with two lines do not wrap the text correctly.

Here is a list of problems, in no particular order, that have been reported with PowerPoint files that have been imported to Keynote. This is by no means a comprehensive list, and you can expect it to change as Apple releases new versions of Keynote that squash bugs and do a better job of working around Windows/Mac cross-platform problems.

- Keynote doesn't seem to like PowerPoint slides that contain Body text with no bullets. Keynote sometimes imports the text with added bullets (**Figure 10.2**).

- PowerPoint supports multiple text boxes on one slide, each of which can contain bulleted text. Keynote can only have one text box with bulleted text per slide. PowerPoint files with multiple text boxes will import with one of the text boxes containing automatic bullets (which can be edited and will keep its bullet style), and the other one as a plain text box with manually placed bullets. Usually, the bullets in the two text boxes will not line up.

- PowerPoint slides that contain hyperlinks will not import correctly, since Keynote doesn't support hyperlinks on slides. The link text will import as body text, and the link information (i.e., the URL) will be discarded.

- PowerPoint slides that contain embedded Excel worksheets will import the worksheet into Keynote as a graphic, not as text, and will lose the link to Excel. Because you can't change the style of the text within the graphic, you might be better off recreating that portion of the slide as a table in Keynote.

Preparing PowerPoint Files for Import

By default (and for compatibility with PowerPoint for Windows) PowerPoint X makes slides sized at 720 x 540 at 72 dots per inch. Because of PowerPoint's auto-resize function, you never notice that it actually resizes your slides during your presentation, so it still looks good when projected at 800 x 600 or larger resolutions. Keynote uses fixed slide sizes, so before importing a PowerPoint file into Keynote, you may want to change the resolution of your PowerPoint file to match the projector resolution and slide size you'll want in Keynote. You change the resolution in PowerPoint in its Page Setup dialog (**Figure 10.3**).

Because PowerPoint uses inches as its unit of measure, and Keynote uses pixels for its slide sizes, you have to do a little math before you can change the Page Setup to match your target slide resolution. Here's a chart to help you with the resolution to page size equivalents:

Resolution	Width	Height
640 x 480	8.88"	6.66"
800 x 600	11.11"	8.33"
1024 x 768	14.22"	10.66"
1152 x 870	16"	12.08"

Simply change the size in the Page Setup of your PowerPoint file and choose to not have PowerPoint fix any margin problems if you get a dialog that offers that option.

Doing this will make it much easier for you to change themes once you are in Keynote, because you won't have to rearrange slide elements quite so much.

Finally, sometimes you'll end up with a slide size of say, 799 x 599 when you import into Keynote. This small amount won't give you problems with slide elements, but Keynote may complain of a size change when you apply a new theme. Just click OK and continue working.

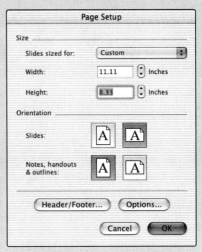

Figure 10.3 Change the resolution in the Page Setup dialog.

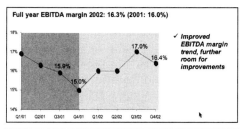

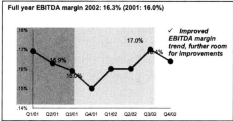

Figure 10.4 This graph in PowerPoint (top), after importing into Keynote, has portions out of place. Note also that the line of the graph imported thicker, and that the text in the text box on the right now wraps differently.

◆ Keynote does not appear to always correctly convert Windows Metafile graphics. Those graphics, which are vector graphics created by many Windows applications including the Microsoft Office programs, may import without a colored background, may appear shifted in relation to other slide objects (**Figure 10.4**), and text spacing within the graphic may be incorrect. In some cases, you can use Keynote's Shape tools to add the background, and you can resize and reposition the graphic to better work on the Keynote slide.

✔ Tip

■ If you are creating a slideshow in PowerPoint that you know will be exported to Keynote, make sure you use PowerPoint's default Title and Bullet boxes. By using these default boxes, the text will translate smoothly to Keynote's equivalents, and you'll be able to take full advantage of Keynote's ability to modify and apply changes in master slides. If you start with a blank slide in PowerPoint and make your own text boxes, you'll have to change all your fonts manually in Keynote.

Importing PowerPoint Files

You can bring PowerPoint files into Keynote in two ways. You can simply open the file, or you can drag the PowerPoint file onto the Keynote application icon.

To open PowerPoint files:

1. In Keynote, choose File > Open.

   The Open dialog appears (**Figure 10.5**).

2. Find the PowerPoint file that you want to open, and select it in the list.

3. Click Open.

   Keynote imports and opens the file as an untitled document (**Figure 10.6**).

✔ Tip

■ If you open the Master Slides Organizer, you'll see that imported PowerPoint files only come with as many master slides as are used in the imported presentation. To add on to the presentation with a different master slide, you'll have to either apply a Keynote theme, or create your own master slides that match the imported presentation.

To import PowerPoint files by dragging and dropping:

1. In the Finder, find the PowerPoint file that you want to open.

2. Drag the PowerPoint file's icon onto the Keynote application icon inside your Applications folder.

   or

   If Keynote is running, drag the PowerPoint file's icon onto the Keynote icon in the Dock.

   Keynote imports and opens the file as an untitled document.

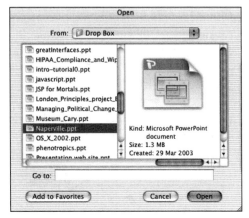

Figure 10.5 Importing PowerPoint files is as easy as opening them in Keynote.

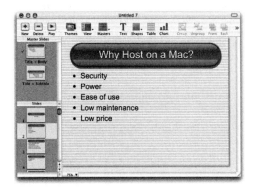

Figure 10.6 PowerPoint files only import with the number of master slides actually used in the presentation.

Tweaking your PowerPoint Presentation

After you import your PowerPoint file into Keynote, you'll usually have to make a pass through the entire file and adjust some text and graphics to make it look and flow better in Keynote.

Adjusting text

Here are some techniques that you can use to tweak and reformat text imported as part of PowerPoint files:

◆ The vast majority of the changes you'll need to make will be to resize text boxes because sometimes the imported text will overflow Keynote's text boxes. Just select the text boxes and drag the grow handles until the text fits. In some cases, you may also have to open the Fonts window, select the text in the text box, and apply a different font size.

◆ Whenever possible, try to resize text boxes, change text sizes, and modify bullet attributes in a master slide, rather than in the individual presentation slides. If you make changes to a master slide before you have attempted to modify individual slides, all the slides associated with that master slide will change when you finish editing the master slide. If you have already made changes to the presentation slides, you can modify the master slide, then switch back to the presentation slide, and choose Format > Reapply Master to Slide. The presentation slide will then take on the attributes of the master slide.

- Sometimes you'll have to cut text out of imported text boxes and paste it back into your slide as a separate text object, so that you can position it precisely. In **Figure 10.7**, the text "The bicycle object" came in from PowerPoint as part of the single body text box on the slide, and it was underneath the graphic of the bicyclist. I selected and cut the text, clicked in a different spot on the slide, and pasted the text, which reappeared as its own text object. I was then able to move the text object where it needed to go.

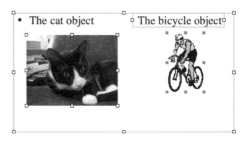

Figure 10.7 After importing, the text "The bicycle object" was part of the overall text box, and didn't lineup correctly with its associated graphic. By cutting and pasting the text back into the slide, you are able to reposition the text box precisely.

Tweaking graphics

- Clipart from Microsoft Office programs is often in Windows Metafile format, and as noted previously, that doesn't always translate well into Keynote. As a workaround, open a PowerPoint or Microsoft Word document, insert the clipart you want from the Microsoft Clip Gallery, then copy and paste the clipart into Keynote. This works better than importing PowerPoint files containing clipart.

- Embedded movie files in PowerPoint presentations will often not translate well (if at all) to Keynote. It is better to place your movie clips directly in Keynote.

- Whenever you have problems with imported graphics not looking right in Keynote, open the file in PowerPoint, copy the graphic, and paste it into Keynote. This simple approach solves a multitude of problems.

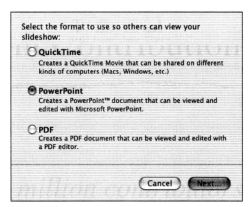

Figure 10.8 Choose a format for exporting the Keynote file.

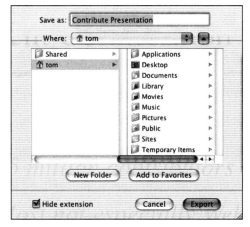

Figure 10.9 Specify a location for the exported file, then click Export.

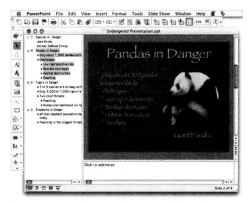

Figure 10.10 The Keynote file opens in PowerPoint.

Exporting to PowerPoint

It's quite easy to export your Keynote presentations as PowerPoint documents. But because there are differences between the two programs, you won't get quite the same results in PowerPoint (especially on Windows) as you get in Keynote. Some graphics may be resized, some text may need a bit of adjusting in PowerPoint, and because some of Keynote's transitions do not exist in PowerPoint, they will be converted into different transitions.

To export a Keynote file in PowerPoint format:

1. Choose File > Export.

   A sheet will slide down from the top of the document window asking you to select a format for the export (**Figure 10.8**).

2. Click the PowerPoint button, then click Next.

   A sheet appears asking you to name the exported file and specify its location (**Figure 10.9**).

3. Name the file, navigate to where you want to save it, then click Export.

   Keynote exports the file (**Figure 10.10**).

✔ Tip

- You'll find information about exporting Keynote files to the other two export formats, QuickTime and PDF, in Chapter 12.

WORKING WITH OTHER APPLICATIONS

You've seen in earlier chapters a bit about how you can use other applications to enhance your Keynote presentations. For example, in Chapter 2, you saw how OmniOutliner can be used to write the text of your presentation. In Chapter 5, there was some discussion about using graphics programs, such as Adobe Photoshop and Macromedia Fireworks to produce presentation images.

But importing and exporting text and pictures doesn't begin to exhaust Keynote's abilities to work with other applications. In this chapter, you'll see how Keynote can import presentations created in AppleWorks' presentation module; use content from Microsoft Word and Microsoft Excel; use Microsoft Office's clipart in your Keynote presentation; and export your presentations to QuickTime movies or PDF (Adobe Acrobat) documents. You'll also see an overview of Keynote's amazing abilities to integrate with, and produce presentations from, database programs.

Importing from AppleWorks

AppleWorks, Apple's integrated software package, is popular in schools, easy to use, and it comes with every iMac and iBook. AppleWorks is made up of several modules, but two are of special interest to Keynote users: the Presentation module and the Draw module.

The AppleWorks Presentation module (**Figure 11.1**) is adequate for the simplest presentations, but it is hardly a competitor to Keynote or PowerPoint. But don't despair if you happen to have a bunch of presentations already created in AppleWorks; the good news is that Keynote will read your AppleWorks presentations and convert them seamlessly.

The AppleWorks Draw module (**Figure 11.2**) is useful to Keynote users because it can create graphic objects that are beyond the capabilities of the simple Shapes in Keynote. For example, AppleWorks can create rectangles with rounded corners, which Keynote cannot. You can then copy the objects in AppleWorks and paste them into Keynote. Because the object was created as a vector shape in AppleWorks, you'll be able to scale and make other adjustments to the object without loss of quality while working in Keynote.

Figure 11.1 The AppleWorks Presentation module isn't very powerful, but it will do for very simple presentations. It's better to use Keynote.

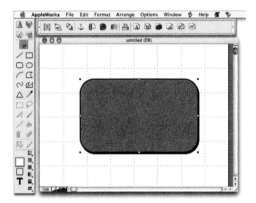

Figure 11.2 The AppleWorks Draw module allows you to build graphic shapes that Keynote can't; this rounded rectangle is one example.

Figure 11.3 You'll need to find the AppleWorks presentation file so that you can open it in Keynote.

Figure 11.4 Here is the AppleWorks presentation in Keynote.

To import an AppleWorks presentation:

1. In Keynote, choose File > Open.

   The Open dialog appears (**Figure 11.3**).

2. Navigate to the AppleWorks presentation file, then select it.

3. Click Open.

   Keynote converts the presentation file and opens it as a new untitled document (**Figure 11.4**).

IMPORTING FROM APPLEWORKS

To use AppleWorks graphic objects in Keynote:

1. Open the Keynote presentation that will receive the graphic object from AppleWorks, and display the slide where you'll want to place the object.

2. Launch AppleWorks.

3. From the Basic tab of the Starting Points palette (**Figure 11.5**), click Drawing.

   AppleWorks opens a new drawing document (**Figure 11.6**).

4. In the new document, create the graphic that you want to use in Keynote.

   You can use any of AppleWorks' graphic tools.

5. Select the graphic that you created.

6. Choose Edit > Copy, or press ⌘C.

7. Switch to Keynote.

8. Choose Edit > Paste, or press ⌘V.

   The graphic appears in Keynote.

✔ Tips

- Besides the rounded rectangle tool in the AppleWorks Draw module, AppleWorks supports many other graphics tools not found in Keynote, such as the polygon, arc, freehand drawing, and Bezier tools.

- Unfortunately, even though AppleWorks' Word Processing module has a fairly capable outliner, Keynote cannot read AppleWorks word processing documents, so you can't use AppleWorks to write your presentations.

- Once a graphic object created in AppleWorks is in Keynote, you can treat it as you would other graphic objects. Using the Graphic and Metrics Inspectors, you can apply a drop shadow; change its opacity; scale it; rotate it and flip it horizontally and vertically.

Figure 11.5 Select the Drawing icon in the Basic tab of the AppleWorks Starting Points palette to begin a new drawing document.

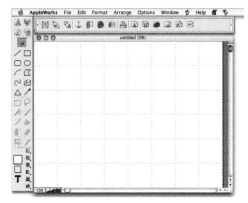

Figure 11.6 AppleWorks' Drawing canvas is ready for you to create the shape that will end up in Keynote.

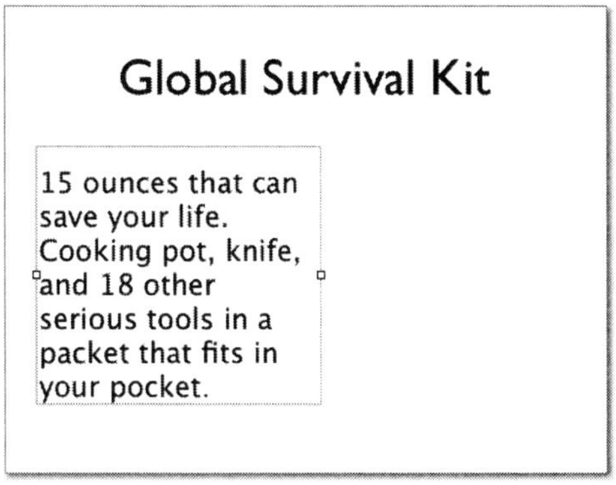

Global Survival Kit

15 ounces that can save your life. Cooking pot, knife, and 18 other serious tools in a packet that fits in your pocket.

Figure 11.7 This text pasted from Microsoft Word appeared in a free text box using 12 point Times, far too small for a slide. I changed the font to a larger size and changed the font face.

Figure 11.8 Begin importing the contents of a Word table by selecting the content that you want to bring into Keynote.

Importing from Microsoft Word

Microsoft Word is the most widely used word processor on the Mac, and indeed in the world. Naturally, at some point you're going to want to use information that you already have in Word in your Keynote presentations. While there are a number of ways you can use Word documents in Keynote, I'm going to focus on using tables and the WordArt feature.

Of course, if all you want to do is move text from Word into Keynote, you can simply copy the text in Word, and paste it into Keynote. The text will appear in a new free text box on the Slide Canvas in the same size font as it was in Word, which you will most likely have to resize in Keynote (**Figure 11.7**).

Using Word tables

If you want to import data from tables that you have in Word documents, you can do so. The obvious reason to do this is so that you don't have to waste time retyping information from Word into Keynote. Another reason is to use some of the table capabilities in Word that Keynote lacks. For example, you can do arithmetical calculations in Word tables. You can move the contents of the table, calculations and all, into a Keynote table.

To import Word tables:

1. In the Word document, select the contents of a table that you want to move to Keynote (**Figure 11.8**).

2. Choose Edit > Copy, or press ⌘Ⓒ.

3. Switch to Keynote.

4. Display the slide where you want the copied content.

continues on next page

5. Click the Table button on Keynote's toolbar.

The default table appears, with three rows and three columns.

6. Using the commands in the Format > Table menu, adjust the number of rows and columns in the Keynote table to match the number of rows and columns in the Word table.

7. Double-click in the upper-left cell of the table to place the insertion point in the Keynote table.

8. Choose Edit > Paste, or press ⌘Ⓥ.

The contents of the Word table are pasted into the cells in the Keynote table (**Figure 11.9**).

✔ Tips

■ If the Keynote table has fewer rows and columns than the Word table, any excess data from Word will be discarded when you paste into Keynote.

■ You can also drag and drop the contents from the Word table into the Keynote table.

■ Unfortunately, when you transfer table data, any formatting you had in Word will be lost. You will need to restyle the text in Keynote (**Figure 11.10**).

Figure 11.9 After you paste the Word table data into a Keynote table, the text appears too small to see.

All Time Top 10 Movies at the US Box Office

Rank	Released	Film Name	Total Box Office
1	1997	Titanic	$600,788,188
2	1977	Star Wars	$460,998,007
3	1982	ET: The Extra-Terrestrial	$431,197,000
4	1999	Star Wars: Phantom Menace	$431,088,297
5	2002	Spider-Man	$403,706,375
6	1993	Jurassic Park	$357,067,947
7	2002	Lord of the Rings: The Two Towers	$337,526,600
8	1994	Forrest Gump	$329,693,974
9	2001	Harry Potter and the Sorcerer's Stone	$317,557,891
10	2001	Lord of the Rings: The Fellowship of the Ring	$313,364,114

Figure 11.10 After restyling, the copied table text is appropriate for use on a slide.

Figure 11.11 WordArt can transform text into graphically interesting images.

Figure 11.12 Some styles of WordArt work fine in Keynote, but other styles do not. These four styles all look fine in Word (left), but the second and fourth examples are misdrawn when they get to Keynote (right).

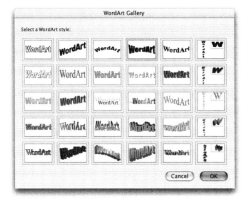

Figure 11.13 Begin creating WordArt by choosing a style from the WordArt Gallery.

Figure 11.14 Enter the text for the WordArt in the Edit WordArt Text dialog.

Using WordArt in Keynote

WordArt is a feature in Word that allows you to take text and turn it into an image that is formatted in graphically interesting ways (**Figure 11.11**). You can use WordArt images as headlines for slides, or as additional graphic touches anywhere on the Slide Canvas.

WordArt comes in many styles, but only some of them will work well in Keynote. In general, the WordArt styles that work better are the simpler ones that have few, if any, 3-D effects. Some styles will paste into Keynote slightly misdrawn, or with a colored background that renders it useless (**Figure 11.12**). The best way to find out what styles will and won't work well is just to try them.

To create and import WordArt:

1. Create a blank Word document.

2. Choose Insert > Picture > WordArt.
   The WordArt Gallery dialog appears (**Figure 11.13**).

3. Click one of the styles to select it, then click OK.
   The Edit WordArt Text dialog appears (**Figure 11.14**).

4. In the Edit WordArt Text dialog, enter your text and, optionally, change the font, font size, and style the text as bold or italic.

5. Click OK.
   The WordArt image appears in your Word document. The image is already selected.

continues on next page

6. Choose Edit > Copy, or press ⌘C.

7. Switch to Keynote.

8. In the Slide Navigator, select the destination slide.

9. Choose Edit > Paste, or press ⌘V.
   The WordArt image appears on your Keynote slide.

10. The WordArt image will probably appear too small and will need to be resized to fit properly on the slide (**Figure 11.15**).

Figure 11.15 After resizing, the WordArt adds a nice flair to your slide.

✔ Tip

- WordArt images can be manipulated in many, but not all, of the ways that you would other images in Keynote. You can scale, flip, rotate, add shadows, and adjust the opacity of WordArt in Keynote, but you can't change the color fill. You can change the stroke color and style, but all that will be affected will be a box around the image, not the edges of the letters in the image, which makes this fairly useless. For more information on the types of adjustments you can make to graphics, see Chapter 5.

Figure 11.16 The Microsoft Clip Gallery contains hundreds of pieces of clip art that you can use in Keynote.

Using Microsoft Office Clip Art

Clip art is essential to liven up your presentations, but Keynote doesn't come with much, just the Objects, Pictures, and Flags documents that you can open by choosing File > Open Image Library. You can purchase clip art collections on CD, of course. But if you own Microsoft Office v. X, you already have a clip art treasure trove waiting for you.

Microsoft Office comes with hundreds of pieces of clip art, and you can use that clip art in your Keynote presentations. In fact, you can even use the downloadable clip art that Microsoft makes available online on their Design Gallery Live site (http://dgl.microsoft.com), as long as you import it into Office first.

You access Office's clip art by using the Microsoft Clip Gallery from inside one of the Office applications. The Clip Gallery is one of the Office helper applications that is shared by Microsoft Word, Excel, and PowerPoint (but not by Entourage).

To import Office clip art:

1. Create a new document in Word, Excel, or PowerPoint.

2. Choose Insert > Picture > Clip Art.
   The Clip Gallery appears (**Figure 11.16**).

3. Click the category in which you want to look for images.

4. Select the image you want to add.

5. Choose Edit > Copy, or press ⌘C.

6. Click Close.

7. Switch to Keynote.

continues on next page

8. In the Slide Navigator, click on the destination slide.

9. Choose Edit > Paste, or press ⌘V.

   The image will almost certainly appear much larger than your entire slide.

10. Use the image's selection handles to resize the image to the size you want on your slide (**Figure 11.17**).

11. Drag the image to where you want it on your slide.

✔ Tips

■ If you try to insert a clip art image into a Word document, copy it from the document, and then paste it into Keynote, it won't work. You'll just get an empty free text box in Keynote. You must copy the image from the Clip Gallery, or from PowerPoint.

■ You can get a nice effect by pasting clip art in, resizing it so that it takes up the whole area of the slide, then sending it to the back, behind your text, thus turning it into the slide background (**Figure 11.18**).

Figure 11.17 The Office clip art will appear in Keynote too large for your slide, but it scales down nicely, with no distortion.

Figure 11.18 Using a piece of clip art as a slide background can make for an attractive slide.

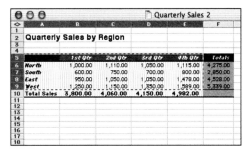

Figure 11.19 Select the Excel worksheet data that you'll want to chart in Keynote.

Importing from Microsoft Excel

You'll use information from Microsoft Excel primarily in conjunction with charts on your slides. You can bring data from an Excel worksheet into the Chart Data Editor if you want to create the chart in Keynote, or you can create the chart in Excel and place it onto a slide.

Importing worksheet data

If you want to create a chart in Keynote from Excel data, you'll need to get that data into Keynote's Chart Data Editor. The only way to do this is by copying the data from Excel and pasting it into the Chart Data Editor.

To import worksheet information:

1. In Excel, open the worksheet that contains your data.

2. Select the cells containing the data (**Figure 11.19**).

    If the data has row and column labels, you should select those, too. If the worksheet includes totals, you should not select them (if you do, the totals will also be charted).

3. Choose Edit > Copy, or press ⌘C.

4. Switch to Keynote.

5. Display the slide where you want to add a chart.

continues on next page

6. Click the Chart button on the toolbar.

Keynote opens the Chart Data Editor and places a placeholder chart on the slide.

7. Double-click the upper-left cell in the Chart Data Editor to select it.

8. Choose Edit > Paste, or press ⌘V.

The Excel data replaces the placeholder data in the Chart Data Editor, and Keynote charts the new data. If you selected row and column labels, they will replace the placeholder row and column labels (**Figure 11.20**).

Importing charts

You'll need to import charts from Excel if you want to use charts that Keynote can't create, such as 3-D charts with transparency, or a stock chart. The process is to create the chart in Excel, copy it, and then paste it into your Keynote slide.

To import an Excel chart:

1. In Excel, open the worksheet that contains the chart.

2. Click the chart to select it (**Figure 11.21**).

3. Choose Edit > Copy, or press ⌘C.

4. Switch to Keynote.

5. Display the slide where you want to add the chart.

6. Choose Edit > Paste, or press ⌘V.

The chart appears on your slide (**Figure 11.22**).

You'll probably have to resize and reposition the chart on the slide.

✔ Tip

■ The Excel chart will appear in Keynote with a white background. You can't change this, so you should use a slide background that will complement the white chart background.

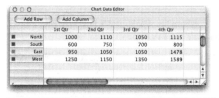

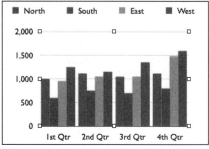

Figure 11.20 Row and column labels from the Excel spreadsheet transfer into Keynote's Chart Data Editor when you paste them in, and Keynote updates the chart.

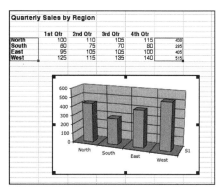

Figure 11.21 To move a chart from Excel to Keynote, first select and copy the chart in Excel.

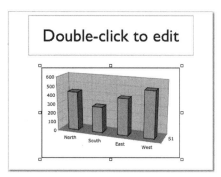

Figure 11.22 The Excel chart appears on the Keynote slide as a single graphic object.

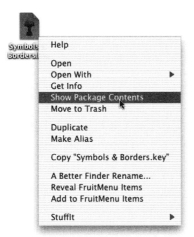

Figure 11.23 You can see the contents of a Keynote document's package by Control-clicking the document's icon in the Finder.

Figure 11.24 The contents of a Keynote document package.

Transferring Keynote Files

When you see a Keynote presentation file in the Finder, it looks like any other file, but you can run into problems when you need to send that file via e-mail or if you want to burn it onto a CD-ROM. The reason for this is that a Keynote file isn't a single file at all; it's a special kind of Mac OS X file called a *package*. The Keynote package file looks like a document icon in the Finder, but it is really more like a folder, containing many other files within.

To look inside the Keynote package file, Control-click a Keynote document file in the Finder. A contextual menu will appear (**Figure 11.23**). Choose Show Package Contents and a Finder window will open and display the contents of the package (**Figure 11.24**).

The possible problems with sending Keynote files via e-mail or burning them onto a CD-ROM are because the e-mail or CD creation program has problems working with package files.

Email

The most common problem when attempting to send Keynote files via email is that the file arrives in the recipient's inbox as a folder, rather than as a file. Email programs such as Qualcomm Eudora and Apple Mail will send or receive package files as folders. Similarly, Microsoft Entourage will receive a package sent from Eudora or Mail incorrectly; the package will arrive as many individual attachments (the contents of the package file), rather than one file.

The solution for sending and receiving problems with package files is to use a compression program such as StuffIt, from Aladdin Systems (www.aladdinsys.com) to compress the package file before you send it. A compression program converts a file or a folder of files into a single smaller file, using a mathematical algorithm to reduce the size of the stuffed file. On the other end, the recipient will need a decompression program to unstuff the file. Some email programs, such as Entourage, have the built-in ability to compress using StuffIt. If your email program does not, you should purchase one of the versions of StuffIt.

✔ Tips

- Mac OS X comes with a free program (you'll find it in /Applications/Utilities/) called StuffIt Expander. That program allows you to decompress any StuffIt file, but not to create StuffIt files. You'll need to get either StuffIt Standard or StuffIt Deluxe to make StuffIt files.

- If you're a .Mac member, check to see if you can get a copy of the DropStuff program, which can make StuffIt files, for free or at a reduced price. In the past, Apple has offered several deals with Aladdin Systems for .Mac members.

- An alternative to using StuffIt to compress packages is to use Mac OS X's Disk Copy program to create a disk image file, then copy your Keynote file or files to the disk image, then send the disk image file as an email attachment.

Figure 11.25 Toast Titanium allows you to burn your own CDs.

Figure 11.26 After you use the New CD button in the Toast window, you can drag in your Keynote files.

Making CDs

Some CD creation programs have problems with package files. One of the most popular, Roxio Toast Titanium, needs to be set up in a particular fashion in order to successfully create CDs with package files such as Keynote documents.

Normally, you add files to the Toast window (**Figure 11.25**) by dragging them in from the Finder. If you do this with a package file, it appears in the Toast windows as a folder, and since it is the only folder on the CD, the package will be written incorrectly. The solution is simple; use the New CD button at the bottom of the Toast window to create a "wrapper," initially called "Untitled CD," for the CD, then drag the Keynote files into the Toast window (**Figure 11.26**).

Mac OS X's disc burning in the Finder seems to work fine with package files.

✔ Tip

- If you put a CD containing Keynote files into a Mac, and the files appear in the Finder as folders rather than as Keynote document icons, check to see if Keynote is installed on that machine. If it is not, you will get folder icons, instead of the proper document icons.

Exporting Presentations to QuickTime

Keynote allows you to export your presentations as QuickTime movies, which can be quite helpful. As a QuickTime movie, the presentation can be played on Macs that don't have Keynote installed. QuickTime movies can also be played on Windows and Linux machines. Keynote files exported as QuickTime movies include all the transitions and animated object builds that you added to the presentation.

Another benefit of a Keynote file exported to QuickTime is that you can create a self-running QuickTime movie, which is useful for unattended presentations, such as kiosks. When you create a self-running QuickTime movie, you can set the duration for object builds and how long a slide is visible.

If you prefer, you can instead create an interactive QuickTime movie, which allows your viewers to advance through the slide builds and slides manually.

To create a self-running QuickTime movie:

1. Open the Keynote file that you wish to export to a QuickTime movie.

2. Choose File > Export.

   The Export sheet slides down from the top of the document window (**Figure 11.27**). By default, QuickTime is selected.

3. Click Next.

   The QuickTime Export sheet appears (**Figure 11.28**).

4. From the Playback Control pop-up menu, choose Self-Playing Movie.

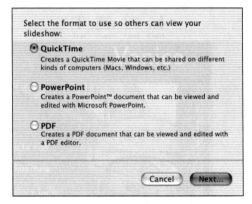

Figure 11.27 Choose an export format in the Export sheet.

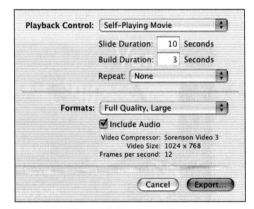

Figure 11.28 The QuickTime Export sheet lets you choose if you want to export a self-playing movie or an interactive movie.

5. If you want to change the slide duration (the length of time a slide is displayed after it is fully built) from its default value of 10 seconds, enter a new value.

A slide's duration does not begin until all of the object builds on the slide are complete.

6. Enter a value in the Build Duration field, if you want to change it from the default duration of three seconds.

There is no delay between the moment a slide first appears on the screen and when the first object build begins. The Build Duration field controls the number of seconds between the beginning of one build and the next. So, for example, when the presentation switches to a slide that has an object build, the first build will trigger immediately, the next build will occur according to the number you chose in the Build Duration field, and subsequent builds will also take that long.

7. From the Repeat pop-up menu, choose one of the following:

   ▲ **None** means that the slideshow will play through only once.

   ▲ **Loop** makes the slideshow play continuously, beginning over again automatically when it reaches the end.

   ▲ **Back and Forth** makes the presentation play through once, then, when it reaches the end, begin to play backwards.

continues on next page

8. From the Formats pop-up menu, choose one of the following presets:

   ▲ **Full Quality, Large** uses the Sorenson Video 3 video compressor, at 12 frames per second (fps), and produces movies that are the same size as your slides. Use this one for the highest quality presentations. The tradeoff is that this option creates the largest files.

   ▲ **CD-ROM Movie, Medium** uses the same video compressor and frame rate, but the movie is half the size, at 512 × 384.

   ▲ **Web Movie, Small** uses the same video compressor and frame rate, but the movie is one-quarter the Large size, at 256 × 192.

9. If you have audio in your presentation, and you want it included in the exported movie, make sure the Include Audio check box is selected.

10. Click Export.

    A Save sheet appears, prompting you for the name of the exported movie and where you want to put it on your hard disk.

11. Click Export.

    The Export to QuickTime window appears, and shows you a preview of the slideshow as it is exported (**Figure 11.29**). When the export is complete, the window disappears.

Figure 11.29 The Export to QuickTime window gives you feedback about the progress of the export process.

✔ Tips

■ The size of the exported file is dependent on the quality you use for export. For example, I exported a small (6 slides) file that had transitions and object builds in the Large, Medium, and Small sizes. Respectively, the sizes of the exported QuickTime files were 10.5 MB, 712 KB, and 116 KB. Especially if you will be using your presentation on the Web, carefully balance the size of your presentation with the quality you need.

■ Depending on the speed of your Mac, the size of the presentation, and the settings you chose from the Formats pop-up menu, the export could take up to several minutes to complete.

To create an interactive QuickTime movie:

1. Open the Keynote file that you wish to export to a QuickTime movie.

2. Choose File > Export.

   The Export sheet slides down from the top of the document window. By default, QuickTime is selected.

3. Click Next.

   The QuickTime Export sheet appears.

4. From the Playback Control pop-up menu, choose Interactive Slideshow.

   The Slide Duration, Build Duration, and Repeat controls will become inactive.

5. From the Formats pop-up menu, choose one of the presets: Full Quality, Large; CD-ROM Movie, Medium; or Web Movie, Small.

   See the previous section for an explanation of these options.

6. If you have audio in your presentation, and you want it included in the exported movie, make sure the Include Audio check box is selected.

7. Click Export.

   A Save sheet appears, prompting you for the name of the exported movie and where you want to put it on your hard disk.

8. Click Export.

   The Export to QuickTime dialog appears, and shows you a preview of the slideshow as it is exported.

✔ Tips

- In the QuickTime Player, you step through an interactive presentation by using the space bar or right arrow key to go forward, and the left arrow key to go back.

- If you have QuickTime Player Pro installed on the machine you are using to play back the presentation, you can play back using the full screen. See "Using QuickTime Pro" in Chapter 6 for more information.

- If you want to embed the QuickTime file into a Web page, you can turn off the movie controller (the part of the window with the Play button) as part of your HTML. The user will still be able to step through the show by clicking on the movie.

EXPORTING PRESENTATIONS TO QUICKTIME

Tweaking Video and Audio Formats

It is possible to change the export settings in the QuickTime Export sheet to more precisely control the video and audio formats used in the QuickTime movie. You can change the type of video compression used (called the video *codec*), and also change the audio codec.

To change these settings, choose Custom from the Formats pop-up menu. The Custom QuickTime Settings dialog will appear (**Figure 11.30**). You can use this to create a custom size for your movie, or you can change the compression scheme by clicking the Settings button in the Video section, which brings up the Compression Settings dialog (**Figure 11.31**). You can then choose a video codec from the pop-up menu at the top of the dialog. Different codecs have different settings that will appear. There is a preview area that will show you the effects of your changes.

Clicking the Settings button in the Audio section brings up the Sound Settings dialog (**Figure 11.32**), which allows you to select an audio codec.

Just because you can change the settings from the presets doesn't necessarily mean that you should, however. The presets produce files that look quite good, and will suffice for the vast majority of your export needs. But if you are familiar with the effects of the different QuickTime video and audio codecs and are confident that you can improve on Keynote's presets, you have the power.

Figure 11.30 You'll use the Custom QuickTime Settings dialog to change the size of the QuickTime movie, and also to apply different video and audio codecs.

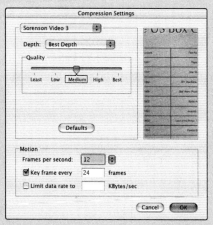

Figure 11.31 The Compression Settings dialog gives you a choice of two dozen different video codecs, each with their own set of adjustments.

Figure 11.32 The Audio Sound Settings dialog lets you choose from 12 different audio codecs.

Figure 11.33 When you export a slide (top) with shadows and transparency (middle), those features will be lost in the resulting PDF file (bottom).

Exporting Presentations in PDF Format

If you need to export your presentation in a format that can be easily transported between computers and that can also be easily printed, the correct choice is to export to PDF (Portable Document Format, also known as Adobe Acrobat format). PDF files can be viewed and printed with the free Acrobat Reader, which is available for a very wide range of computer platforms, including Macintosh (Mac OS X and Classic Mac OS); Windows (3.1 through XP); Linux and other versions of UNIX; and even some handheld computers, such as Palm and Pocket PC. On Mac OS X, PDF files can be read by either Acrobat Reader or by the Preview application.

Keynote slides that are exported to PDF generally look pretty good, but you should be aware of some limitations. For example, files exported to PDF will lose transparency and shadows on text and graphic objects, apparently due to a bug in Keynote's PDF exporting routines (**Figure 11.33**). Graphics in Keynote often turn out to look more jagged (less smooth) when exported to PDF. These difficulties may improve in a future version of Keynote.

To export a presentation to PDF:

1. Open the Keynote file that you wish to export to a PDF file.

2. Choose File > Export.

The Export sheet slides down from the top of the document window.

3. Click PDF.

4. Click Next.

A Save sheet appears, prompting you for the name of the exported PDF file and where you want to put it on your hard disk.

5. Click Export.

The Export to PDF window appears (**Figure 11.34**), and shows you the progress of the export.

✔ Tip

■ Presentation files exported to PDF can be quite large, especially if you have many photographic images in the slideshow. Large files are often not convenient to send via e-mail, or to post on the Web for downloading. If you need to create PDF versions of your presentations on a regular basis, you might consider purchasing a utility program that optimizes and shrinks the size of PDF files. One example is Apago, Inc.'s (www.apago.com) PDFShrink, a $125 program that can shrink a PDF file up to 10% of its original size, depending on the content of the PDF file and the desired resolution of graphics in the optimized version. The same company also offers PDFShrink Lite for $35, which reduces the resolution of all color and grayscale images to 72 dpi, which is acceptable for viewing on a computer screen.

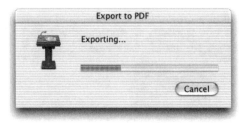

Figure 11.34 The Export to PDF window shows you the progress of the export.

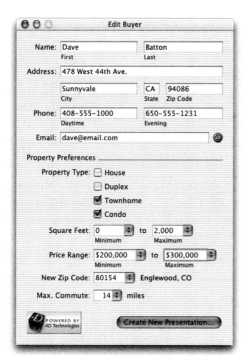

Figure 11.35 The data entry screen from the sample application for the 4D Keynote Builder allows you to choose a variety of criteria for a real estate buyer.

Working with Databases

When Steve Jobs introduced Keynote at his presentation at Macworld Expo in January 2003, he referred to the possibility of using Keynote in conjunction with a database program to create presentations that utilized up-to-the-minute data. That tantalizing possibility remained unfulfilled until April 2003, when two database makers introduced Keynote integration tools for their products. In this section, you'll see a brief overview of these tools, and get a glimpse of their potential.

4D Keynote Builder

4th Dimension is a powerful relational database program that provides a potent development environment for database software developers. With 4D, developers can build custom database solutions for clients that include data entry forms, menus, and other customized user interfaces. A custom 4D application can look indistinguishable from any other Mac OS X application. 4D also has strong querying features and report generators that allow users to extract and use information in the database.

The 4D Keynote Builder is a free developer tool that 4D developers can build into their own applications to easily produce Keynote presentations (http://www.4d.com/2003/integration.html). The sample application that 4D has distributed along with the tool shows how you can use the combination of 4D and Keynote to extract data from a real estate database that is customized for a particular buyer. The user (in this case presumably a real estate broker) enters the buyer's information and buying criteria, then clicks Create New Presentation (**Figure 11.35**). The application searches for homes in the real estate database that match the criteria,

continues on next page

WORKING WITH DATABASES

then shows you a summary of what it found (**Figure 11.36**). Another click creates the Keynote presentation file, using a custom theme (**Figure 11.37**).

Because 4D understands how to read other kinds of files, developers can now use 4D and 4D Keynote Builder to create Keynote presentations based on other data sources, including text files, Web pages, Excel spreadsheets, and many more.

Figure 11.36 The summary screen shows what matching data was retrieved from the database.

Figure 11.37 This slide from the generated presentation uses a custom theme.

Figure 11.38 The FileMaker to Keynote Tool lets you build Keynote presentations from a variety of data.

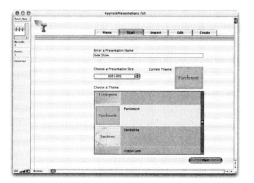

Figure 11.39 The first thing that you'll need to do is name your presentation and select a theme.

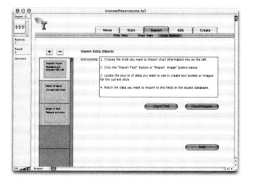

Figure 11.40 The next step is to import slide text and images.

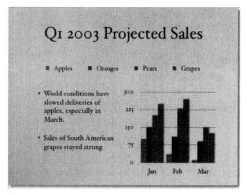

Figure 11.41 The resulting presentation built with the FileMaker to Keynote Tool includes title text, a chart, and bulleted text.

FileMaker to Keynote Tool

FileMaker, a subsidiary of Apple, produces FileMaker Pro 6, a relational database designed for easy development and ease-of-use. FileMaker Pro comes with dozens of database templates that allow you to get started quickly, and you can use these templates as a starting point for your own database designs. FileMaker Pro is designed more as an end-user program for individuals and workgroups than as a professional database development environment, but developers can purchase advanced versions, such as FileMaker Developers 6, that allows developers to create custom FileMaker solutions.

The FileMaker to Keynote Tool (**Figure 11.38**) is an example set of databases that shows how you can use FileMaker Pro to gather text and images from a variety of sources, including FileMaker databases and text and image files on your hard disk, then have FileMaker build a presentation from the data (`http://www.filemaker.com/xml/xslt_library.html`). The database works by providing the user with an application that steps through building a presentation. The user is first prompted to name a new presentation and select a Keynote theme (**Figure 11.39**), then to fill the presentation with text and images (**Figure 11.40**). The resulting presentation brings all of the information together (**Figure 11.41**).

XML: The Universal Solvent

Extensible Markup Language (XML) is a markup language for documents containing structured information. Structured information contains content and an indication of what role the content plays in the document. For example, the images or text in a document are the document's content. But where the text is placed in the document also has meaning; section headers mean something different than the body text and figure captions, and images have their own meaning.

Virtually all documents have some sort of structure, and XML is a very flexible language that can be used to describe the structure of almost any kind of document. As a result, XML has gained a tremendous amount of popularity amongst software developers, because it can be used as a file format that can be easily read and used by many software programs.

Where this connects with Keynote is that the main file in a Keynote package is the `presentation.apxl` file, which is an XML file. Apple has published the schema (think of it as the roadmap for the Keynote XML file format) that is freely available at `http://developer.apple.com/technotes/tn2002/tn2067.html`.

Programs that understand and can write XML files can use the Keynote schema to create their own Keynote files. Database developers, such as 4D and FileMaker, have used the schema to build tools for their database products that take information in the database, and then create a Keynote presentation file that includes the data, nicely formatted.

If you're interested in working with Keynote and XML, you might find the Keynote developer tools mailing list to be of interest. It's at `http://www.opendarwin.org/mailman/listinfo/keynote-tools`.

GIVING THE PRESENTATION

The funny thing about presentations is that you do a bunch of work to create your presentation and make it look good, and at the end of the process the real job hasn't even started yet—you still have to give the presentation. For some people, giving a presentation (and public speaking in general) ranks in popularity just this side of dental surgery. Other folks like nothing better than to be standing in front of an audience. Most of us, however, fall somewhere between the two extremes.

Luckily, people have been speaking in front of groups for thousands of years, and there is a lot of received wisdom about how you can make giving a presentation a comfortable experience for both you and your audience. Besides the nuts and bolts of giving a presentation with Keynote, I'll include some speaking tips in this chapter that should help improve your presentations.

You'll also learn how to handle giving presentations with laptops and external monitors or projectors; discover some cool hardware and software extras for presentations; and print your presentation so that your audience can bask in the glory of your presentation long after you've disappeared into the night.

Preparing to Present

The more presentations you give, the better speaker you will become. The key to giving a good presentation is to be prepared, pay attention to the details, and have plenty of practice. Here are some tips that can help your overall presentation.

- Before the presentation, get a friend or coworker to read through your presentation. You'll be surprised at how often they'll find a typo that you missed.

- If you can, get to the presentation venue early. Sit or stand where you will be when you're speaking, and make sure that your seating (or the podium) is adjusted the way that you want it. Take a moment to adjust the microphone and work with the venue's audio technician to get the levels right before the audience arrives. Make sure you have a spot to place a cup of water. Getting comfortable with the physical space and the facilities helps a lot.

- If you have the opportunity to greet some of the audience members as they enter the room, you should do so. It's easier to speak to people you know, even if all you've done is say hello.

- Before you begin, visualize yourself giving a successful presentation. Imagine that you've spoken very well, and see in your mind the audience's involvement in your talk. Hear their applause, and picture audience members coming up to congratulate you after the show. It sounds a bit silly, but visualizing success works.

- Concentrate on your message, not on the audience. If you focus on what you're saying, you will distract yourself from being nervous.

- If you are nervous, never apologize for it. Except in extreme cases, most audiences don't notice that speakers are nervous, and it doesn't help your case to point it out.

- Always keep in mind that your audience wants you to succeed. People don't go to a presentation thinking, "I sure hope this guy does a lousy talk and wastes my time." They want to get something out of your presentation as much as you do.

- Unless you are a professional comedian, keep the jokes to a minimum, or skip them altogether. A joke that falls flat isn't a good way to start a show.

- Don't read straight from a script. Very few people can read from a script without putting their audience to sleep; we call those people actors (and professional speakers).

- Don't read your slides out loud word for word. Your slides should be signposts and reminders of what you want to say. Using your slides as your teleprompter is another way to lose audience interest. If you need prompting for your topics, use your Speaker Notes.

- It's a good idea to put a summary slide at the end of your presentation. Not only does it bring your talk to a natural end, but it helps to once again drive your argument home to your audience.

- Try hard not to run over on time. It's always a good idea to practice your presentation, and when you do, use a clock or a stopwatch to see how long your presentation really is. It's better to cut slides before the presentation than to run out of time and not be able to finish at all. On the other hand, if your presentation is running short, it's better to find out before you're in front of a bunch of expectant faces.

- After the presentation is over, thank your audience and make yourself available for questions. As you are chatting with people, get feedback from them so that you can improve the next show. Simply asking them if there was anything they would have liked you to cover can yield useful information.

Cool Presentation Gear

As already noted in this book, what matters is what you're saying in your presentation. But there is a variety of hardware and software that can make giving the presentation easier, more convenient, or both.

Cool hardware

The first bit of hardware that should be on your list is a **laser pointer**. These handy items are perfect for drawing the audience's attention to a part of your slide, and are essential if you will be doing a demonstration on the computer as well as the slideshow. They are widely available for as little as $10. But the $100 lasers with a green beam are especially cool.

One of the drawbacks to doing presentations with a computer is that you are usually tied to the location of the computer. For some presenters, especially people who are more comfortable if they can move around as they speak, a **remote control** is the answer. These units consist of a handheld control and some kind of receiver that usually connects to your computer via the USB port. Some remote controls use infrared as the connection between the handheld unit and the receiver, and others use RF (Radio Frequency). Infrared remotes require a line of sight between you and the receiver, and the remote can control your computer from a distance of between 20 and 30 feet. RF controllers can work even if you can't see the computer (they can even work through walls), and have a slightly greater range, up to 40 feet.

There are many remote controls available, starting at about $50 and zooming up to as much as $120. The two remote controls most commonly used in the Mac market are both made by Keyspan (www.keyspan.com). The $50 infrared Digital Media Remote (**Figure 12.1**) can control almost any application on

Figure 12.1 The Keyspan Digital Media Remote lets you control Keynote, among many other programs.

Figure 12.2 Keyspan's Presentation Remote has a touchpad that allows mouse movement, and includes a laser pointer.

the Mac, including Keynote, but also iTunes, the DVD player, PowerPoint, and many more. The Keyspan Presentation Remote (**Figure 12.2**), an RF device that sells for $80, has a joystick-like touchpad that provides full mouse control, and includes a laser pointer.

You might already have a remote control for your Mac in your pocket, without even knowing it. If you have a Sony Ericsson **cellular phone** with Bluetooth capability, you can use it as a remote control for Keynote and many other programs on your Mac with the help of a terrific software package called Salling Clicker (see the software section below). Bluetooth connections are good for about 30 feet from your Macintosh, and they do not require line of sight.

If you need to transport your presentation between computers, you can burn it onto a CD, or you can use a **USB flash drive**. These units are about as long as your thumb, and plug into any USB port. They provide between 32MB and 1GB of storage, with no moving parts, and are powered by your computer. When you plug the flash drive into your computer, it shows up on the desktop, just as any other drive does. I put my presentation files on mine as a backup, so I know that even if my PowerBook dies, the show can go on.

Cool software

There are a few software packages that can enhance the presentation process or work around some of Keynote's limitations:

◆ **Salling Clicker**, from Salling Software (www.salling.com), is a great program that allows you to use your Sony Ericsson mobile phone with Bluetooth to remotely control a wide range of applications, including Keynote and PowerPoint. The program uses AppleScript to control programs, so the more scriptable an application is, the more that Salling Clicker can do with it (**Figure 12.3**). The included scripts for Keynote let you play a presentation, go to the first, last, previous, or next slide; or toggle the screen to black.

The nice thing about using your cell phone as a remote control, of course, is that you don't have to carry around a separate remote control. You can even get a little laser pointer that snaps onto some Sony Ericsson phones. Talk about multitasking!

◆ **Keypress**, a free program from GutterFMA.com, is a simple program that uses AppleScript and Apple's GUI Scripting System Events (www.apple.com/applescript/GUI/) to play a presentation automatically (**Figure 12.4**). The program uses AppleScript to press the right arrow key at a specified number of seconds, which tells Keynote to advance through slides and object builds. You can download Keypress from www.keynoteuser.com.

◆ **KeyWebX** doesn't help you give a presentation, but it can help you share the presentation with people who are unable to make it to your talk (**Figure 12.5**). It is a small utility that takes PDF or QuickTime files generated by Keynote, then slices them into separate JPEG images and builds simple HTML pages that you can then use on the Web.

✔ Tip

■ The GUI Scripting System Events package helps control Keynote a little, but it is no substitute for real AppleScript support built into Keynote. Let's hope that a future version of Keynote will allow scripters to really achieve the opportunities that scripting support would bring.

Figure 12.3 Salling Clicker lets you use your Bluetooth-enabled mobile phone as a remote control.

Figure 12.4 Keypress lets Keynote presentations play automatically—something that Keynote can't do on its own.

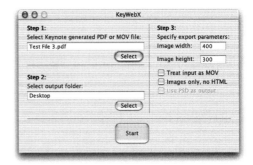

Figure 12.5 You can turn your presentations into simple Web pages with KeyWebX.

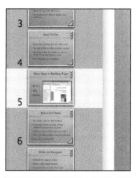

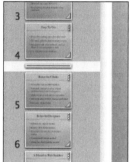

Figure 12.6 After selecting a slide in the Slide Navigator (top), and setting it to be skipped, Keynote shows the slide as a line (bottom) and renumbers the subsequent slides.

Skipping Slides on Playback

There are times when you have your presentation ready to go, and you arrive at the venue and realize that you don't want to show some of the slides in your presentation. Perhaps your company's product line has changed, and you want to skip the slide that shows the fabulous Wonder Widget, because it will soon be replaced by a new model (probably the Ultra Wonder Widget). Sometimes even news reports are a reason to remove slides from your presentation; for example, you probably wouldn't have wanted to give a presentation with a picture of a sinking ship the day after the *Titanic* went down.

You must select slides to be skipped before you begin the presentation; you can't choose to skip a slide while you are playing the presentation.

To set slides to be skipped:

1. Open your presentation.

2. Choose View > Navigator, or choose Navigator from the View pop-up menu in the toolbar.
   The Slide Navigator appears.

3. In the Slide Navigator, click to select the slide that you want to skip.
   You can select multiple slides by clicking on the first slide that you wish to select, holding down the Shift key, and clicking the last slide in the selection. You can select discontiguous slides by selecting the first slide, holding down the Command key, and then selecting subsequent slides.

4. Choose Slide > Skip Slide.
   Keynote collapses the thumbnail image of the slide in the Slide Navigator to a line (**Figure 12.6**).

✔ Tips

■ You can also skip a slide by Control-clicking the slide thumbnail in the Slide Navigator, and choosing Skip Slide from the resulting contextual menu.

■ To restore a skipped slide to your presentation, select the slide thumbnail in the Slide Navigator, and choose Slide > Don't Skip Slide.

Viewing the Presentation

Most presentations are viewed by being projected onto a large screen, but you can also show them on your computer screen, or on a second monitor connected to your computer. When you're using a second display (either a second monitor or a projector) you can choose to use *video mirroring*, where the picture on the presentation computer and the second display are identical, or *dual displays*, where the slideshow plays on the second display, and your display shows you your Speaker Notes.

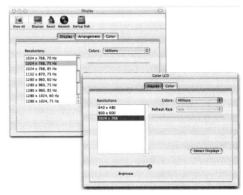

Figure 12.7 When you have two displays connected, there are two windows for the Display pane of System Preferences.

When you're using a portable Macintosh to give your presentation, such as a PowerBook or an iBook with a video-out port, you can use video mirroring with either kind of portable. But if you want to use dual displays, you must have a PowerBook, because iBooks are limited to video mirroring. You will use the System Preferences Displays pane to control the two monitors and choose either video mirroring or dual displays.

Exterior displays, whether a monitor or projector, should be VGA compatible, and capable of displaying at either 800×600 or 1024×768 resolution.

To set up video mirroring:

1. Connect the second display to your computer.

2. Choose Apple > System Preferences.
   The System Preferences application opens.

3. Click Displays.
   The Displays preference pane appears. Because there are two displays, there will be a second window with the controls for the second display (**Figure 12.7**).

4. Set both displays to the same resolution and color depth.
   Use the Resolutions list and the Colors pop-up menu in both screens.

✔ Tips

- It's usually a good idea not to run Keynote while you're setting up video mirroring or dual displays. Sometimes the change in video modes confuses Keynote, and you have to quit and relaunch it to make things work again.

- If your laptop doesn't sync with the projector (the image doesn't appear on the projector or is distorted), shut down, then restart the computer with the projector connected. This usually fixes the problem.

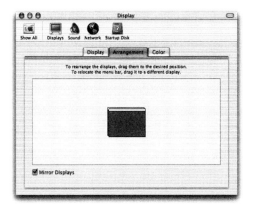

Figure 12.8 The Arrangement pane lets you turn on video mirroring.

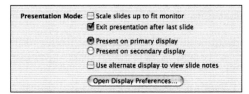

Figure 12.9 If you want to show your Notes on a separate screen from the presentation, you'll need to set the preference in Keynote.

5. One of the windows will have an Arrangement tab. Click it to display the Arrangement pane (**Figure 12.8**).

6. Click Mirror Displays.

The same image appears on both screens.

✔ Tips

- Some portable Macs go into video mirroring mode by default when you connect a second display, so you don't need to go through these steps. Even then, you may want to adjust the resolution and color depth on both displays.

- The Arrangement tab may have a slightly different name (such as Arrange) in some versions of Mac OS X.

Using dual displays

In order to set up your displays so that you can view Speaker Notes on one screen (usually the screen of your portable Mac) and show the presentation on the other, you must first let Keynote know that you will be using dual displays.

To set dual display preferences:

1. Connect the second display to your computer.

2. Choose Keynote > Preferences.

The Preferences window opens.

3. In the Presentation Mode section of the window (**Figure 12.9**), click either "Present on primary display" or "Present on secondary display" to specify the display the on which the presentation will be shown.

The primary display is the one that contains the menu bar.

continues on next page

4. Select "Use alternate display to view slide notes."

If you don't click this option, the alternate display will be black during the presentation.

5. Click Open Display Preferences.

The System Preferences application opens and the Displays preference pane appears.

Because there are two displays, there will be a second window with the controls for the second display.

6. One of the windows will have an Arrangement tab. Click it to display the Arrangement pane.

7. If it is selected, clear the Mirror Displays checkbox.

The pane will change to show the arrangement of the two displays (**Figure 12.10**). If you chose to view slide notes during the presentation, when you play the presentation, you will see the presentation on one display, and on the other you will see the Keynote window with the Notes field open. The Keynote window will be inactive, allowing you to only view Notes.

✔ Tip

- During the presentation, the Notes field isn't scrollable, so if you have a lot of notes, make sure to open the Notes field all the way, and to set the Zoom pop-up menu in the Keynote window to Fit in Window, so that you can still see the entire slide on your screen (**Figure 12.11**).

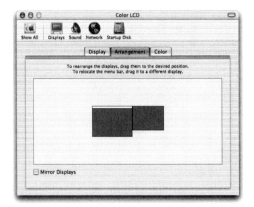

Figure 12.10 When you use dual displays, the desktop spans both displays, and the Arrangement pane lets you move the relative positions of each display, and even lets you change the display where the menu bar resides.

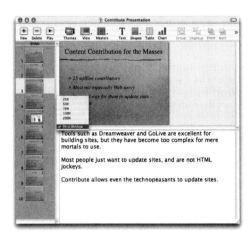

Figure 12.11 Make sure that you open the Notes field all the way before you begin your presentation.

Table 12.1

Keyboard Controls during Presentations	
ACTION	KEY(S)
Play the presentation	⌘ Option P
End the presentation	Esc
	⌘ . (period)
	Q
Next slide or object build	Mouse click
	Space
	Right arrow
	Down arrow
	Page down
	N
Next slide (with no transition)	+ (plus key on keyboard or numeric keypad)
Previous slide or object build*	Left arrow
	Up arrow
	Page up
	P
Previous slide (with no transition)	− (minus key on keyboard or numeric keypad)
First slide	Home
Last slide	End
Jump to a given slide by number, where # is the slide number.	# Enter
Jump forward # slides, where # is the number of slides to jump.	# + (plus key)
	# = (equals key on numeric keypad)
Jump backwards # slides, where # is the number of slides to jump.	# − (minus key)
Toggle black screen	B

* These keys will not step backwards through each object build stage. For example, if you have three lines of bulleted text that build, and you press a previous key after the second line appears, all of the bulleted text disappears, and it is as if you just switched to the slide. Pressing previous again returns to the previous slide. Also, transitions and builds do not play backwards; if going forward, the slides dissolve from one to another, going backwards, the slides will simply switch to the previous slide.

To run your presentation:

1. In Outline or Navigator View, click to select the first slide in the presentation.

2. Click Play in the toolbar.

   or

   Choose View > Play Slideshow.

   or

   Press ⌘ Option P.

   The slideshow begins. Click the mouse button, or use the right arrow key to advance through your slides.

3. To end the slideshow, press Esc, or ⌘ . .

Keyboard controls during the show

When you're running the slideshow, Keynote gives you some control over the show's progress by pressing keys on the keyboard, and by clicking the mouse. See **Table 12.1** for a list of controls.

VIEWING THE PRESENTATION

Printing Your Presentation

Most of the time, your presentation will come to life on a monitor or when projected for your audience. But it's quite common to be asked to provide your presentation in printed form, as well. Printed presentations are often used as audience handouts. Keynote allows you to print your slideshow in several different ways to meet a variety of needs. You can print just your slides; your slides with your speaker notes; a *producer script*, which is a dual column layout that prints four slides per page, with plenty of room for handwritten notes; or you can print the slideshow's outline.

Printing slides is a good way to proof your presentation. Presentations look different on paper than on-screen, so proofing printouts allows you to catch errors that you otherwise might have missed.

To print your slides:

1. Open the presentation you want to print.

2. Choose File > Print Slides.
   The Print dialog opens (**Figure 12.12**).

3. Choose Keynote from the Copies & Pages pop-up menu.
   The dialog changes to Keynote-specific options (**Figure 12.13**).

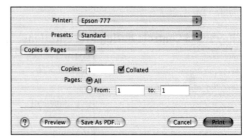

Figure 12.12 The Print dialog lets you set the number of copies and the page range for the print job.

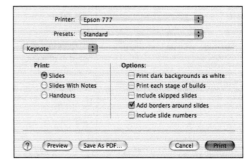

Figure 12.13 Set the Keynote-specific print options in this dialog.

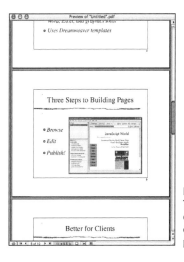

Figure 12.14
The Slides option prints one slide per page.

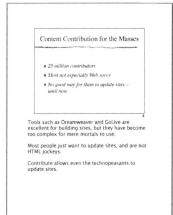

Figure 12.15
Slides With Notes includes the slide and your speaker notes.

Figure 12.16
Handouts prints four slides per page, with plenty of room for handwritten notes.

4. In the Print section, choose one of the following:

▲ **Slides** prints one slide per page (**Figure 12.14**).

▲ **Slides With Notes** prints one slide per page, with your speaker notes below the slide (**Figure 12.15**).

▲ **Handouts** prints four slides per page, and leaves room for handwritten notes (**Figure 12.16**).

5. Select the print formatting options that you want:

▲ **Print dark backgrounds as white** reverses the slide colors to improve the readability of the slide on paper. Dark backgrounds will print white; lighter-colored text will print black. If you are printing to a color printer, colored graphics on slides will print in color.

▲ **Print each stage of builds** prints a separate page for each stage of the object builds on a slide. If the slide has four stages to the object build, four slides will print.

▲ **Include skipped slides** prints all slides in the Slide Navigator, whether or not they are marked as skipped.

▲ **Add borders around slides** puts a thin border around the edges of each slide.

▲ **Include slide numbers** adds a number below each slide.

6. (Optional) If you want to see a preview of your slides before they go to the printer, click the Preview button.

The preview will open in whatever program you have set to view PDF files (usually Preview or Acrobat Reader).

continues on next page

PRINTING YOUR PRESENTATION

7. (Optional) If you want to save a copy of your slideshow as a PDF file, click the Save As PDF button.

   Keynote will present you with a Save dialog so you can choose where to save the PDF file.

8. Click Print.

✔ Tips

- It's almost always a good idea to preview the slides on screen (see step 6) before you print them.
- Printing to a PDF file is different from exporting as PDF (see Chapter 11), which will give you edge-to-edge renditions of your slides. Printing to PDF gives you slides with white space around them.
- Unfortunately, you cannot customize Keynote's print layouts. So if you want a layout with three slides to a page, and with lines for audience notes, you're out of luck, at least printing from Keynote. One alternate possibility would be to create such a custom layout by taking screenshots of each slide, then creating the layout in a page layout program such as Adobe InDesign or QuarkXPress.
- You can use the Pages controls in the Print dialog to print all slides, or a range of slides.
- If you output the presentation as a PDF file, you can use the full version of Adobe Acrobat to add annotations, hyperlinks, and other enhancements.

To print the presentation outline:

1. Open the presentation you want to print.
2. Choose File > Print Outline.

   The Print dialog opens.
3. Click Print.

   Keynote prints the presentation outline (**Figure 12.17**).

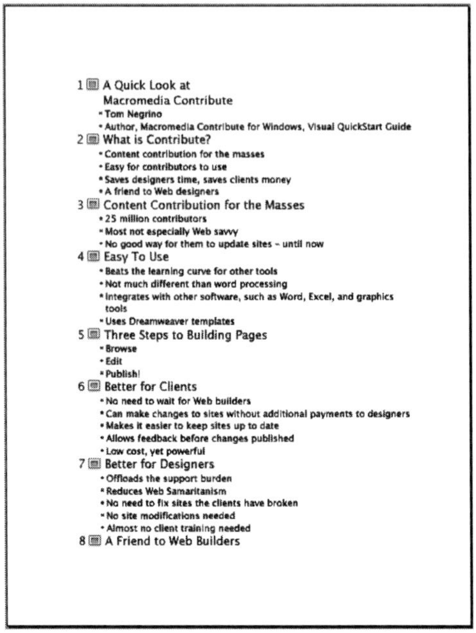
1 A Quick Look at
Macromedia Contribute
- Tom Negrino
- Author, Macromedia Contribute for Windows, Visual QuickStart Guide

2 What is Contribute?
- Content contribution for the masses
- Easy for contributors to use
- Saves designers time, saves clients money
- A friend to Web designers

3 Content Contribution for the Masses
- 25 million contributors
- Most not especially Web savvy
- No good way for them to update sites – until now

4 Easy To Use
- Beats the learning curve for other tools
- Not much different than word processing
- Integrates with other software, such as Word, Excel, and graphics tools
- Uses Dreamweaver templates

5 Three Steps to Building Pages
- Browse
- Edit
- Publish!

6 Better for Clients
- No need to wait for Web builders
- Can make changes to sites without additional payments to designers
- Makes it easier to keep sites up to date
- Allows feedback before changes published
- Low cost, yet powerful

7 Better for Designers
- Offloads the support burden
- Reduces Web Samaritanism
- No need to fix sites the clients have broken
- No site modifications needed
- Almost no client training needed

8 A Friend to Web Builders

Figure 12.17 When you print the Presentation Outline, you're not distracted by slide thumbnails.

CREATING CUSTOM MASTER SLIDES

Whether you are creating a theme from scratch or just want to customize an existing theme to better meet your presentation needs, you will need to learn to customize master slides. Custom master slides can make creating presentations much easier, especially if you need a different look for your presentations than those provided by the theme that you have chosen.

Custom master slides are also useful if you need a kind of master slide that isn't covered by Apple's standard eleven master slides. For example, let's say that you have many slides that will contain large photographs. None of Apple's master slides have big photo cutouts that take up most of the slide. You can create your own master slide with a giant photo cutout and use it in your presentations.

In this chapter, you'll learn how to modify and create master slides; set default slide layouts and backgrounds; and set default styles for objects, text, and tables.

Building Master Slides

Master slides are where Keynote stores its definitions for all slide attributes. Changes that you make to master slides will be reflected in the presentation slides that are based on those master slides. For example, when you click the Table button on the toolbar, Apple's themes create a table with three rows and three columns. If you tend to need a table with four rows and four columns, you can change the table default on the master slide, and from then on in the presentation file, tables will appear your way.

If you modify a master slide in a particular theme in a presentation file, your changes will affect just that file, and will not be reflected in other presentations made from the theme. If you want the changes to work in other files, you must save the changes as a custom theme. See Chapter 14 for more information about building custom themes.

Master slides provide the definitions for the following slide attributes:

◆ Background graphics

◆ Photo cutouts

◆ Text box layouts

◆ Default bullet styles for bulleted text

◆ Default font settings

◆ Line and fill styles for objects and tables

◆ Chart types and styles

◆ Default slide transition

◆ Placement of alignment guides

When you create a custom master slide, you can go about the job in two ways. You can modify one of the existing master slides in your presentation file. Or you can make a duplicate of the existing master slide that has the closest attributes to what you want

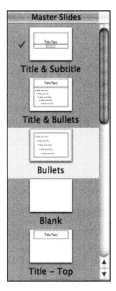

Figure 13.1 You'll make most of your changes to master slides in the Master Slide Navigator.

Figure 13.2 When you create a new master slide, Keynote automatically gives it a name, which you'll probably want to change.

to create, make changes to the copy, and then rename it. If you have previously created the master slide, you can also import it into your current file from another presentation file.

To duplicate a master slide:

1. Choose View > Show Master Slides.

   The Master Slide Navigator appears (**Figure 13.1**).

2. Click to select the master slide that has the most similar attributes to the attributes of the master slide that you want to create.

3. Choose Slide > New Master Slide.

   or

   Press ⌘ Shift N.

   or

   Click New in the toolbar.

   Keynote creates a new master slide under the one you selected, with the name Master #*x*, where *x* is a number one larger than the current number of master slides (**Figure 13.2**). The new master slide will be a duplicate of the originally selected master slide.

✔ Tip

■ You can also duplicate a master slide by selecting it in the Master Slide Navigator, then pressing Return.

To rename a master slide:

1. Select a master slide in the Master Slide Navigator.

2. Double-click the master slide's name.

   The name is selected.

3. Type the new name, then press Return, Enter, or click anywhere else in the Keynote window.

To import a master slide from another presentation file:

1. Open the Keynote file that will be the destination of the imported slide.

2. Open the Keynote file (the *source file*) that contains the master slide that you want.

3. Arrange the two windows so that you can see both of them on your screen.

4. Select the slide you want from the source file, and drag it into the Slide Navigator of the destination document.

   Keynote creates a copy of the slide in the destination file's Slide Navigator, and also creates a new master slide in the destination document that is a copy of the slide from the source document (**Figure 13.3**).

✔ Tips

- The slide from the source file can't be a master slide; it must be a presentation slide.

- As you can see, this technique can also be used to copy slides between presentation files, not just master slides.

- You can't drag the slide into the destination file's Master Slide Navigator, only the Slide Navigator. If all you wanted was to import the master slide, and you don't want a new presentation slide in the destination file, you can delete the presentation slide.

- The new master slide in the destination file will have the same name as it had in the source file. If that name is already present in the destination file, the master slide name will have "copy" appended.

- If you apply a new theme after importing or customizing a master slide, the theme settings will override your customizations, unless you click the "Retain changes to theme defaults" checkbox in the theme sheet before you click Choose Theme (**Figure 13.4**).

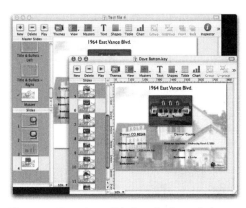

Figure 13.3 Dragging a slide from the front window into the Slide Navigator of the rear window created both a new presentation slide and a new master slide in the rear window.

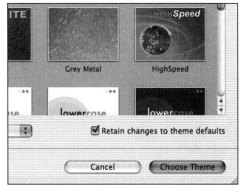

Figure 13.4 If you don't want your custom changes to be overwritten, make sure that you click "Retain changes to theme defaults" in the theme sheet.

Figure 13.5 Begin changing backgrounds in the Master Slide Inspector.

Setting Default Backgrounds and Layouts

Backgrounds, more than any other element of the slide, serve as the unifying element for your presentation. You'll most often use the same background throughout your presentation, but there's no reason that you have to. You might instead want to use a slightly different background on some of the master slides. For example, if you have a long presentation that is delineated into distinct sections, you might want to use different backgrounds for each section, and create a set of modified master slides for each section. From a design standpoint, you probably don't want wildly different backgrounds; it's best to err on the slide of subtlety.

You add and change backgrounds to master slides in the Master Slide Inspector (**Figure 13.5**), and with the rest of Keynote's tools. Backgrounds can be color fills, gradient fills, or image fills, and you can also choose to have no background at all. Besides the fill options, you can also place any objects you want as background elements for the master slide. These elements can include an image (such as a logo), text, drawn objects, or even charts and tables.

To add or change a background to a master slide:

1. Click the Inspector button in the toolbar, then click the Master Slide Inspector button.
   The Master Slide Inspector appears.

2. Choose View > Show Master Slides.
   The Master Slide Navigator appears above the Slide Navigator.

3. Select the master slide for which you want to change the background.

continues on next page

4. In the Background section of the Master Slide Inspector, choose the kind of fill you want for the background from the pop-up menu (**Figure 13.6**).

The settings here for the different kinds of graphic fills are the typical Keynote options for graphics. See Chapter 5 for more information about applying graphics fills.

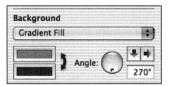

Figure 13.6 The Background section of the Master Slide Inspector allows you to apply color, gradient, and image fills to the slide background.

5. Use any of the Keynote tools to place additional background elements on the slide.

For example, you might want to use objects from the Shapes pop-up menu on the toolbar, or place a free text box with a copyright notice on the slide, or bring in your organization's logo from a graphics program. You can also add QuickTime movies, Flash movies, or sound files to the master slide. See Chapter 6 for more information on working with such media files. Any objects that you add to the master slide will appear on all slides based on that master.

Figure 13.7 Normally, when you select an object you see its selection handles (left). Locked objects change the selection handles to indicate that the object can't be moved.

✔ Tips

■ Once you have placed objects on the master slide, you can choose Arrange > Lock to keep them from being accidentally moved as you continue working (**Figure 13.7**).

■ The rest of the options in the Arrange menu are available to you while you're working on the master slide background. You can layer, align and distribute, and group and ungroup objects. See Chapter 5 for more information about these arrangement options.

■ You can choose whether or not you want objects on the master slide to be able to layer with objects on the presentation slides. You see this most often with photo cutouts on master slides. Photo cutouts are graphics with a transparent part of the graphic that you can then put images behind.

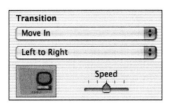

Figure 13.8 Set default slide transitions in the Master Slide Inspector.

Setting default slide transitions

You can set any slide transition as the default for your master slide. Setting a slide transition in the master slide is convenient because you don't have to remember to set transitions later in the presentation slides. However, if you do set transitions in the presentation slides, those settings will override the default transition settings in the master slide.

To set the default slide transition:

1. Open the Inspector window, then click the Master Slide Inspector button.

2. Choose View > Show Master Slides.

   The Master Slide Navigator appears above the Slide Navigator.

3. Select the master slide for which you want to change the default slide transition.

4. From the Transition pop-up menu in the Master Slide Inspector (**Figure 13.8**), choose the transition style you want.

   After you choose a transition, Keynote displays a thumbnail preview of the transition in the Slide Inspector.

5. Some transitions can be set to move in a direction that you specify. If the transition you have selected does, choose a direction from the Direction pop-up menu.

   The directions listed in this pop-up menu will change, depending on the transition style you have selected. If the style doesn't support a direction, the menu will be inactive.

6. Drag the Speed slider to the right to make the transition occur faster, or to the left to make it happen slower.

✔ Tips

■ For more information about slide transitions, see Chapter 9, where you'll find a list of transitions in Table 9.1.

■ It's a good idea to create a presentation slide with the master slide, then check out the transition by playing the presentation, to make sure that the transition looks the way you want.

Customizing Titles and Body Text

Title text boxes and body text boxes can be turned on or off in the Master Slide Inspector. The default style for a body or title text box gets defined on the master slide where the text box appears. To set those style defaults you turn the title and text boxes on, and then select the text in the boxes and set the text attributes using the Fonts and Colors windows and Inspector panes. This works in the same way as editing or changing any text on a slide; see Chapter 4 for more information on text attributes.

To customize title and body text boxes:

1. Open the Master Slide Inspector.

2. In the Master Slide Navigator, select the master slide that you want to change.

3. In the Layout section of the Master Slide Inspector, turn on (or off, depending on what you want) the Show Title and Show Body options (**Figure 13.9**).

   The title and body text boxes will appear (or not) on the master slide in the Slide Canvas.

4. Resize and reposition the text boxes as needed on the master slide.

5. Select the placeholder text in the title or body text box, and format it using the Fonts and Colors windows and with the Text Inspector.

6. (Optional) If you're setting attributes for bulleted text, set the tab positions for each of the bulleted text levels.

   See Chapter 4 for more information on setting bullet tabs.

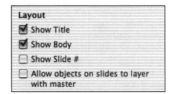

Figure 13.9 The Layout section of the Master Slide Inspector lets you turn on or off the Title and Body text boxes.

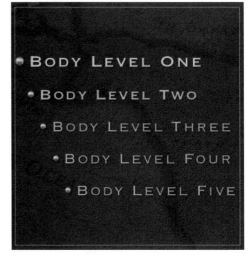

Figure 13.10 You can set the font attributes for each level of bulleted text separately, as shown here.

✔ Tip

■ You can define the font attributes for up to five levels of bulleted text, and each level can be set differently, if you prefer (**Figure 13.10**). You might consider giving custom bullet images to each level.

CUSTOMIZING TITLES AND BODY TEXT

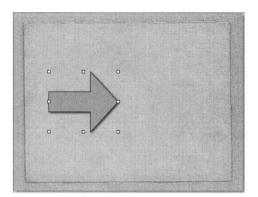

Figure 13.11 Begin setting a shape's defaults by placing a shape on the Slide Canvas.

Setting Default Object Styles

You can set the default styles for all kinds of objects that you place on slides, including shapes, free text boxes, and imported graphics. When you set the defaults, you place a placeholder object on a slide, set its attributes (such as colors, shadows, fonts, etc.), use the commands in the Format menu to tell Keynote that you want to use those attributes as a default, and then delete the placeholder object from the slide. Keynote remembers the defaults you set. You can set defaults on a master slide or on a sample presentation slide. It's usually best to do it on a sample slide, because it is easier to see how your settings will interact with the rest of the slide's elements.

To set default object styles:

1. In the Slide Navigator, click New to create a new slide.

   A new presentation slide appears in the Slide Navigator and the Slide Canvas.

2. Use the Masters pop-up menu in the toolbar to apply the formats from the master slide you are working on.

3. Place a free text box or a shape onto the Slide Canvas (**Figure 13.11**). If you are placing an imported graphic, go to step 7.

   See Chapter 4 for more information about free text boxes; see Chapter 5 for more details about using shapes.

4. If you placed a free text box, type some placeholder text into the box, then select it and set its attributes.

   or

   If you placed a shape, select it and set its attributes.

   continues on next page

SETTING DEFAULT OBJECT STYLES

5. Define the new attributes for the object as the default by choosing one of the following:

▲ Choose Format > Define Defaults for Master Slides > Define [Object] for Current Master (**Figure 13.12**).

[Object] will be replaced by either the words Text or Shape, depending on what type of object you have been working with. This menu choice defines the text box or shape properties for only the master slide you are working on.

▲ Choose Format > Define Defaults for Master Slides > Define [Object] for All Masters.

This menu choice applies the text box or shape properties to all the master slides in the theme you're working in.

6. Skip to step 10.

7. Place an imported graphic onto the Slide Canvas.

8. Select the image, then set its attributes. You can set the stroke (outline), shadow, and opacity for imported graphics using the Graphic Inspector (**Figure 13.13**).

9. Define the new attributes for the image as the default by choosing one of the following:

▲ Choose Format > Define Defaults for Master Slides > Define Image for Current Master.

This menu choice defines the image's properties for only the master slide you are working on.

▲ Choose Format > Define Defaults for Master Slides > Define Image for All Masters.

This menu choice applies the image's properties to all the master slides in the theme you're working in.

10. Delete the placeholder object from the slide.

Figure 13.12 With the commands in the Format menu, you can define the shape for the Current Master or for All Masters.

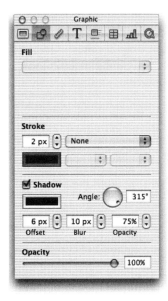

Figure 13.13 You can set stroke, shadow, and opacity defaults for imported graphics using the Graphic Inspector.

✔ Tip

■ When you're placing graphics on your slides (either master slides or presentation slides) that contain text boxes, sometimes the text boxes can be a distraction. You can temporarily turn them off by clearing the Show Title and the Show Body check boxes in the Slide Inspector or the Master Slide Inspector. Don't forget to turn them back on.

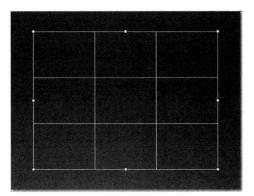

Figure 13.14 This is the original default table, before customization.

Creating Table Defaults

Creating table defaults is much like creating the defaults for other objects. First, you design a placeholder table the way you like it, setting all of its attributes, define it as the default for the current master slide or all master slides, and then delete the placeholder table. After you have created the table defaults, click the Table button in the toolbar to make the custom table that you designed appear.

The nice thing about setting up a custom table as a default is that you can associate it with a particular master slide, then use that master slide whenever you need your table. The table can contain all the customization that you can create in Keynote, including the number of rows and columns, line styles and colors, textiles, shadows, and merged or split cells.

Once again, it's best to set table defaults in a presentation slide, so you can see how the table will work against the background and other objects included in the master slide.

To set table defaults:

1. In the Slide Navigator, click New to create a new slide.

    A new presentation slide appears in the Slide Navigator and the Slide Canvas.

2. Use the Masters pop-up menu in the toolbar to apply the formats from the master slide you are working on.

3. Click the Tables button in the toolbar.

    A table appears on the Slide Canvas (**Figure 13.14**).

4. Set the attributes for the table, using the Table Inspector, the Fonts window, the Colors window, and Keynote's other tools.

    continues on next page

5. Resize and position the table on the Slide Canvas so that it looks the way you want it to look (**Figure 13.15**).

6. Select the table, then define the table's attributes as the default by choosing from one of the following:

   ▲ Choose Format > Define Defaults for Master Slides > Define Table for Current Master.

   This menu choice defines the table's properties for only the master slide you are working on.

   ▲ Choose Format > Define Defaults for Master Slides > Define Table for All Masters.

   This menu choice applies the table's properties to all the master slides in the theme you're working in.

7. Delete the placeholder table from the slide.

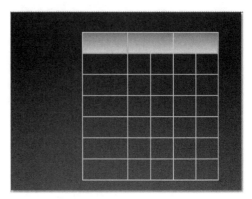

Figure 13.15 After customization, this table, with the gradient fills and additional rows and columns, appears when you click the Table button on the toolbar.

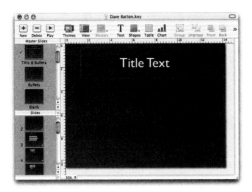

Figure 13.16 You need to show the rulers before you can place alignment guides.

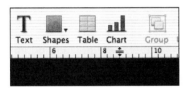

Figure 13.17 The alignment guide cursor appears when you click in one of the rulers.

Setting Alignment Guides

Alignment guides that you set on the master slides do not automatically appear on the presentation slides. Rather, they are "hidden" until you move objects around on the Slide Canvas; the guides appear whenever the center or edge of the object aligns with the center or edge of another object, or with the center of the Slide Canvas.

You can create your own default vertical or horizontal alignment guides on master slides. See Chapter 5 for more details about using alignment guides.

To set default alignment guides:

1. Choose View > Show Rulers, or press ⌘ R.
   The rulers appear in the Slide Canvas (**Figure 13.16**).

2. In the Master Slide Navigator, select the master slide for which you want to set alignment guides.
   The master slide appears in the Slide Canvas.

3. To create a horizontal alignment guide, click in the ruler at the top of the Slide Canvas.
   The cursor turns into the alignment guide cursor (**Figure 13.17**).

4. Drag down into the Slide Canvas.
   A yellow alignment guide, the width of the slide, appears.

continues on next page

SETTING ALIGNMENT GUIDES

5. Drag the guide to where you want it on the Slide Canvas.

As you drag, a position tag appears with the guide to help you precisely place the guide (**Figure 13.18**). The number in the position tag uses the same units as the ruler (in the figure, the units are inches). The label "y" indicates that the measurement is from the top of the slide, where you dragged from.

6. To create a vertical alignment guide, click in the ruler at the left side of the Slide Canvas.

The pointer turns into the alignment guide cursor.

7. Drag to the right into the Slide Canvas.

A yellow alignment guide, the height of the slide, appears.

8. Drag the guide to where you want it on the Slide Canvas.

The position tag will appear as you drag the guide. This tag will have an "x" label, indicating the distance from the left edge of the slide.

✔ Tips

■ You can place as many alignment guides on the Slide Canvas as you want.

■ The numbers in the position tags use the units set in the Ruler Units section of Keynote's Preferences (**Figure 13.19**).

Figure 13.18 Use the position tag to place the alignment guide at an exact place on the slide.

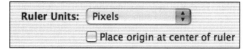

Figure 13.19 Use Keynote's Preferences window to set the units you want the rulers to use.

SETTING ALIGNMENT GUIDES

CREATING CUSTOM THEMES

Now that you are comfortable creating slides, presentations, and master slides in Keynote using Apple's themes, you are probably going to want to try creating your own themes. A custom theme allows you to brand your presentation as your own, and provides the audience with an experience that is unique to your presentation.

All the tools you need to assemble a custom theme are provided within Keynote. You may find though, that you want to create some of your theme graphics in another application with better graphics capabilities, such as Adobe Photoshop, Macromedia Fireworks, OmniGraffle, AppleWorks, or Adobe Illustrator.

In this chapter, you'll learn how to use Keynote, in combination with other graphics programs, to create and save your own custom Keynote themes.

Theme Planning

A good way to save yourself lots of time in creating your theme is to plan ahead. If you jump into theme building without a plan, it might take a lot longer than you anticipate.

There are several questions you should ask yourself before you begin building a new theme. Among them:

◆ What kind of background do you want (dark, light, gradient, photographic)?

◆ What kind of "dressing" do you want for your slides? Do you want boxes and shapes behind the titles, special logos or images added to the slides, or just backgrounds and text?

◆ What color scheme will you use? You'll need to decide on the colors for all of the elements in your theme.

◆ What type of graphics do you want to use (vector-based PDF images, bitmapped photos, or a combination of both)?

◆ What fonts do you want to use for the text in your theme?

◆ What size will your theme be? Most themes come in two sizes, 800 × 600 pixels and 1024 × 768 pixels. If your theme will be only for your own use, you can use whatever size works best for your needs. If you are going to distribute your theme on the Internet, it is a good idea to offer both sizes.

✔ Tips

■ Using fonts that are provided with Mac OS X will insure that your theme will look the way that you intend on any Mac you use to play your presentation.

■ If you plan to distribute your theme and you wish to include a special font with it, make sure you get permission from the font creator to distribute it, or include a URL with your theme so others can find the font easily.

Good Theme Design

Many of the themes that Apple includes with Keynote have two different backgrounds, one dark and one light. Usually the Title and Photo Cutout slides are darker or have a special texture or background to them. The inner, or bulleted slides, have a lighter or even solid white background.

Don't feel pressured into conforming to Apple's standard theme design, but take some lessons from it. You can experiment with different styles and techniques as you build your themes, but don't forget what Keynote was built for—giving presentations. You can create a beautiful masterpiece of design and art, but if the message gets cluttered up in a mess of colors and fluff, no one will take the time to read the content on your slides. One good way to get inspiration for theme creation is to purchase a design magazine from your local bookseller. Look at the different printed pieces and get a sense of color and shape. Borrow ideas from printed pieces and see if they fit into your theme, but try not to lose touch with the final goal, presenting your message in a clear, clean, and concise manner.

Figure 14.1 Apple includes eleven master slide layouts in every theme, but you do not have to use all of them in your custom themes.

Creating a Theme from an Apple Theme

Starting with one of the Apple Keynote themes makes creating your own theme much easier because you have a foundation of master slides to build from. From there, you can simply add graphics on top of the existing theme, or use it as a starting point for your own custom work.

Apple includes eleven master slide layouts in each of their themes (**Figure 14.1**). Sticking with those layouts and names to begin with is usually a good idea, because it makes things easier for the user: they can switch themes in the middle of building a presentation, and as long as the master slide names match, the user's slides will use the equivalently named master slides in the new theme. You can add more master slides to your custom theme.

The Apple theme you might want to choose as a starter theme is the White theme. This theme is basically a blank slate, and it provides an excellent framework for your custom work.

Before you get started, you need to understand an important fact about Keynote files. There are two types of files: *presentation files* and *theme files*. These two types of files have different file extensions: .key and .kth, respectively. In earlier chapters, you've been working with .key files. Now, you will begin the process of creating the custom theme file in a presentation file. At the end of the process, when your theme is complete, you will save the presentation file as a theme file. Keynote can then recognize the new theme file as a template from which to build new presentations.

Keep in mind that when you are creating a theme file, all of your modifications must be made to the *master slides*, not to the presentation slides in the file. If you make your changes to the presentation slides, your custom theme will not work.

continues on next page

241

To choose your starting theme:

1. Choose File > New, or press ⌘N.
   The Theme sheet appears.

2. Click on the theme you want to use as your starting point.

3. From the Presentation Size pop-up menu, choose the size theme you want to start from.

4. Click Choose Theme.
   Keynote takes a moment to build the theme, then creates the new document window, using the first master slide in the theme.

5. From the View pop-up menu in the tool-bar, choose Show Master Slides.
   The master slides appear in the Slide Navigator (**Figure 14.2**).

6. Click on the master slide called "Title & Subtitle."
   This is the master slide where you will start making your custom modifications.

✔ Tips

■ Chart colors and textures are two of the most finicky parts of creating themes. Starting with a theme that already has chart colors (or textures) you want to use can save you time as you build your theme.

■ If you plan to make your theme in both sizes, you can create slide images sized at 1024 × 768 and just shrink them in Keynote to 800 × 600. Shrinking things gives you better results than scaling them larger. Otherwise, you might have to create two versions of every image.

Figure 14.2 To edit a theme, you'll have to display and work in the master slides, not the presentation slides.

Building More Than One Size of a Theme

If you plan to create both theme sizes, you can start with the larger size first and then take screen shots of your finished slides. Save a copy of your large theme and change the slide size to 800 × 600 using File > Slide Size. You can then place these screen shots inside Keynote as a guide to line up all the elements of the smaller version; it's almost like tracing the larger version. When you're done, you should delete the guide image. If you want to use mathematics and be exact in your theme creation, the smaller 800 × 600 theme size is exactly 78.125% smaller than the 1024 × 768 version. So each of the elements in the 800 × 600 version of your theme will need to be 78.125% of the equivalent elements in the 1024 × 768 version. You can scale images in your image editor using these figures, and they will be correct.

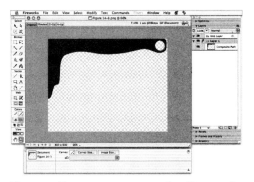

Figure 14.3 You can use programs such as Macromedia Fireworks to create custom bitmapped backgrounds for your theme.

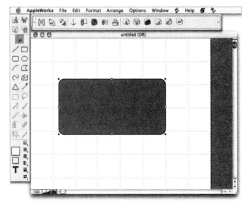

Figure 14.4 AppleWorks is a good, quick way to make shapes to use in your theme, such as this rounded rectangle.

Preparing Your Graphics

Keynote imports quite a few different image types (see **Table 6.1** for a list). This lets you create theme graphics in a number of ways using different graphics programs.

A tutorial on using the different graphics programs is beyond the scope of this book, but I can make suggestions as to what programs are appropriate for different graphic tasks. You'll want to think your theme through before jumping in, as you can save time and effort if you know what kind of program you need to create the type of images you wish to use.

What are my image creation options?

◆ Use Adobe Photoshop or another image editor to prepare photos and photographic backgrounds.

◆ Use Macromedia Fireworks to create bitmapped images that appear to be vector based (**Figure 14.3**). Fireworks is a great tool for making photo cutouts.

◆ Use Macromedia FreeHand or Adobe Illustrator to create vector-based PDF images and backgrounds. These will be fully scalable, and as a result you can use the same objects for every size theme you make.

◆ Use AppleWorks to create basic objects such as rounded boxes and copy and paste them into Keynote (**Figure 14.4**).

◆ Use a cheaper drawing program such as the Omni Group's OmniGraffle (www.omnigroup.com) or Purgatory Design's Intaglio (www.purgatorydesign.com) to create objects and save them as PDF images, or copy and paste them into Keynote.

continues on next page

These are just a few examples of the programs and image types that you can use in Keynote. If you aren't a graphic designer or artist and you don't have some of these higher-end programs, I suggest you start out with something like AppleWorks or OmniGraffle for creating objects, and use iPhoto or Adobe Photoshop Elements for preparing photos.

✔ Tips

■ Since AppleWorks can't be set to work in pixels, changing the Page Setup to US Legal and changing the page orientation to Landscape can give you more room to work with on your page.

■ If you are using the AppleWorks page grid as a guide, try keeping your objects less than 11 squares (or inches) wide by about 8 squares high. Your 800 × 600 pixel presentation comes out to be 11.11 inches wide by 8.33 inches high if you convert it from pixels to inches at 72 dots per inch.

■ Some programs export PDF files at a regular page size, so don't be alarmed if the resize handles of your imported object are a lot bigger than the object. To avoid this, make your document's page size close to the same size as the image in the document.

Figure 14.5 You add your custom bullet images in the Text Inspector.

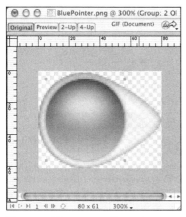

Figure 14.6 You can use Photoshop or a similar photo editor to create photographic bullets. Just make sure your background is transparent before saving. The checkerboard pattern indicates transparency.

Using OmniGraffle for Bullets

If your Mac came with a free copy of OmniGraffle (PowerBooks and G4 towers do), put it to good use. OmniGraffle is one of the easiest programs you can use to create custom bullets. Just create an object, then select it and choose File > Export. Make sure you use the PDF format, and turn on the Transparent Background option (**Figure 14.7**).

Figure 14.7 OmniGraffle is a great tool to use when creating custom bullets. When you save the bullet in OmniGraffle, be sure to save the file as a PDF with a transparent background.

Creating custom bullets

Bullets are a little different than other images in Keynote. Because Keynote does not let you paste bullet images into the Custom Image box in the Text Inspector (**Figure 14.5**), all custom bullets must be created outside of the program and imported, not pasted, into Keynote.

Here are some suggestions as to which programs are best for creating custom bullets:

◆ If you use a vector-based program such as OmniGraffle or Adobe Illustrator to make your bullets, they will be fully scalable and won't lose quality if you decide to make them bigger.

◆ You can also create photographic or bitmapped bullets in Photoshop (**Figure 14.6**) or Fireworks. Just make sure you leave the bullet on its own layer and create your file with a transparent background or your bullet will end up with a white rectangle behind it.

◆ AppleWorks doesn't export objects as PDFs (printing as a PDF gives you the whole page, not just the object), and exporting them as PICT images does not give you a smooth anti-aliased edge, so it's best to use another program for creating bullets.

✔ Tip

■ It often isn't a good idea to create your bullet with a shadow behind it. When you use Keynote to add a shadow to text containing bullets, a shadow is also added to your bullet. If your bullet already has a shadow as part of the image, you'll get a double shadow and it may not look good.

Importing Graphics into Keynote

There are several ways to get images into Keynote. Depending on how your image was made, you'll use a combination of techniques to import images (see Chapter 5 for more on importing graphics):

◆ While you can copy and paste objects into Keynote from certain applications, it's not a good idea to copy and paste objects that have semi-transparent portions (such as shadows) or aren't rectangular in shape. Pasting a semi-transparent image into Keynote usually results in an image that is 100% solid, badly dithered, or a combination of both (**Figure 14.8**).

◆ You can drag and drop images from the Finder into Keynote. This gives you the same results as choosing Edit > Place > Choose. Using this method will ensure that your semi-transparent images work properly (**Figure 14.9**).

◆ You can drag and drop images from some applications into Keynote. This usually works in applications that also support using copy and paste. Dragging and dropping images this way can give unexpected results. Sometimes the image comes into Keynote properly, other times you get the same type of result as when using the copy and paste method.

◆ Using Edit > Place > Choose works for any image type that Keynote supports, and it can come in handy if your screen is cluttered and you can't easily get to an image in the Finder or in another application.

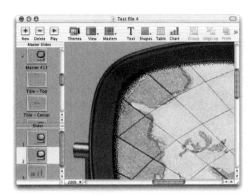

Figure 14.8 Copying and pasting photo cutout images doesn't always work correctly. Here the soft transparent edge in the cutout has been replaced with a dither pattern with lots of small dots.

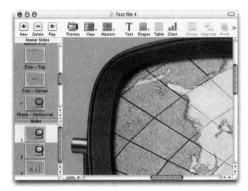

Figure 14.9 Dragging and dropping a photo cutout file from the Finder retains the soft edge of the cutout properly.

✔ Tips

■ Some programs, such as Macromedia FreeHand, do not support drag and drop or copy and paste in Keynote; instead, you must export your graphics as PDF images.

■ You can't edit the fill or stroke on graphics imported into Keynote. If you want to modify them, you'll have to edit the original and re-import it.

■ When scaling imported objects, remember that the thickness of the stroke of the object will scale with it.

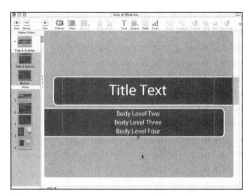

Figure 14.10 Here's a typical Non-bulleted layout. Notice the body text is centered and does not contain bulleted lines.

Begin by Deleting Slides

Some designers prefer to delete all but one master slide from the Slide Navigator and create all the slides from scratch, copying and pasting slides that are similar in style and then renaming and redesigning them. The benefit of doing it this way is that it's easy if you have many slides that have similar title and body settings or similar layouts. The drawback is that you must remember all 11 theme names and layouts, or open a reference theme once in a while to make sure you are using all the names and layouts correctly. If you're a beginner, I recommend using each pre-existing master slide as a basis for your new slide. You can then copy and paste similar master slides and delete extra master slides as you go along.

Laying out Master Slides

Once you've gotten your objects into Keynote, it's time to start laying out your master slides. You'll be laying out graphics (including background images) and text boxes on the master slides in your presentation file.

There are basically three kinds of master slides in Keynote: Bulleted, Non-bulleted, and Photo Cutout. While the Bulleted and Non-bulleted slides are very similar, you can save yourself a lot of bullet formatting if you think of them as different types. See Chapters 3 and 13 for the details on how to layout your master slides.

Non-bulleted master slides

The first type of master slide is a Non-bulleted slide. These are all the slides that have body text boxes set to only display text by default, not bulleted text. An example of this is the Title & Subtitle master slide (**Figure 14.10**). Once you have created one slide of this type it is easy to copy and paste your slide elements to the others, or to copy and paste whole master slides and just make a few adjustments, then rename them. Here are some layout tips:

◆ Don't be afraid to move the text boxes around. Just because Apple put them in a certain place, doesn't mean they need to stay there on your slides.

◆ While Keynote can't create rounded rectangular objects, it does have some basic drawing tools. Use them when you can, and your theme's file size will be smaller, because the built-in shapes don't require much space. Besides, it's easier to do as much as you can in Keynote, rather than fiddling with other programs.

◆ If two master slides you are creating have a similar layout, copy one of them and paste it back into the Master Slide Navigator, then change the copy. Doing this can save you some time over creating the second master slide from scratch.

Bulleted master slides

Bulleted master slides are similar to non-bulleted slides, except that the body text boxes on them are set up to display bullets automatically. Here are tips for working with bulleted master slides:

◆ Don't be afraid to create bulleted slide layouts that aren't exactly like your non-bulleted slides; the contrast can be attractive. Add extra objects behind the bullet boxes to dress up the slide, such as the rounded rectangle in **Figure 14.11**.

◆ Copy and paste bulleted slides to save layout time.

◆ Use custom bullets to spice up your theme (**Figure 14.12**). See the "Creating custom bullets" section earlier in this chapter.

Inserting custom bullets

Once you have imported all your images and constructed your slides, you may want to insert some custom bullets into your bulleted lists.

To insert a custom bullet:

1. Switch to the Text Inspector.

2. On the master slide, select the bulleted text box containing your bulleted list.

3. In the Bullets & Numbering section of the Text Inspector, choose Custom Image from the pop-up menu (**Figure 14.13**). Keynote displays an Open dialog.

4. Find and select the file with the custom bullet, and click Open.
   The bullets change to the custom bullet image you selected.

5. Make any sizing and spacing adjustments you want to the bullets in the Spacing section of the Text Inspector.

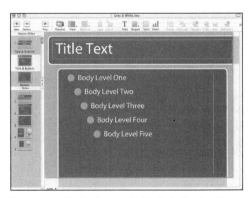

Figure 14.11 Placing images behind a bullet list, like the rounded rectangle here, can add a little more life to a bulleted slide. Make sure you don't use colors that make the bulleted list hard to read.

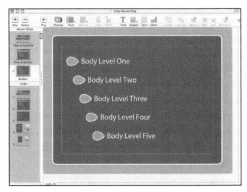

Figure 14.12 Using custom bullets is a good way to add value to your theme if you plan to distribute it.

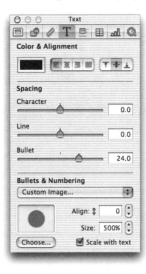

Figure 14.13 Choose Custom Image from the Bullets & Numbering pop-up menu to choose your custom bullet.

Multiple Bullet Styles in a List

You can assign different custom bullets and even different fonts and font sizes to each subline of your bullet box by using this process on each bullet instead of the whole bullet box. Just select each bullet line and follow the process described on the preceding page (**Figure 14.14**).

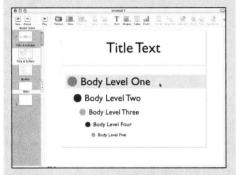

Figure 14.14 You can set different bullets and font styles for each bullet line by clicking on the line and making your changes in the Text Inspector.

Transparent area

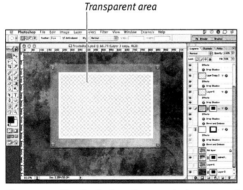

Figure 14.15 The checkerboard pattern in the center of this photo cutout represents the transparent area that your photos will show through when you place them behind it.

✔ Tips

■ The Align field in the Bullets & Numbering section of the Text Inspector allows you to shift the bullet above or below the baseline of the bulleted text.

■ The Size field in the Bullets & Numbering section of the Text Inspector will only allow you to scale a bullet image up to a maximum of 500%.

Photo cutouts

The third type of master slide is a photo cutout. This slide consists of an image with a transparent hole cut in it placed above the background of the slide. The user then places an image on top of the cutout layer, and sends it to the back. The image ends up behind the photo cutout, but in front of the background, completing the framed effect of the cutout.

Because of the nature of Apple's photo cutout master slides, you cannot simply change the size of the cutout in Keynote. You can, however, use a program such as Adobe Photoshop to create your own photo cutout backgrounds, then bring them into Keynote. Here are some tips if you choose to use Photoshop to create your photo cutouts. You can adapt these ideas to your preferred photo editor:

◆ Photo cutouts created in Photoshop must have fully transparent areas and have no background layer (**Figure 14.15**).

◆ Use the selection tools to select and permanently delete portions of your layers so they are fully transparent. Or, you can use the Save Selection and Layer Mask functions to mask sections of your layers without permanently deleting anything.

continues on next page

◆ Take a screen shot of your actual slides in Keynote and bring them into Photoshop to create cutouts. You may need to turn off the Photoshop Color Management settings (choose Photoshop > Color Settings) to make sure you don't get any color shifting (**Figure 14.16**).

◆ Always save a copy of your original layered Photoshop file in case you need to edit it.

◆ Use the Merge Visible Layers command to merge all your Photoshop layers into one, while maintaining the transparency.

Once you have created your photo cutout, you need to decide what format to save it in. Here are a few pointers on file types:

◆ PNG format files hold transparency really well and compress the image down to a good size for Keynote files. You can use Macromedia Fireworks to create PNG files for your themes (**Figure 14.17**).

◆ PDF files work well for images with hard-edged photo cutouts because Photoshop's PDF format lets you use JPEG compression to shrink the image's file size.

◆ Photoshop PDFs do not work well for images with semi-transparency inside your photo cutout (like a soft shadow). Upon saving and importing into Keynote, the semi-transparent areas have a white tint and do not work properly (**Figure 14.18**). Saving a Photoshop file as a PDF gives you a working PDF file, but it is not the same as a vector PDF file. Photoshop PDF files are bitmapped in nature and will usually not scale up very well.

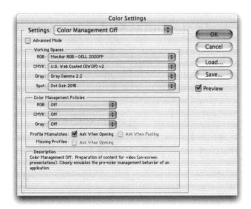

Figure 14.16 Turning off Photoshop's Color Management settings can keep colors from shifting if you are using screen shots of your slides to build photo cutouts.

Figure 14.17 Saving this photo cutout as a PNG file kept the shadow semi-transparent so that it still looks like a shadow when the photo is placed behind it. You can see the shadow at the top and left edges of the cutout.

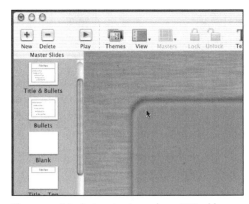

Figure 14.18 A photo cutout saved as a PDF adds a white edge to the shadow, messing up the effect.

LAYING OUT MASTER SLIDES

Figure 14.19 You can be pretty creative with photo cutouts once you understand how they work.

Creating Vector-based Cutouts

You can create vector PDF photo cutouts in any drawing program that supports "punch" or "mask" functions. Adobe Illustrator and Macromedia FreeHand work well for this type of cutout. Here are a few tips when making vector photo cutouts in Illustrator or FreeHand:

◆ Make sure you change your measurement units into pixels.

◆ Make your document the same size as your theme (800×600 or 1024×768 pixels).

◆ Use the Punch or Mask feature in your program to punch holes in another object. This works well if you create an image the size of the entire slide and use a different shaped object to punch a hole in it.

◆ Any punched holes or blank areas of the document become transparent areas when exported as a PDF. Review your design by moving a large colored object to the back layer of your document to see where the object is visible. This way you won't end up with holes where you don't want them.

◆ TIFF files can hold transparency properly, but Keynote only supports compressed TIFFs using the LZW scheme, so they aren't as small as other file types. Generally PNG files turn out smaller than TIFF images.

◆ PSD (Photoshop) files hold transparency properly, but don't compress as well as other formats. If you aren't planning to distribute your themes, you can actually use your original, fully layered PSD files as your final photo cutout—it will just cause your theme to be larger than normal.

◆ It's not a good idea to use JPEG or GIF for photo cutouts. The JPEG specification does not support transparency, so it can't be used as a photo cutout. GIF images only support 256 colors and do not have translucent capabilities, so you are really limited if you decide to use GIF.

As you can see, there are many ways to create photo cutouts. With a little patience and imagination, you can create some stunning photo cutouts to go along with your custom themes (**Figure 14.19**).

Placing photo cutouts

Now that you've created your photo cutouts, you need to place them on your master slides. You can't choose a photo cutout in Keynote as a normal background using the Slide Inspector; instead you place the cutout on the actual master slide and send it to the background.

To place a photo cutout:

1. In the Slide Navigator, select the master slide to which you want to add a photo cutout.

   If you are using an existing theme as a starting point, make sure you clear off any old cutout by clicking on the slide background and choosing Arrange > Unlock (**Figure 14.20**). You must then press Delete to remove the old cutout.

2. Drag the new photo cutout file from the Finder onto your slide.

   or

   Choose Edit > Place > Choose, then select your photo cutout from the Open dialog.

   Keynote places your photo cutout image over the slide, covering the contents of the slide (**Figure 14.21**).

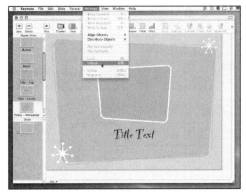

Figure 14.20 You must first unlock a photo cutout before you can delete it from a master slide.

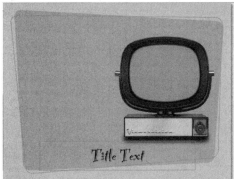

Figure 14.21 After you add the photo cutout, you may have to adjust the position of the master slide's text boxes. The text box on this slide was moved from the middle of the slide to below the antique television.

Figure 14.22
Use the numeric settings in the Metrics Inspector to make sure your photo cutout is placed correctly over the entire slide.

Figure 14.23
Turn on the "Allow objects on slides to layer with master" setting to ensure your photo cutouts work properly.

3. Move your photo cutout so that it fits exactly over the entire slide.

   Enter zeros in the Position fields on the Metrics Inspector if you can't get the photo cutout to line up perfectly (**Figure 14.22**).

4. Choose Arrange > Send to Back and then Arrange > Lock to move your photo cutout to the back of the slide and lock it down.

5. If it isn't already on, turn on the "Allow objects on slides to layer with master" checkbox on the Master Slide Inspector so the photo cutout works properly (**Figure 14.23**).

✔ Tip

- Once you lock down your photo cutout, you may need to move the text boxes on the master slide to work better with your new cutout. Look at the position of the text boxes in **Figure 14.21** for an example.

Adding Custom Charts

With the graphics and layouts all in place, you'll want to focus on modifying some of the settings that make your theme appear more professional. Charts in Keynote can use color or image fills, and they have many settings you can customize to match your theme.

To customize a chart with your own colors or images:

1. Select the Blank master slide in the Master Slide Navigator.

2. Choose Edit > Copy, or press ⌘C.

3. Choose Edit > Paste, or press ⌘V.

   Keynote creates a duplicate of the Blank master slide, called "Blank copy."

4. Click on the Chart icon in the toolbar, or choose Edit > Place > Chart.

   Keynote gives you a new chart with two sample data series, opens the Chart Inspector, and opens the Chart Data Editor (**Figure 14.24**).

   continues on next page

Figure 14.24 When you create a chart the Chart Inspector and the Chart Data Editor open.

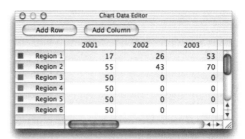

Figure 14.25 Entering placeholder data in the Chart Data Editor makes Keynote create bars in the chart, which you can then customize with your own chart fills.

Hacking Apple's Colors

If you are adventurous, you can save a lot of time by tinkering around inside your Keynote file and editing Apple's tile image files. Using this technique saves you from having to color every column of every type of chart one by one in Keynote. Remember though, this is not for the faint of heart. You could destroy your Keynote file if you are not careful. Always work on a copy in case something goes wrong. Here are a few advanced techniques that professional theme builders use:

◆ Control-click on the Keynote file in the Finder and choose Show Package Contents from the pop-up menu. Open and edit the tile files in the package and resave them. Make sure you leave the file names the same, as you could ruin the Keynote file if you don't.

◆ Edit the tile files and change the names to reflect the new content. Then edit the Keynote XML file (called "presentation.apxl") by opening it in TextEdit and using Find/Replace to replace the old names with the new ones.

◆ Create completely new tile images and remove the old files from the package. You'll need to move the new image files into the package window by copying and pasting them in the Finder; you can't just drag them in. Then edit the XML file.

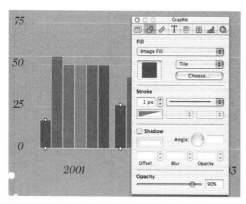

Figure 14.26 Use the Fill options on the Graphic Inspector to change your chart fills.

✔ Tips

■ While Keynote lets you choose an image as a chart fill, try to stick with square, tiled images. If you use, for example, an object image as a fill, you can choose to tile the image, but Keynote does not have the ability to use an object to "build" a chart column correctly. Your object may appear to "stack" properly (i.e., it would work vertically), but it will also tile horizontally, giving you strange-looking results in many cases.

■ You are not limited to six chart colors. You can add as many colors as you want by adding more Data Series to your chart and continuing the process mentioned earlier. Also, if you use, for example, only 2 colors, you can get an alternating color effect as Keynote will start at the beginning of the color series after it uses all the colors you've set.

5. In the first column of the Chart Data Editor, add 4 more items under Region 2. If you want you can name them Region 3, Region 4, Region 5 and Region 6. The names aren't important; you just need placeholder data series.

   The idea is to add more regions so that you will be able to apply chart fills for up to six data series. The fills will serve as the defaults for charts made from this master slide.

   Your chart should now have six colored rows in the 2001 column (**Figure 14.25**).

6. Now we need some data in those regions so that they appear in our chart. In each of the regions in the 2001 column, starting with Region 3, double-click on each cell and enter the number 50. Again, it doesn't really matter what number you enter here; you just want some sample data. (This should be directly under the number 55 in the Chart Data Editor.)

7. In your chart, starting with the left-most chart column, double-click the column so that small white dots appear at the top and bottom of the column, indicating that it has been selected.

8. Switch to the Graphic Inspector.

   Notice that you can fully edit both the fill and stroke of the column. You can choose from solid colors, gradients, or even image fills of your choice. There are also several tiling options for image fills, which change the behavior of the fill inside the chart columns (**Figure 14.26**). For more information about tiling options, see "Using Color and Gradient Fills" in Chapter 5.

9. Repeat step 8 for the other five columns until you have all of the columns set up with your custom color or fill.

Setting chart defaults

Now that you have customized the colors of your chart, change the other settings on this chart to fit your theme (see Chapter 8 for more information). You can modify the grid lines, fonts, and legend to your liking. Then you'll need to set the chart defaults, that is, lock down the settings for this chart and finish the rest of the charts. You can assign chart defaults to your entire theme, or you can choose them for each individual master slide. If you are setting them up for individual master slides, make sure that the slide you use to build your chart has had the correct master slide applied to it before you lock down any chart settings.

To set the chart defaults:

1. Select your chart and choose Format > Define Defaults for Master Slides and pick from one of the following choices:

   ▲ If your theme will use different chart colors for different master slides, then choose Format > Define Defaults for Master Slides > Define Chart for Current Master, and do this on every master slide you wish to use this chart on.

   ▲ If you wish to use this chart style on every master slide, choose Format > Define Defaults for Master Slides > Define Chart for All Masters. This will lock this particular chart style down for every master slide.

   If the menu items are grayed out, the chart was inadvertently deselected. Try clicking on the slide background, then on your chart, and try the menu again.

Figure 14.27 You can decide what type of chart is created when the Chart button in the toolbar is clicked by changing the default chart type in the Format menu.

2. To set the default chart size and placement for your theme, choose Format > Define Defaults for Master Slides > Set Size and Placement for All Charts for All Masters to lock it down for every master.

or

You can lock down the default chart size and placement for only the master you are currently using by choosing Format > Define Defaults for Master Slides > Set Size and Placement for All Axis Charts for Current Master. If you're working on a pie chart, the menu choice changes to Set Size and Placement for Pie Charts for Current Master.

If the chart already seems to have a good size and placement on the slide, you do not need to use this setting.

3. The last setting, Format > Define Defaults for Master Slides > Make *charttype* Chart the Default Chart Type, allows you to decide which type of chart will be created when you click the Chart button while using your theme.

Charttype represents whichever chart type you have selected when you bring up this menu item. For example, if you wanted to make the pie chart the default chart type, you simply make sure you have a pie chart on your slide, select it, and choose Format > Define Defaults for Master Slides > Make Pie Chart the Default Chart Type (**Figure 14.27**).

Once you have finished one chart type and set the defaults for that chart, you will need to repeat these steps again for all eight chart styles. Keynote is smart enough to keep the colors or fills you assigned to the first chart when you switch chart types in the Chart Inspector, so it is best to work your way through all the chart types by just changing the current chart to a new type, making your settings changes and locking in the defaults for that chart type.

ADDING CUSTOM CHARTS

Finishing Your Theme

So you've got your slide masters finished, your photo cutouts installed, your charts all set. You're almost done, but there are a few small things you can do to add that extra professional touch to your theme:

◆ Set your table defaults. See Chapter 7 for information about creating a table to match your theme. Then follow the steps in Chapter 13 to lock down the default table settings for your theme, so that when the Table button is clicked in the toolbar the table you created is built automatically. Don't forget to set the font and font styles for the table.

◆ Set the default style for free text boxes by following the steps in Chapter 13 on changing and locking the default text style.

◆ Because the file you are using to create your theme is (until you save it as a theme file) just a regular Keynote file, there is always a "regular" slide in the Slide Navigator under the bar marked "Slides." Set up this first slide as the preview image that will appear in the theme sheet (**Figure 14.28**). Place the name of your theme on the slide and make it as large as you can since the preview that is built from it will only appear as a 120 × 90 pixel image in the theme sheet (**Figure 14.29**).

◆ Create a .key file that contains objects filled with your colors or tiles so other users can copy their styles to their own objects.

◆ Create a file of extra images that match your theme and can be pasted into a presentation. Doing this can take time, but it can add value to your theme, especially if you plan to sell it.

◆ Create a full presentation of your theme before saving it. This is a good way to test it, and the presentation can be included as a sample file if you distribute it.

Figure 14.28 Set up the first "regular" slide in your theme file as a preview image of your theme.

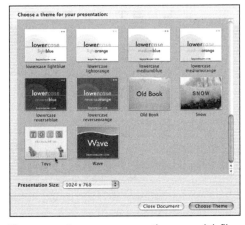

Figure 14.29 Once you save your theme as a .kth file and install it, Keynote will use the preview slide you created as a thumbnail in the Themes sheet.

Figure 14.30 If you save your theme in the proper place, it will appear in the Keynote Themes sheet.

Saving Your Theme as a Theme File

Once you have finished setting up the backgrounds and object defaults, built your preview slide, and tested the theme, it's time to save the Keynote file as a theme file.

Before you save, however, you might want to look through Appendix B, "Theme Creation Checklist," to make sure that you've covered all the bases.

To save your custom theme:

1. Choose File > Save Theme.

   A Save dialog will appear.

2. Choose the location where you want to save your theme. Keynote may default to your *username*/Library/Application Support/Keynote/Themes folder. If you'd rather take a look at the theme file you created, or plan to save copies of it elsewhere, you might want to save it to the desktop instead of this default location (**Figure 14.30**).

3. Name your theme.

   It is vital to use the proper naming scheme, which is "*name*_8x6.kth" with *name* representing the name you want the theme to display in Keynote's theme sheet, and the 8 and 6 corresponding to the actual size of your theme. If your theme was 800×600 and called Green Circles, the name of your theme file would be Green Circles_8x6.kth.

   If the theme size is 1024×768, the proper form is *name*_10x7.kth. Another important rule is that the "x" in the theme name must be lowercase.

4. Click Save.

✔ Tip

- If you are creating only a single theme in a single size, you are not required to add the _8x6 or _10x7 tags to your theme name. If you make a theme in both sizes, you need these tags so that Keynote knows they both belong to the same theme. If you get the naming scheme wrong, you'll likely either see the tags visible in the Themes sheet, or you'll end up with two different theme previews showing in the Themes sheet, instead of one theme preview with two sizes in the Presentation Size menu (**Figure 14.31**).

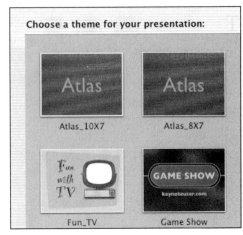

Figure 14.31 If you don't follow Keynote's naming scheme, you'll get multiple copies of your theme in the Themes sheet. In this case, the second instance of the Atlas theme mistakenly says 8x7, rather than 8x6, which makes it appear separately in the sheet, rather than as a size in the Presentation Size pop-up menu.

KEYNOTE RESOURCES

But wait, there's more!

Beyond the covers of this book, there are many resources that can help you learn more about Keynote and creating good presentations; sources for additional themes besides the ones that ship with the program; and places where you can purchase presentation hardware.

Most of these resources will be found on the Web. There are at least three good sites where you can get your Keynote questions answered. Some sites are now selling packages of Keynote themes. And of course, there are themes that people have created that are free for the downloading.

Find it Online!

You'll find an updated list of the sites listed in this appendix at this book's companion Web site, located at www.negrino.com/keynote/. I'll keep the Web site current with a list of Keynote-oriented sites, and if eagle-eyed readers spot any errors in the book, I'll note them on the site, too.

As usual with products that can be found on the Internet, Web sites come, go, and change addresses with alarming regularity. The sites listed here were in existence when this book went to the printer (Spring 2003) and may be available when you check them out, or may not. I'm just reporting the URLs; I have no control over them. If you find a link that has become stale, I'd appreciate it if you would drop a note to keynote@negrino.com so that I can update the next edition of the book.

Community and Training Sites

Almost as soon as Keynote was announced, people began gathering online to discuss the program and help each other with how to use it. You can now find several Web sites, a mailing list or two, and discussion boards where you can go to slake your thirst for all things Keynote.

Apple's Keynote Discussion Page

http://discussions.info.apple.com/webx/keynote/

Apple's discussion board (**Figure A.1**) allows you to send feedback to the Keynote team at Apple (they read it, but they won't reply), and lists Frequently Asked Questions (FAQ) and their answers. You can also post your own questions, and chances are a Keynote expert will have an answer for you within a few hours.

One politeness rule to follow on this board: Before you post your question, use the Search function to see if your question has been asked and answered before. In many cases it has, and there's no need to take up people's time answering the same old questions again and again.

KeynoteUser.com

http://www.keynoteuser.com

This site, produced by Brian Peat of The Peat Group, Inc., provides Keynote news and reviews of Keynote-related products, including presentation hardware and themes from companies other than Apple (**Figure A.2**). You'll also find tips, tutorials, and links to other Keynote sites around the Web.

This site is a good source for themes that you can download. There is a nice selection of themes available for free from several creators. Peat also creates his own high-quality themes, both for sale and as free downloads from the site.

Figure A.1 Apple's Keynote Discussion page is an excellent place to get your questions answered.

Figure A.2 KeynoteUser.com has a good mix of news, themes, and reviews.

Figure A.3 The Keynote Yahoo! Group delivers Keynote talk to your email box, or you can read the discussion on the Web.

Figure A.4 Keynote HQ is chock-full of tips, downloadable themes, and a user forum.

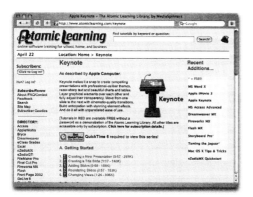

Figure A.5 Atomic Learning's Keynote tutorials can be viewed in just a few minutes each.

Keynote Yahoo! Group

`http://groups.yahoo.com/group/`
`applekeynote/`

KeynoteUser.com sponsors a Yahoo! Group devoted to Keynote, which is primarily used as a mailing list for Keynote aficionados (**Figure A.3**). The mailing list can be delivered via email, or you can read and post messages from the Web site. The site also has a Files area, which contains some tutorials contributed by the group's members, and a selection of free themes.

Keynote HQ

`http://www.keynotehq.com`

This was the first of the Keynote sites to appear, and it is one of the best (**Figure A.4**). You'll find Keynote tips, themes, tutorials, and a forum where you will find friendly people who can answer virtually any question you might have about Keynote or presentations.

Atomic Learning

`http://www.atomiclearning.com/keynote/`

This Minnesota-based company produces training classes broken up into bite-sized QuickTime movies for a number of products, including Keynote (**Figure A.5**). Each of the 49 Keynote movies is between thirty seconds and two minutes long, and covers just one topic. You won't find advanced techniques here, but the basics are well covered.

The site provides access to all of its contents (not just the Keynote stuff) for a yearly individual subscription of $50, with reduced rates for schools, organizations, and businesses. If you have training needs that span several programs (on both Mac and Windows), it's worth a look.

Where to Find Themes

Once you begin making presentations, you can get tired of the twelve built-in themes pretty quickly. Sure, you can create your own master slides and themes (see Chapters 13 and 14 for more information), but many of us don't have the time, or the artistic talent to do a great job. Luckily, there are other folks that have both the time and talent.

Free themes

The Keynote community has grown quite quickly, and you can find a number of themes that people have created and are giving away. The best places to find them are at the two Keynote community sites, Keynote HQ (`http://www.keynotehq.com`) and Keynote-User.com (`http://www.keynoteuser.com`). There is some overlap between the sites, but each site seems to have free themes that are not available at the other.

There are some themes that look like refugees from a zillion boring PowerPoint presentations, but some of the themes are quite high quality, especially given that they are being given away for free. For example, the Old Book theme, created by Gerry Straathof, has a nice antique book page look (**Figure A.6**). Another good-looking theme, Snow, by Bart Alexander van de Biezen, uses black-and white snow scenes for a successful, slightly impressionistic effect (**Figure A.7**).

Figure A.6 This free theme, Old Book, has an authentic antique paper look, because it's made from photographs of, well, an old book.

Figure A.7 The Snow theme, another free theme, is minimalistic, but effective.

WHERE TO FIND THEMES

Themes for sale

If you're going to pay money for Keynote themes, here are some things to look for. Not all of them may be present, but a great theme will include many of these items.

- **Good graphic design.** Do the slide masters look good? Is the slide well designed? Are the slide backgrounds distinctive, yet not so busy that they would detract from your bulleted text?

- **Extra slide masters.** Apple provides eleven styles of slide masters, and a custom theme should provide a selection at least as large. Better themes provide master slide designs above and beyond Apple's themes. For example, you can have themes with extra-large photo cutouts, or ones with alternate text layouts.

- **Good text design.** The placement of text boxes and the choice of fonts are vitally important, as it is the text that you'll mainly be using to get your points across to your audience.

- **Extras.** This can include anything from custom bullets (higher marks if the theme includes alternate bullet styles for second and lower-level bullets), to a selection of custom color chips for chart fills, to interesting graphic shapes that you can use to dress up your presentation. It's also nice, but not essential, if the themes come in both the 1024 x 768 and 800 x 600 sizes.

WHERE TO FIND THEMES

Here are six sites, presented alphabetically, that offer Keynote themes for sale (prices and offerings are, of course, subject to change):

♦ **Jumsoft** (`http://www.jumsoft.com`), a Lithuanian company, produces a number of themes at cut-rate prices (at press time, they were offering 10 themes for $10 for the 90 Mb download, or $25 for the themes on a CD). Some of these themes are quite nice, such as their Old Paper theme (**Figure A.8**), which has a great manila envelope look. Others are more pedestrian. Some of the themes are a bit busy, and they generally stick with the standard eleven slide masters, with few extras. Still, the Jumsoft themes are a good value for the money, even if you don't end up using all of them.

♦ **Keynote Gallery** (`http://www.keynotegallery.com`), hailing from Canada, makes a number of well-designed premium themes, including the whimsical Jeans theme, which looks as if it were made out of denim (**Figure A.9**). The themes are available in both 1024 × 768 and 800 × 600 sizes, and they contain custom image bullets and several bonus master slides. This site seems to be adding new themes on a regular basis, so check back often.

♦ **Keynote HQ** (`http://www.keynotehq.com`), offers several theme packs, each with three themes bundled for $10. Some of these themes would be good for business presentations, but many are rather plain, such as a corkboard layout (**Figure A.10**), or a few themes with simple backgrounds and colored frames around the entire slide. Some of the themes include extras, such as extra images for bullets.

Figure A.8 Jumsoft's Old Paper theme is one of their best.

Figure A.9 The Jeans theme, from Keynote Gallery, uses denim pockets as photo cutouts, and the custom bullets are pictures of buttons and rivets.

Figure A.10 The Corkboard theme, from Keynote HQ, is simple and direct.

Figure A.11 Keynote Theme Park's Granite theme features beveled edges for the photo cutouts, a good example of their attention to detail.

Figure A.12 Filmmakers and television producers should get a lot of mileage out of the PitchBoard theme, from KeynotePro, which allows them to use Keynote for storyboards. Of course, as shown here, Keynote can't do anything about the quality of your movie.

◆ **Keynote Theme Park**
(http://www.keynotethemepark.com), from Wow You Design, produces a good selection of beautifully designed themes. The themes all include custom bullets and chart fills designed especially to match the theme, and they also come with a total of 18 master slides. The themes have some very attractive graphical touches, such as feathered or beveled edges for photo cutouts (**Figure A.11**) and slides with an inverse color scheme, which give you a different look while still being in character with the rest of the theme.

These attractive and innovative themes are a bit more expensive than the themes on other sites, but they are very high quality.

◆ **KeynotePro**
(http://www.keynotepro.com) appeared just before this book went to press, showcasing two stunning themes, with more on the way. Their PitchBoard theme lets film and video producers use Keynote to create storyboards for television and film projects (**Figure A.12**). The theme comes in Classic and Pro versions; the Classic version has master slides with photo cutouts in 4:3 and 3:2 aspect ratios, and the Pro version contains additional masters with aspect ratios for high-definition television, feature film, and IMAX.

continues on next page

Where to Find Themes

◆ **KeynoteUser.com**
(http://www.keynoteuser.com) sells a few
excellent premium themes that come
with tons of extras. The site's Lowercase
Blue (**Figure A.13**) and Lowercase
Orange themes come with an incredible
31 master slides, three color variations,
unique photo cutouts, and seven pages
of extra color chips, and graphic objects.
The attention to detail is excellent. The
themes use Apple's Installer to put them
in the correct folders for Keynote's use,
and there's even a sample presentation
file that shows you how to use the theme's
special features.

KeynoteUser.com's themes are reasonably
priced, especially considering all of the
extras that come with each theme. Highly
recommended.

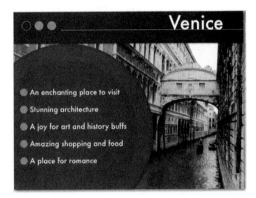

Figure A.13 The Lowercase Blue theme, from
KeynoteUser.com, comes with innovative photo
cutouts, like this full-screen effect, and many
extras, such as color chips and graphic objects.

THEME CREATION CHECKLIST

There are a lot of steps involved in creating a custom theme, and you'll want to make sure you haven't forgotten anything before you save your Keynote file as a theme. With so many different settings and layouts to remember, it's good to have a reference chart or checklist to follow so you don't forget anything in your theme.

Just as airline pilots use a pre-flight checklist to make sure everything is set up properly before take-off, think of this as your theme-building pre-flight checklist.

Things to check before saving your Keynote presentation file as a theme file:

❑ Master slide names match Apple master slide names, at least for the basic eleven layouts.

❑ Master slide names are the same for custom master slides across different versions of your own themes. This makes it easier for the user to switch themes.

❑ Master slide backgrounds are properly set up (there should be no leftover backgrounds from the theme you used as the starter theme).

❑ Background images placed on master slides cover the entire slide (with no edges showing).

❏ Turn on "Allow objects on slide to layer with master" for slides with photo cutouts.

❏ Check photo cutouts to see that they work and don't have transparency problems.

❏ If you will be using bleed type photo cutouts (cutouts where the photo extends off the edge of the slide), test the master slide with the Cube or Push transition for proper alignment across slides.

❏ Check and lock table settings for *all* slide masters, or at least for those slide masters that may contain tables. Make sure you set font settings when you create table settings.

❏ Set default object styles throughout the theme.

❏ Set default text font and styles throughout the theme.

❏ Check font settings on blank slides and slides with no Body or Title box checked, so that if the user decides to turn on the Body or Title box, it will match the styles used in the rest of the theme.

❏ Check fonts in all charts for proper color, size, and shadow settings.

❏ If you are using custom chart grid colors, turn on and check both axes of chart grids, even if one set will be turned back off before you save the theme.

❏ Set up the *first* regular slide of your .key file as the Theme Preview image.

If you will be distributing your theme:

❏ Check that fonts used are included in Mac OS X, or were included with Keynote. If you use custom fonts, make sure that fonts are included with the theme with permission of the font's creator, or, if the font is freely downloadable, that the font's URL is included.

❏ Test the theme on a screen or projector for contrast and other visual problems.

❏ (optional) If the presentation will be shown on TV rather than a computer monitor or projector, test that the theme does not have overscan problems. Because TV screens have a smaller resolution than computer screens, themes composed for computer screens can have part of their edges cut off.

After saving the Keynote theme file:

❏ Be sure the theme name follows the "*name*_8x6.kth" or "*name*_10x7.kth" naming scheme. Notice the *lowercase* "x" between the size numbers. A space works *in* the name, but not *after* it.

❏ Make your chart colors accessible for the user to reuse in other presentations. You can do this by including a special Keynote file with your theme that contains color chips, i.e., objects filled with your chart colors, so that users can copy the styles onto their own objects.

For advanced theme builders (after saving the Keynote theme file):

❏ Remove extra bullets from the theme package and confirm that the XML file has been modified using Find/Replace (otherwise, extra bullets tend to duplicate when using custom bullets).

❏ Check inside the theme package for left-over objects from the original theme. If you created your own chart fill files and replaced Apple's, make sure you didn't leave an old Apple file inside your theme.

❏ Change the names of Apple's chart tiles and use Find/Replace to check this XML file. (If you changed the colors of the chart fill files, but left the old names, it looks better to have names that match your theme.)

INDEX

INDEX